A Place to Write

NCTE Editorial Board

Steven Bickmore
Catherine Compton-Lilly
Deborah Dean
Antero Garcia
Bruce McComiskey
Jennifer Ochoa
Staci M. Perryman-Clark
Anne Elrod Whitney
Vivian Yenika-Agbaw
Kurt Austin, Chair, ex officio
Emily Kirkpatrick, ex officio

A Place to Write

Getting Your Students out of the Classroom and into the World

Rob Montgomery
Kennesaw State University

Amanda Montgomery
*Park Street Elementary School
Marietta, Georgia*

National Council of Teachers of English
340 N. Neil St., Suite #104, Champaign, Illinois 61820
www.ncte.org

Staff Editor: Bonny Graham
Manuscript Editor: The Charlesworth Group
Interior Design: Jenny Jensen Greenleaf
Cover Design: Pat Mayer

Cover Images: Front: iStock.com/IrisImages, iStock.com/SrdjanPav, iStock.com/empire331, iStock.com/shylendrahoode, iStock.com/michelmond, iStock.com/VistaVision, iStock.com/SeanPavonePhoto, iStock.com/Nate Hovee, iStock.com/ziggy1, iStock.com/BackyardProduction, iStock.com/m-image photography, iStock.com/Thi Soares; Back: iStock.com/kostsov, iStock.com/liujiachuan, iStock.com/powerofforever, iStock.com/rclassenlayouts

NCTE Stock Number: 35457; eStock Number: 35464
ISBN 978-0-8141-3545-7; eISBN 978-0-8141-3546-4

©2021 by the National Council of Teachers of English.

All rights reserved. No part of this publication may be reproduced or transmitted in any form or by any means, electronic or mechanical, including photocopy, or any information storage and retrieval system, without permission from the copyright holder. Printed in the United States of America.

It is the policy of NCTE in its journals and other publications to provide a forum for the open discussion of ideas concerning the content and the teaching of English and the language arts. Publicity accorded to any particular point of view does not imply endorsement by the Executive Committee, the Board of Directors, or the membership at large, except in announcements of policy, where such endorsement is clearly specified.

NCTE provides equal employment opportunity to all staff members and applicants for employment without regard to race, color, religion, sex, national origin, age, physical, mental or perceived handicap/disability, sexual orientation including gender identity or expression, ancestry, genetic information, marital status, military status, unfavorable discharge from military service, pregnancy, citizenship status, personal appearance, matriculation or political affiliation, or any other protected status under applicable federal, state, and local laws.

Every effort has been made to provide current URLs and email addresses, but, because of the rapidly changing nature of the web, some sites and addresses may no longer be accessible.

Library of Congress Cataloging-in-Publication Data
Names: Montgomery, Rob, 1973- author. | Montgomery, Amanda, 1987- author.
Title: A place to write : getting your students out of the classroom and into the world / Rob Montgomery, Kennesaw State University, Amanda Montgomery, Park Street Elementary School.
Description: Champaign, Illinois : National Council of Teachers of English, [2021] | Includes bibliographical references and index. | Summary: "Explores opportunities for writing in a different real-world setting (such as museums, public places, natural places, and virtual spaces) by providing a range of practical K-12 classroom activities in a variety of commonly taught genres"—Provided by publisher.
Identifiers: LCCN 2020037793 (print) | LCCN 2020037794 (ebook) | ISBN 9780814135457 (trade paperback) | ISBN 9780814135464 (adobe pdf)
Subjects: LCSH: English language—Composition and exercises—Study and teaching. | Creative writing—Study and teaching. | Language arts—Correlation with content subjects.
Classification: LCC LB1576 .M656 2021 (print) | LCC LB1576 (ebook) | DDC 428.0071—dc23
LC record available at https://lccn.loc.gov/2020037793
LC ebook record available at https://lccn.loc.gov/2020037794

Rob dedicates this book to his students—current, past, and future. But he owes a special debt of gratitude to five former student teachers from Kennesaw State University whom he's now proud to consider colleagues—Casey Black, Stephanie Coggins, Katie Ferguson, Melissa Oliver-Pridgen, and Emily Wynn. You were the first to say, "Hey! You should turn this place-based writing stuff into a book!" Thanks to all of you. You lit the fuse, and just look what happened.

Amanda would like to dedicate this book to her inquisitive students, who motivate her each day to find new and different ways of highlighting their voices in writing.

Contents

ACKNOWLEDGMENTS ix

INTRODUCTION xi

CHAPTER 1 Foundations and Frameworks 1
    The Current State of Writing Instruction: Where Are We—
        and Do We Want to Be There? 1
    Authenticity: What Does Anything Mean, Anyway? 4
    Place-Based Writing: The World as Classroom 7
    The Potential of Place-Based Writing 15

CHAPTER 2 Place-Based Writing in Action 24
    The Plan: A Garden as Research Project 26
    Writing about the Past through Future Eyes 33
    Conclusion and Next Steps 36

CHAPTER 3 Writing in School Places 37
    But First, a Note about the Flexibility of Place-Based Writing ... 37
    Writing in (or near) School Locations 39
    Extended Lesson Idea: Ethnographic Thick Description 41
    Writing about Literature and Other Texts 48
    Writing Arguments 53
    Writing Narratives, Poetry, and Scripts 58
    Writing for Research and Inquiry 61
    Writing for Change 63
    Further Considerations 65

CHAPTER 4 Writing in Museums 68
    Extended Lesson Idea: Exploring Local History 70

    Writing about Literature and Other Texts 78
    Writing Arguments 81
    Writing Narratives, Poetry, and Scripts 84
    Writing for Research and Inquiry 89
    Writing for Change 90

CHAPTER 5   Writing in Public Places 94
    Extended Lesson Idea: Rooting Narrative in Place 98
    Writing about Literature and Other Texts 106
    Writing Arguments 109
    Writing Narratives, Poetry, and Scripts 113
    Writing for Research and Inquiry 115
    Writing for Change 121

CHAPTER 6   Writing in Natural Places 125
    Extended Lesson Idea: Protecting Our Wild Places 128
    Writing about Literature and Other Texts 134
    Writing Arguments 139
    Writing Narratives, Poetry, and Scripts 141
    Writing for Research and Inquiry 144
    Writing for Change 146

CHAPTER 7   Writing in Virtual Places 151
    Extended Lesson Idea: Creating a Virtual Tour 153
    Writing about Literature and Other Texts 161
    Writing Arguments 165
    Writing Narratives, Poetry, and Scripts 169
    Writing for Research and Inquiry 171
    Writing for Change 175

FINAL THOUGHTS 179

APPENDIX: Garden and Composting Research Project 181

NOTES 189

WORKS CITED 197

INDEX 205

AUTHORS 213

Acknowledgments

Amanda and Rob want to thank Kurt Austin, Bonny Graham, and the books team at NCTE for helping shepherd us through this process, patiently answering many questions rookies probably should have known better than to ask. We also want to specifically acknowledge the inspiration we have received from National Writing Project teachers near and far. Many of the activities described in this book saw their genesis in the Kennesaw Mountain Writing Project Summer Institute during our time as codirectors, and we appreciate our colleagues' generosity in allowing us to fumble through their early stages. Both of us consider the National Writing Project to be our home (philosophically and pedagogically speaking), and it is in the company of other Writing Project teachers that we feel most comfortable. Thanks for the vital work you do every day, and we hope you find *A Place to Write* to be at least partial recompense for all your efforts in helping students become more confident and sophisticated writers.

Introduction

"We're taking a tour of the school," Mr. Schaffer said. "Grab your notebook and a writing utensil. Leave everything else behind. You are *not* to talk. You're simply to observe. Use your senses. Look, listen, smell, touch. And taste, if you're brave. Take notes of what you experience, but *do not talk*. When we get back to the classroom, I'll tell you why we're doing this."

This was 1989, when Rob was in tenth grade. Mr. Schaffer—his otherwise formula- and grammar-driven English teacher—surprised everyone by beginning class this way, and, without another word, heading out the door. Twenty-five 15- and 16-year-old students, surprised into silence, hesitantly followed him on a guided tour of the building.

They traveled down early-morning hallways that smelled faintly of ammonia, into the cafeteria already pungent with cut-rate tomato sauce, and through the gymnasium where a class was playing basketball, the squeaking of tennis shoes on hardwood competing with the full-bodied bouquet of sweat and leather suffusing the sticky air. Pine shavings in woodshop. Formaldehyde in the biology classroom. A riot of neon on paint-spattered canvases in the art room. Crying and laughing children in the day care annex located at the rear of the building. The click-clacking of electric typewriters in the main office. And, underneath it all, the faint buzz of lecture and discussion that would rise in volume as the students approached each classroom and then Doppler into silence as they continued down the hall.

When they returned to the classroom, Mr. Schaffer instructed his class to conceive a story that incorporated as many different details as possible from the notes they took during their tour. "Be creative. Don't feel like it has to be set in a school. But think about how you can take those sensory images and use them to bring life to an original story."

Rob, struck by the dual inspirations of a talking Teddy Ruxpin doll he'd seen cast aside in the day care center and the faint but unmistakable odor of cigar smoke as the class passed the custodian's office, concocted a story about a cigar-chomping teddy bear who came to life in an effort to be like the students he saw passing the day care center each day.

It was not a great story.

But it *was* the one time Rob remembered feeling engaged and inspired in a school year that was otherwise saturated with five-paragraph essays, rigidly formatted explications of dusty canonical texts, and hastily constructed "research" papers about literary figures that were mainly exercises in plugging the required number of direct quotes into paragraphs of summary. It's not that Rob disliked English. He was an avid reader and writer from an early age. It's just that English—as it was taught—seemed to have very little to do with *him*. The rules, and templates, and strictures, and even the lockstep way he and his classmates were expected to use The Writing Process, none of it seemed to have anything to do with what he already understood writing to be: a mode of expression that could be personal, and experimental, and *fun*.

And as Rob continued to reflect on this experience as he became a high school English teacher and eventually a teacher educator, he realized that, if this was the effect a traditional approach to writing was having on *him*, someone who generally enjoyed writing, what effect was it having on his former classmates and current students who didn't see the value of writing and didn't consider themselves good at it?

Why did Mr. Schaffer's "School Tour" activity work as well as it did? Rob didn't have the lingo at the time to articulate it, but what he and his classmates had been asked to engage in was a simple and accessible version of *place-based writing*. And now, thirty years after the fact, it's this approach to teaching writing that could help save traditional writing instruction from itself.

What Place-Based Writing Is, What This Book Isn't (and Is)

But we are getting ahead of ourselves. Ending that anecdote with such a hyperbolic and potentially off-putting statement is quite a cliffhanger with which to start things off, especially considering we haven't even explained why this topic matters in the first place. We promise not to be so bombastic throughout the remainder of the book, but we also think it's important not to undersell the transformative potential inherent in place-based writing. So, with that in mind, what exactly *is* place-based writing, and what are you getting yourself into with this book?

While a detailed explanation of place-based writing and its benefits takes up a large chunk of real estate in Chapter 1, here's a brief (and admittedly simplistic) definition that might prove helpful at the outset: if you're getting your students out of the classroom for the purpose of writing about the world beyond it, you're engaging in some form of place-based writing.

Let's look at that definition in the context of Rob's story about Mr. Schaffer. The act of asking the students to do something as simple as touring the school (in silence!), taking notes, and writing a story free from the rigid parameters of the essay format managed to be both engaging and liberating. It allowed Rob a degree of agency in the way he suddenly found himself with sole ownership of his story. He had to consider his audience, or else he ran the risk of boring Mr. Schaffer (something he had frankly never considered a problem before). And at the heart of it all was the unusual challenge of incorporating commonplace details from around the school into an original story, which gave Rob a purpose he hadn't previously experienced with more conventional forms of academic writing. The activity asked him to look at the school in a way he hadn't previously considered and notice details he was usually too hurried to catch. True, Rob could have written a story *without* the tour. He'd written stories before. But the sheer novelty of the guided tour created an experience that stuck with him for decades. Writing that is restricted to the classroom can certainly also be authentic and meaningful for students. But what we hope to convince you of in *A Place to Write* is that asking students to write in the world outside the classroom *about* the world outside the classroom uniquely positions them to do authentic, meaningful work in a way other writing often struggles to achieve.

So, if that's what place-based writing is and what it can do (at least in its most introductory form), what exactly can you expect to find in this book? To begin, this isn't the right place to visit if you're primarily looking for the theory behind place-based writing. Theory is valuable and necessary, and we're not opposed to it; we recognize the importance of understanding why certain ideas are valuable and certain strategies are effective. As Blau (2003) reminds us, "without a set of principles or a theory to frame demonstrated practices, the practices . . . would easily lose their originating focus and pedagogical purpose" (pp. 14–15) as they are adapted and modified for different classes and students. As a teacher educator, Rob works regularly to help his students articulate the connection between theory and practice in order to understand why certain strategies and activities seem worth using, especially so they can advocate for themselves in their first years in the classroom, before they have developed a professional reputation with administrators and parents. Theory matters, and we haven't shirked our responsibility in explaining it here.

But we have always been most drawn to those books that emphasize the practical and provide just enough theory to contextualize the activities described within. We're thinking specifically of books like Beers and Probst's (2012) *Notice*

& *Note*, Blau's (2003) *The Literature Workshop*, Kittle's (2008) *Write beside Them*, Crovitz and Devereaux's (2016) *Grammar to Get Things Done*, Anderson's (2005) *Mechanically Inclined*, and McCann et al.'s (2006) *Talking in Class*. These authors are not theory averse, but they recognize—in proper National Writing Project fashion—the value of teachers sharing good ideas with one another, as opposed to having "good ideas" handed down in a mandate from above or sold to them in an expensive box. These books represent what Hillocks (1995) tells us is the necessary flip side of being familiar with the theory that serves as our instructional foundation: "Theories of discourse, inquiry, learning, and teaching are useless if we cannot invent the activities that will engage our students in using, and therefore learning, the strategies essential to certain writing tasks" (p. 149). In books like those mentioned above, theory serves as the appetizer, but the description of practice is the entrée and (to continue an admittedly silly metaphor) actually seeing that practice succeed with similar activities you've created for your own students is the dessert.

So this is not a book about place-based writing theory.

What this book *is*, then, is a resource and a tool kit (a how-to manual would be a close genre equivalent) you can rely on as you consider the kind of place-based writing you want to conduct with your own students. One thing that sets this book apart from other texts dealing with place-based writing is the inclusive angle we've tried to take. Many existing texts dealing with place-based writing do so from a specifically environmentalist standpoint. Encouraging students to engage with, and become advocates for, the environment is desperately relevant work (which we will discuss at various points), but what we found missing from the existing literature is a text that helps teachers see how place-based writing can serve a variety of instructional purposes that may or may not be exclusive to environmental advocacy (or even be ideological at all). As we worked with practicing and preservice teachers at our school sites, in conference presentations, and as former codirectors of the Kennesaw Mountain Writing Project's Summer Institute, the question we heard most frequently was this: "Is there a book describing a variety of different place-based writing activities?" Our short answer was always "no." We've been able to point teachers toward edited collections consisting of case studies of individual place-based teaching experiences (which, again, tend to focus on environmental education or sometimes community advocacy).[1] However, what seemed to be missing from the professional conversation was a catchall text establishing place-based writing as a valuable instructional approach for a wide range of learning goals accompanied by descriptions of easily modified lesson ideas.

To that end, in each chapter (see the next section for more details), we provide you with a variety of authentic place-based writing activities you can modify based on the specifics of your community and curriculum, as well as a description of how and why place-based writing is appropriate and effective for the topic in question. And, if we're going to be completely honest, the best use of this book is to familiarize yourself with the promise inherent in place-based writing to such a degree that you can actively seek out ways to design meaningful and authentic new activities that are specific to your context, beyond those we present in the pages that follow.

A Brief Word about Structure and Location

What we hope sets this book apart is that it is, at heart, a book about *place*. We take up writing forms and genres in ways that we hope are serious and helpful to you. We've made this book easy to navigate, so, if you're interested in exploring ideas for teaching argument, for example, you can find them without any trouble. But this is, first and foremost, a book that celebrates place and the opportunities it presents for your students to do writing that matters.

To begin, though, some necessary organizational legwork is in order. Chapter 1 provides an overview of place-based writing and the concept of authenticity in student writing (while also discussing the traditional pedagogical practices for which place-based writing can be a remedy) and lays out the framework we've designed to help you develop your own place-based writing activities. Chapter 2 presents two extended activities Amanda facilitated with her fourth-grade students. The role of this chapter is to introduce you to the practicality of place-based writing by sharing the entirety of two complete units, one that took place on Amanda's school site and one that was conducted at a local national park. This should help you start thinking about what you can do with place-based writing in your own school and community as well as how readily activities can be adapted and modified for different grade levels and subject areas. For anyone a little intimidated by the thought of taking your students outside, we also wanted to start with these examples so you could rest assured that place-based writing needn't be expensive, extravagant, or—maybe most important for your first experience—chaotic.

Beginning with Chapter 3, the remainder of the book divides place-based writing into the following different general locations to help you think about the range of experiences that are possible for your students:

- Chapter 3—School locations. If you're looking for a small-scale, low-key way to try place-based writing that's still engaging and authentic, your own school site likely has a wide range of productive spaces. The cafeteria, the outdoor classroom, the gym, the courtyard, the hallways, and more—they're all fair game for place-based writing.

- Chapter 4—Museums and other learning centers. The sterile nature of many museums may initially make them seem like odd places to pursue authentic writing. However, we believe the curated nature of their exhibits gives us a unique way of teaching a range of English language arts–related content, from literature study to argument to research and beyond. In Chapter 4, we explore how a variety of museums—art, science, history, etc.—can be a useful middle ground between writing at your school site and venturing into the great outdoors.

- Chapter 5—Public places. When was the last time you were moved to write by the sight of an office building? For obvious reasons, the seemingly mundane places we routinely occupy are oft-neglected sources of writing inspiration. Yet spaces such as public squares, parks and playgrounds, public art installations, city buildings, and even malls and shopping areas can provide our students with easily accessible settings in which to explore a variety of real-world applications for writing. These are also places where we can begin to explore with our students such important topics as gentrification and community identity.

- Chapter 6—Natural places. While the order of these chapters is not hierarchical, we nonetheless feel that writing in natural places can be seen as the most idealized version of place-based writing. It is certainly where some of your most vital work will be accomplished if one of your goals is to promote environmental advocacy or stewardship. In Chapter 6, we broaden our scope to explore the ways in which writing can be used to strengthen our students' connections to the environment as well as how the natural world can result in a variety of narrative, argument, and research writing lessons.

- Chapter 7—Virtual places. Throughout the book, we try to be sensitive to the fact that financial resources and other logistical issues can often curtail teachers' ambitions. Fortunately, technology has advanced to the point where a reasonable facsimile of place-based writing can be re-created in a classroom setting. In Chapter 7, we explore some of the opportunities provided by different computing applications and platforms to capture the spirit of place-based writing even if it isn't physically possible to get your students into the world beyond the school grounds.

We begin each of these chapters by more fully describing the type of place and explaining why we think it can be valuable and productive for your students. We continue each chapter with an extended description of a related series of writing lessons you could teach in this type of place, followed by practical examples of activities and assignments that align with the kinds of writing (and students) you are likely to encounter in your classroom. These chapters will contain the following sections with one or more corresponding activities in each:

- writing about literature and other texts
- writing arguments
- writing narratives
- writing for research and inquiry
- writing for change.

Following the description of each activity, we also include a brief discussion of the way(s) in which it can be modified for additional authenticity, as well as how teachers can make interdisciplinary connections. We close each chapter with some suggestions for how students with special needs and English language learners can be supported in these activities.

The practical examples we provide in each chapter can mostly be found in our backyard, which is the metro Atlanta area. Our goal, however, is to generalize our descriptions as much as possible so you can consider similar resources in your own area. For instance, just because we base an activity at the downtown square in Marietta, Georgia, doesn't mean you have to fly cross-country to do it if you live in Tucson, Arizona. A range of comparable locations will work just as well, and it is ultimately our goal to ensure that, for any activity we describe, you can quickly and easily see how it could be translated to meet your own circumstances and needs.

Finally, the elephant in the room is the fact that we're writing this introduction in the middle of a pandemic, when the structure and complexity of schooling has been, for the time being at least, dramatically altered. There is some indication, however, that the approach to writing described in this book could have a natural appeal to educators struggling with ways to keep their students healthy while still seeking out meaningful educational practices. With COVID-19 spreading less easily in outdoor spaces (Centers for Disease Control and Prevention, 2020), teachers may find it safer, as well as more engaging and authentic, to take students outside to write. In fact, some teachers are already finding this to be the case, with the Toronto (Canada) District School Board "encouraging teachers to take classes outside whenever possible this year" (Bridge & Common, 2020, para. 16). Our unprecedented situation could actually prove to be the catalyst by which students can be encouraged to safely engage with the larger world in order to write more honestly and authentically.

Happy writing (and exploring)!

Foundations and Frameworks

The Current State of Writing Instruction: Where Are We—and Do We Want to Be There?

Before digging into the benefits of place-based writing, it's worth spending a few pages taking stock of where we are so we have a better sense of where place-based writing can take us. However, talking about the shortcomings of current writing instruction is a discomfiting proposition. We know and have worked with (and, in Rob's case, taught) dozens of teachers who are out there in the thick of it, spending their days helping their students become more confident, competent, and sophisticated readers, writers, and thinkers. And those teachers are everywhere, not just in our backyard. If you've taken the time to pick up this book, there's an above-average chance you're one of them. And, of course, we know from our own experience as teachers that writing instruction may very well be the most complicated pedagogical undertaking there is. But make no mistake: as much as we love writing teachers and consider ourselves to be part of the club, writing instruction itself needs, if not saving, then at the very least an intervention.

Not too long ago, Applebee and Langer (2011) presented a sobering picture of the state of writing in middle and high schools. One of the conclusions of their study of 260 classrooms was that, even though what we consider to be "good" writing instruction has changed since a similar study was conducted in 1979–1980, most classrooms don't actually engage their students in it. In Applebee and Langer's estimation:

> [The kind of writing students are asked to complete] looks much the same [as it did in 1979–1980], with students completing many more pages of exercises and copying than they do of original writing of even a paragraph in length. And even some of the extended writing that students do complete is constrained as

practice for on-demand, timed assessments where the instruction that occurs is focused on successful test performance rather than on the development of the skills and strategies that will serve a student well in the varied tasks that make up the larger domain of writing. (2011, p. 24)

This finding has been echoed by many of Rob's student teachers since 2009, with nearly all of them to one degree or another reporting tension between what they have been taught effective writing instruction looks like and how it is actually enacted in the schools in which they are completing their senior-year field placements.

Even though many of their mentor teachers make overtures toward such worthwhile strategies as fostering a culture of revision, incorporating collaborative writing activities, or teaching students to write in real-world genres, the emphasis in many schools (as mandated by site and district administrations, and often with the reluctance of the teachers themselves) has increasingly become achieving satisfactory end-of-year test scores. And these scores are of course inevitably tied to the measures of effectiveness by which teachers are judged. As a result of the pressure caused by such external evaluation, teachers somewhat understandably resort to teaching almost exclusively the kind of writing that will appear on these tests. This aligns with Applebee and Langer's (2011, p. 18) finding that teachers "reported making frequent use of rubrics or scoring systems similar to those that will be used on the exam, and of incorporating the types of writing from the exam in the regular curriculum." They also found that, by allowing testing to drive instruction, there was unavoidably "a very direct and limiting effect" (p. 18) on how writing was actually taught.

It bears mentioning that these findings neatly align with those arrived at by Hillocks (2002) nearly a decade earlier. In *The Testing Trap*, Hillocks studied how standardized testing influenced writing instruction in five states (Illinois, Kentucky, New York, Oregon, and Texas). His first step was to analyze three texts: the states' writing prompts, the student-written benchmark essays provided by the state as instructional models, and the scorers' commentary on those benchmark essays. This analysis yielded a view of what each state considered to be quality writing. Hillocks's (2002) distressing findings were that, not only did teachers overwhelmingly use the states' test-focused resources to guide their instruction, but those resources—and especially the benchmark essays—"exemplif[ied] vacuous thinking" (p. 201) and were ultimately used to the detriment of student writers. Applebee and Langer's (2011) discovery that little had changed in the intervening years should trouble us all.

Now let's fast-forward a further nine years. In Rob's current classroom experiences with preservice teachers, standardized tests are still being used to guide instruction, and that has led teachers to adopt all manner of questionable practices, from a reliance on simple formulas (such as the musty old five-paragraph model or its Jane Schaffer variation) to an emphasis on responding to the kind of stilted, inauthentic prompts only found on tests. These approaches have also filtered to the younger grades. In Amanda's experience working with local teachers through the Kennesaw Mountain Writing Project, she's seen districts attempt to raise standardized test scores by mandating the use of packaged, scripted writing curricula without recognizing when it is developmentally inappropriate for students of varying backgrounds. We mention this not to turn this book into a polemic on American testing culture.[1] We also don't want to be seen as piling on, when so much of the current rhetoric about education (and specifically public education) revolves around the supposedly lousy job teachers are doing. As we said earlier, we know many, many teachers who strive every day to provide their students with meaningful experiences, and we also know administrators who rightfully recognize their faculty as expert practitioners and provide them with the flexibility and autonomy to do what's best for their students, regardless of testing.

However, if we're going to discuss at length the promise place-based writing has for students, we would be remiss if we didn't point out the forces that actively work against it and can problematize, or at least complicate, its use. We aren't sure if it says more about the tests or the schools (or maybe both?) that the response to state testing has largely been to constrain and standardize the teaching of writing. Wiggins (2009) reminds us that, if a school has implemented a robust writing curriculum that encourages meaningful work from its students, the results will unavoidably show up on the required tests in the same way that living a healthy life will result in a good showing on your yearly physical. In his analogy, what schools are currently doing—using various formulae and asking students to write by the narrow and artificial terms of the standardized test—is "akin to practicing all year for the doctor's annual physical exam instead of working all year to be healthy" (p. 36).

With all this in mind, it is crucial to remember at this juncture that, if what we're really after in our classrooms is to see our students become thoughtful, sophisticated users of language who will be likely to continue to write after they leave our classrooms, and if we want for ourselves as teachers to embody the healthy writing instruction about which Wiggins writes, the current emphasis on obviously test-centric writing is not the way to do it. What's missing, then? In a word, authenticity.

Authenticity: What Does Anything Mean, Anyway?

The clear dividing line between place-based writing and the kind of writing described in the previous section deals with the inauthenticity of most conventional writing instruction—what Whitney (2011) refers to as "the schoolishness of school" (p. 55). For instance, in writing to a formula or for transparently standardized test–based reasons, there's no getting around the fact that this writing exists only *in* schools *for* school-based purposes. Even if some of the broad skills, such as critical thinking or formulating an argument, may have a degree of transfer to the world outside school, it's virtually impossible to make the writing itself authentic in the same way as the writing our students will choose to take up on their own.

So, if *authenticity* is a hallmark of place-based writing, what do we mean by that word (which we use repeatedly throughout this book) and can such a thing even exist in schools? Even though the fine points of different authors' definitions of authenticity (and authentic writing) may differ slightly, they all tend to circle around two central ideas: the topic has personal relevance, and it serves a purpose beyond receiving a grade. For example, Whitney (2017) tells us writing feels authentic "when it is useful, important, or necessary to get a job done" (p. 16). Rodesiler and Kelley (2017) argue that one of the linchpins of authentic student writing is that it "target[s] audiences beyond the teacher" (p. 22). Duke et al. (2006) pinpoint authentic activities as existing "outside of a learning-to-read-and-write context" with a "true communicative purpose" (p. 346), while Gallagher (2011) homes in on authentic writing as a vehicle through which students can experiment with composing for real-world motives. Kirby and Crovitz ambitiously define authentic writing as "involving . . . writing for real audiences (not just the teacher) about a topic important to you . . . for a reason important to you . . . to communicate a real message . . . in a form . . . that enhances your message" (2013, p. 124). Kixmiller (2004) similarly characterizes authentic writing as a blend of personally relevant topic, audience, and purpose, but also emphasizes the power such writing has to "help students make sense of their world while advocating for change" (p. 29). Wiggins (2009) boils it down to ensuring that "students have to write for real audiences and purposes, not just the teacher in response to generic prompts" (p. 30), and, most recently, Lindblom and Christenbury (2018) have described authentic writing as "real writing, written for a real audience, for a real purpose, in a real forum" (p. 30).

We could continue in this vein for some time, but even a brief sampling of the research surrounding authenticity makes two points immediately clear. The first is that authentic writing is, for the writer, *real*. In contrast to traditional school writing—wherein all the students in the class are handed a single topic that has been devised by the teacher, usually for the teacher's own purposes (even if those purposes are well intentioned)—authentic writing has meaning for the student that exists outside of and beyond school. Whether it's a journal entry reflecting on the day, an indignant letter protesting an unjust policy, or song lyrics voicing frustration about being turned down for a date, the writing hasn't been mandated from above, there's no rubric attached to it, and there will never be a letter grade. This writing is, essentially, a selfish act, even when eventually presented to an outside audience.

And the key point to underline about audience—the other issue that shows up repeatedly in the research about authenticity—is that, like the writing's purpose, it is *real*. Rob's current students (all preservice teachers at a public university) almost universally report that the model they experienced most frequently in their own high school English classes was that they would write an essay in isolation (usually in response to a teacher-created prompt), submit it to the teacher, receive the teacher's grade, briefly peruse the teacher's comments, and file it in a binder or drop it in the trash on the way out the door. We suspect such a process is familiar to you, the reader, as well. It certainly is to us.

That closed-circuit model of writing is, in many ways, the antithesis of authentic writing. Students have no voice in the topic about which they are writing; they receive no meaningful formative feedback from other writers, such as their classmates or the teacher; no one but the teacher sees the finished product; and any important summative feedback is artificially constrained to a letter grade or a total number of points derived from a rubric. Even in instances in which students receive narrative feedback in the form of comments, they are rarely given direction or opportunity to learn from them in subsequent writings. Please note that we are not trying to shame teachers who have engaged in any of these practices. It is common, and we have all done it at one time or another, perhaps due to expedience, or mandate, or lack of any better ideas. What we argue throughout this book, though, is that we need to do better.

So, if authenticity means students are choosing topics, purposes, audiences, and forms that are relevant and meaningful to them, is it actually possible for writing in schools to *ever* be 100 percent authentic? It's a reasonable question, and there is an understandable undercurrent of despair to it. After all, even when we incorporate activities that *look* authentic—Whitney (2011) uses the example of students asked to replicate a colonial newspaper—they're often *not* authentic. In Whitney's example, the newspaper is an assignment dictated by the teacher, the students aren't colonists, and neither are the people who will be reading their newspaper. Even in instances in which students are given carte blanche to write an argumentative essay about any issue that matters to them, the assignment still originated with the teacher, which, by the metric we've just described, would seem to render it inauthentic. The same can be said for other writing assignments where students have some latitude in determining topic or form. Romano's (1995) multigenre research project—arguably the assignment over which students can take the most ownership, choosing as they do their own topics and the genres through which they will present their research—is still teacher assigned and will presumably be assessed through a rubric or scoring guide that has been created at least in part by the teacher. The very nature of school seems to eliminate the possibility of complete authenticity—so, should we just throw up our hands and reconcile ourselves to the fact that our work with students will, despite our best intentions, always be suspect?

Our answer (after encouraging you to take a few deep breaths) is an emphatic "no!" Instead, we find it beneficial to rethink authenticity in the context of how that term is taken up in real-world settings, and what it says to us about the work we do in schools. Take, for instance, the book you are reading. As part of Rob's job description as a tenured professor, he knows he has to conduct and publish research—such as a book on place-based writing. That requirement has been mandated (or assigned) to him by the University System of Georgia. If, in light of the previous discussion, we are to take any writing that has been assigned by an external entity as somehow inauthentic, that makes this very book (or any other job-related research and writing Rob completes) inauthentic. Which doesn't seem accurate to us, since this is a topic about which we're passionate, written for an audience we deeply respect and admire, for a purpose in which we believe, and in a form that we think will be most useful to its audience. The fact that it was in some ways originated by a faceless academic entity is beside the point.

A more helpful way to think about authenticity, then, is to subscribe to what Kohnen (2013) refers to as "the latent-functional authenticity spectrum." In her conception, authenticity exists on a continuum. One end of that continuum is *latent authenticity*, where the genre in which the students are writing "may exist in the real world" (p. 32), but its purpose as a writing act never transcends the classroom. Instead, teacher goals drive assessment of the students' work with little or no attention paid to how well their writing actually maps onto the real-world demands of the genre in question. A practical example of this from Rob's own life came during tenth grade, when the class was required to write a review of a local community theater production of Thornton Wilder's *Our Town*. Rob's well-written but scathing review was greeted with the teacher comment, "Very creative, but very biased." The notion of an unbiased review seems to contradict the real-world purpose of the review genre, casting this particular assignment at the latent end of the spectrum. This example isn't meant to imply that assignments at that end of Kohnen's continuum are without merit. Lindblom and

Christenbury (2018) refer to these assignments as "pseudo-authentic," and they can still be helpful in the classroom in the way they "approximate an authentic writing situation and raise valuable discussion" (p. 50).

Pseudo-authentic assignments can be particularly helpful as models or exemplars as we move students toward the other end of the spectrum, which Kohnen (2013) refers to as *functional authenticity*. In these assignments, the genre "exist[s] outside of school . . . [and] the classroom draws on its real-world qualities," with the students' writing "assessed according to teacher goals *and* genre goals" (p. 32, emphasis in original). In other words, one of the expressed purposes of this kind of assignment is to help students think more clearly and thoroughly about the real-world demands of the genre—its formal characteristics, as well as the audience that is likely to read it—in addition to any of the more "schoolish" demands that are the hallmarks of classroom assignments. In Chapter 2, Amanda describes such an assignment: an authentic inquiry project based in her school's garden and compost area that culminated in a how-to book written by her fourth-grade students to be read by the second- and third-grade science classes.

All our writing assignments likely exist somewhere on this continuum, from the letter to the editor that never actually gets mailed (at the latent end) to the real-world grant proposal written by students in the hope of acquiring more young adult titles for the school library (at the functional end). If we shift our thinking about writing from the conventional, classroom-bound essay to the skills we're trying to teach and assess *through* that essay, we'll realize that it's easier than we thought to bring authentic writing into the classroom, in forms that are likely more engaging than the essay. In that shift we also move the question from a panicked "Is it even possible to be authentic?" to "Just how authentic have I allowed this particular assignment to be?"

That's where place-based writing comes in.

Place-Based Writing: The World as Classroom

It's probable you've asked your students to do place-based writing without even realizing it. Like students who figure out on their own when to effectively use *however* or *nevertheless* in their writing without being told those words are technically called conjunctive adverbs, you've probably asked your students to write somewhere other than your classroom without needing to be told that what you were doing was technically called place-based writing. Moving the act of writing outside the classroom is deceptively simple—you're in your classroom, and then you aren't—but, in terms of what it can accomplish, place-based writing has a variety of potential benefits for students and can be modified to bring in a wide range of written genres, including those that have been privileged through their inclusion in your state's content standards (Common Core or otherwise).

The idea behind place-based writing—or place-based education in general—is hardly new, which reveals an important point: we've realized, for more than one hundred years, how artificial school can be. The educational reformer John Dewey notes this artificiality in a speech originally delivered in 1899:

> From the standpoint of the child, the great waste in the school comes from his inability to utilize the experiences he gets outside the school in any complete and free way within the school itself.... When the child gets into the schoolroom, he has to put out of his mind a large part of the ideas, interests, and activities that predominate in his home and neighborhood. So the school, being unable to utilize this everyday experience, sets painfully to work ... to arouse in the child an interest in school studies. (1899/1902/1990, p. 73)

In many ways, this still sounds familiar. Rather than accounting for who our students are and leveraging that knowledge to teach writing authentically, school frequently divorces writing (and reading, too) from the lived experiences of its students. Instead, the school (which could simply mean the classroom teacher, but might also, depending on the context, refer to site or district administration or even state or federal departments of education) decides what is worth teaching and how it's worth teaching it. This is similar to the argument Beach et al. (2012) make in favor of taking a literacy practices approach to teaching,[2] noting how the inauthentic instructional frameworks frequently used in schools "share a common limitation.... They do not focus first on issues, topics, or themes that emerge from students and the world" (p. 32). In their view, "one of the critical tasks of the English language arts teacher is the creation of meaningful events that foster rich, complex literacy practices. Often this involves thinking about how students interact in literacy events outside the classroom" (p. 36).

Designing these events is trickier than it sounds. Teachers (including your authors) have often taken up the call for authenticity in superficial ways, grafting a traditional assignment onto something we *imagine* resembles our students' existing literacy practices. "Kids love technology!" we shout, and then, to assess their understanding of characterization, we design an assignment in which our students have to create a Facebook page for *The Catcher in the Rye*'s Holden Caulfield. Such an assignment isn't particularly "rich" or "complex" as literacy practices go, it doesn't actually analyze an author's methods of characterization in any meaningful way, and it completely ignores the fact that many adolescents don't even use Facebook anymore (Sweney & De Liz, 2018), which calls the assignment's presumed authenticity into question. Instead, teachers need to dig more deeply into what actually matters to students, particularly as it pertains to their communities. Place-based writing is a natural fit for such an approach, and we return to its application later in this section.

The point in bringing up both Dewey and the literacy practices framework is to emphasize just how much we should place our focus on what students are already doing in terms of literacy in their lives outside the classroom. Our students spend much of their time in places other than school, and they probably won't spend much time in schools after they graduate (unless they become teachers themselves). Yet school, as Dewey points out, often treats learning as something that happens best—and only—in the classroom. Jardine et al. (2006) characterize this as *curricular scarcity*, whereby school subjects "become necessarily bounded in ways that make it possible to control, predict, [and] assess" them (p. 3). The richness, messiness, and vitality of life are frequently omitted in the drive to standardize and assess. In other words, there's what students do in school and what students do at home, and never the twain shall meet.

But, of course, the twain *should* meet—and meet in compelling ways. In an English classroom especially, we have the opportunity to routinely explore how the school subject and the outside world intersect, in the process, treating the curriculum as a vast web with innumerable valuable connections to be made between the curriculum, the students, and the world in which they spend most of their time. Teachers who adopt this perspective necessarily have to take their students' interests, backgrounds, and existing literacy practices into account. After all, if you don't know who your students *are*, how do you make those important connections? The next logical step, once you know your curriculum and your students, is to consider how they intersect in the real world. And, if it makes good instructional sense to do *that* (and we're betting you think it does, or you wouldn't have read this far), it stands to reason that we make place-based writing an integral component of our teaching.

While research about the various strands of place-based writing has a rich tradition that extends from nature writing and ecocriticism (Armbruster & Wallace, 2001; Berry, 1977; Buell, 1995), to ethnographic thick descriptions (Geertz, 1973), to writing for community engagement and reclamation (Brooke, 2003; Critchfield, 1991; Robbins & Dyer, 2005; Theobald, 1997), to a synthesis of place and critical pedagogy (Gruenewald, 2003), for our purposes, it's Sobel's (2004) definition of place-based education that seems most useful: "the process of using the local community and environment as a starting point to teach concepts in language arts" (p. 7). Relying on such a simple definition shouldn't imply that there isn't room for other, more complex views of place-based writing. For example, just because we aren't granting centrality to Theobald's (1997) theory of intradependence[3] doesn't mean we're discounting it. Rather, the very idea of place-based writing is so fundamentally basic that it can encompass a wide range of purposes and perspectives, all dependent on an individual teacher's aims.

The malleability of place-based writing makes a good deal of sense when you consider the concept of "place" is itself rather slippery. Cresswell (2015) defines *place* as "a meaningful location" (p. 12), but he also points out that its ubiquity—references to place are everywhere, and we often refer to place without consciously realizing we're doing so—makes it both simple and complicated. We inherently know what place means, but it can mean so many different things. "Place" can reflect geography (where we live, work, or vacation), social hierarchy ("the right side of the tracks"; uptown vs. downtown), community (as in a lived-in place, such as San Francisco's Chinatown, or a meeting place like a church), history (your college dorm room or the first house you owned), and so on, but this connotative flexibility can actually work to a teacher's advantage. "Place," as an idea, has a variety of functions, so it stands to reason that a teacher can choose to take it up in a variety of ways.

But, before moving into the specifics of place-based writing, it might be helpful to clarify what Cresswell means by "a meaningful location," a definition that certainly informs the way we think about place in the context of writing. Agnew (1987) pinpoints three crucial aspects that, for want of a better expression, makes a place *a place*. The first is *location*, that is, the actual physical location of the place (e.g., a physical address or map coordinates, even if those coordinates shift, in the case of a moving ship). The second is *locale*, or all the individual features that make up a location. We live near Atlanta, but Atlanta—as a place—is made up of a variety of neighborhoods (Little Five Points, Midtown, Buckhead, Inman Park, Poncey-Highland, etc.) that, along with the features that make up each neighborhood, collectively give the city its sense of identity. And it's that sense of identity—or *sense of place*, as Agnew (1987) calls his third characteristic—that imbues individual places with the emotional attachments that make them resonate with people. It is perhaps this third characteristic that makes place so potentially meaningful for writing instruction. By situating our activities in real places, we're moving writing from the often abstract or artificial environs of the classroom into concrete locations whose particulars must be reckoned with.

Let's think about those second and third aspects of place for a moment, especially the promise they hold for bridging the rural and the urban. Place-based education was originally seen as an offshoot of outdoor or environmental education (Woodhouse & Knapp, 2000), a way in which to counteract "young people's diminished encounters with the natural world" (Smith & Sobel, 2010, p. 38). As a practice, place-based education was traditionally rooted in ecological concerns. In recent years, however, place-based education has come to be recognized as a valid way to do some of the work typically associated with critical pedagogy. That stance's connection to place-based education grows out of Freire's (1970/2000) contention that people exist "in a situation," which we can read broadly as the particular context in which each of us lives. Geography—place—is part of that situational context, and Freire sees it as incumbent upon all of us to not just "critically reflect" upon it, "but critically act upon it" (p. 109). If we take place-based education's emphasis on the natural world and transpose it into settings occupied by people, it makes sense that some of the tenets of critical pedagogy have a natural home within the broader umbrella of place-based education. We can look at an exploration of place as being especially valuable in the classroom when it comes to recognizing injustice and inequity, identifying power structures that oppress marginalized populations, and "nam[ing] and recover[ing] those aspects of community life that truly contribute to the well-being of all people and the places they inhabit" (Gruenewald, 2003, p. 10). Similarly, Owens (2001) sees a discussion of place as being critical for promoting a philosophy of sustainability, or "meeting today's needs without jeopardizing the well-being of future generations" (p. 1). He proposes one distinct way to promote this thinking:

> Creating a space where students write and share stories about where they live, a space where they might come to see ways in which their needs and desires reflect the conditions of those communities, and, hopefully, begin to see their local environments not as separate incidental landscapes but as extensions of themselves. (p. 75)

By helping students discover "the kind of self-worth that comes from being amazed at one's local worlds" (p. 69), Owens believes we can help students see the value in preserving environments that are central to their identities.

This sentiment is echoed in Kinloch's (2010) work in a rapidly gentrifying Harlem neighborhood where she saw the many ways in which place—and especially, in Agnew's (1987) terms, its locale and sense of place—is inextricably linked with identity. Because "youth stories of place, belonging, struggle, culture, and identity are often devalued in schools" (Kinloch, 2010, p. 104), Kinloch argues that we need to find ways for students to engage with their home communities in the classroom in order to create counternarratives that honor their cultures and more accurately reflect their lived experiences. In short, place-based education shouldn't be seen solely as a way of connecting students with their natural environments (although that is certainly one of its most commendable goals). If we extend our definition of *place* to incorporate our human environments, too, we open up possibilities for exploring issues of justice and equality as they relate to the physical places we (and others) inhabit. Even if you don't subscribe to taking an overtly political stance in your classroom, it's worth remembering this simple equation from eco-writer Terry Tempest Williams: "place + people = politics" (2001, p. 3). If we intend to tackle place and people in our teaching, we'd also better be ready to address politics when they inevitably arise.

Before going any further, addressing an elephant in the room will help contextualize our own goals for the rest of this book. You might have noticed from the last few pages that place-based writing is often ideological in nature. Indeed, this is a subject we take up multiple times in the ensuing chapters. From promoting environmental advocacy, to tackling the fallout of gentrification, to reclaiming a sense of identity through place-based storytelling, to becoming involved in a form of participatory action research (PAR) (Dyrness, 2011), all of these approaches encourage students to become more engaged citizens. The ability to discourage passivity is one of place-based writing's greatest strengths.

But, as valuable as these approaches are, there are certain blind spots frequently omitted from the research that describes them. From a purely practical standpoint, some teachers may not have the resources or the administrative support to facilitate activities encouraging environmental stewardship or community engagement. For instance, we have learned that teaching in the South—even just outside a major metropolitan area—often means teaching on eggshells. The slightest whiff of "agenda pushing" can result in parent phone calls and visits to administration. Similarly, in a data-driven educational climate such as the one in which we're all currently living, administration can be loath to part with financial resources to embark on a writing assignment that may not obviously seem to translate into higher test scores. The unfortunate truth is that not all schools, not all teachers, and not all students have the resources or opportunities for place-based community engagement or environmental advocacy.

However, while place-based writing has traditionally been treated as primarily ideological in nature, *it doesn't have to be*. If your teaching situation allows you to take on an ideological project, like the "Wild Places" assignment we describe in Chapter 6, that's great. If, on the other hand, the primary benefit of place-based writing for you is to use it to teach craft lessons (such as Chapter 5's extended narrative assignment), that experience will be no less valuable for your students. The danger in pitching an instructional approach as mainly valuable for ideological means is that, in doing so, we immediately overlook its other possible benefits. What we're trying to do with this book is bridge the gap between the ideological and what we might call the more traditionally academic. And to say, in effect, you can have it all.

For one teacher, place-based writing was the ideal avenue for students to research their communities and produce public service announcements that drew attention to issues of local interest, in the process helping students to "realize their ability to make a difference, however small, and achieve specific goals in writing" (Esposito, 2012, p. 76). For another teacher, however, tenth-grade students conducted research at a cemetery near their school to get a better sense of local history and "discover . . . things about one another and [their] community that [they had] never known before" (Walker, 2005, p. 82). The former project would likely be said to be the more ideological of the two (focusing as it did on local issues and the creation of public service announcements), but the cemetery visit could have had just as much impact on students in the way it encouraged them to conduct authentic research about local history. Whether the goals are modest or extravagant, there is almost certainly a place-based activity that can be designed to meet them.

This malleability also underscores one of the other potential pitfalls in taking a purely ideological approach. No matter what you're doing with place-based writing, assignment design and instructional objectives matter. While, in our experience, it's true that place-based writing is a more immediately engaging form of writing, we can't (and shouldn't) fall back on engagement as the end goal and simply trust our students to meet some ill-defined objectives that deal vaguely with "writing outdoors." As with any other work we ask our students to complete, we need to be honest with ourselves in terms of the specific goals we want to meet through the act of writing outdoors. What are the skills or knowledge we want our students to come away with? How do we know the writing we're asking our students to complete will accurately gauge their learning? And how do we teach those skills or that knowledge in between the date we introduce the assignment and the date our students submit it? This might seem like (and probably is) Teacher Education 101. We mention it here anyway so that you enter into place-based writing from a place of thoughtfulness, but also to further bolster place-based writing's viability as an instructional approach. You might encounter the attitude from some who haven't tried it that place-based writing is merely fun time, with no more academic value than reading a book on the lawn.[4] However, whether you're designing an assignment that encourages students to promote change in their communities or taking them on a tour of the school to help them use descriptive language more vividly, you should always think clearly and specifically about your goals and how you're going to support your students in meeting them. Simply going outside isn't enough of an objective.

We should talk about one more potential instructional hurdle. The tricky thing about place-based writing is that, like our earlier discussion about authenticity, just because an activity *looks* like place-based writing—and might even meet the official definition of it—that doesn't mean it's accomplishing all it could. Think back to Whitney's (2011) example of the student-created colonial newspaper. As an assignment, it's certainly more authentic than merely asking students to fill in a template with the components of a newspaper article, but it's not the *most* authentic method of engaging students with news writing. In the same way, if you take your students outside to compile a list of sensory images that they'll then use to write a descriptive paragraph of at least one hundred words that contains a topic sentence and uses at least five images from their list, you're technically engaging them in place-based writing. You got your students out of the classroom, and, by asking them to engage with the natural world, they're certainly doing something more authentic than sitting in class and just imagining what it's like outside that day. As an assessment, it also gives you some indication of how well your students can write descriptively, as well as the degree to which the class as a whole understands topic sentences. The activity's constraints (the length, the form, the number of words), however, limit the benefits students might otherwise gain from an assignment that starts with the same premise—generating descriptive words and phrases from their own observation—but offers them more flexibility in the execution (such as writing a story, poem, or script).

In case it isn't obvious, we wrestled at length with the question, "What makes place-based writing what it is?" In order to foreground the chapters that follow, we wanted to generate a list of traits you could use to determine if you were, in fact, engaging your students with place-based writing in the ways we describe. But every time we sat down to create the list, we realized there *was* no list. The truth is, the sole hallmark of place-based writing is only that the act of writing originates outside the classroom. That's it. Are your students outdoors[5] writing *about* the outdoors or *inspired by* the outdoors? If so, congratulations. They're doing place-based writing.

In the process of trying to generate this list, we realized we were overcomplicating a practice that is, at its core, a model of simplicity. As we created and discarded possible criteria for the list-that-was-never-to-be, we realized instead that it was perhaps more helpful to think not about what place-based writing is, but what it *can be*. The more useful conversation (at least as we see it) deals with place-based writing's nuances, those *can be*s that determine its potential for students. So, this won't be a list that defines place-based writing (remembering that we're using Sobel's [2004] earlier definition as our foundation) as much as it establishes place-based writing's possible curricular benefits. These benefits are not unique to place-based writing; after all, thoughtfully designed writing activities that take place entirely in the classroom can also embody some or all of these characteristics. But what *is* unique to place-based writing is the way in which it requires students to experience—and grapple with—the world firsthand, in the moment, lending it a degree of authenticity that more classroom-bound forms of writing will find hard to match.

The Potential of Place-Based Writing

In the chapters that follow, we use the following five characteristics to ground our discussion about how you can use place-based writing in a variety of contexts to meet a variety of educational needs.

Place-Based Writing Can Be Personal (and Purposeful)

In the same way that our interaction with a written text will depend on the prior knowledge and experiences we bring to our reading (see, e.g., Probst, 2004; Purves et al., 1995; Rosenblatt, 1995), the way we interact with the world around us is a highly individual endeavor. If Amanda were to meet you at a specific place on a particular date and at a definite time, and, on that date and during that time, the two of you sat for thirty minutes and took notes of your observations, you would still have very different accounts of the experience. No two people will see and experience a location in the exact same way, even if they're sharing that space together. For that reason, it seems unfair to repeatedly ask our students to write about topics that often reflect the goals and interests of a single, external person (usually the teacher, but we can also throw test-based writing into the mix here, too).

Traditional school writing, wherein students are usually responding to a tightly constrained and defined prompt, is about as impersonal as it comes. Place-based writing, on the other hand, can allow students the opportunity to experience the world on *their* terms and report on it in ways that accurately and thoughtfully reflect that experience. As our classrooms become more and more diverse—with a wide range of backgrounds, home cultures, home languages, and learning needs increasingly becoming the norm—it is even more important that our students feel welcome to share their experiences in writing. And this isn't just a simple matter of classroom engagement. For students of color especially, it's a matter of honoring identities and communities that have traditionally been marginalized (or erased altogether) in public schools. Or, as San Pedro (2017) puts it, "validat[ing] who we are and who we are becoming" (p. 113). In this way, place-based writing aligns with Paris's (2012) tenets of culturally sustaining pedagogies, especially the notion that our instructional practices "support young people in sustaining the cultural and linguistic competence of their communities" (p. 95). If we want to look for ways that our classrooms can "center cultural, linguistic, and literate pluralism as part of schooling for racial justice and positive social transformation" (Paris & Alim, 2017, p. 13), it is essential that we look for ways in which those local communities, cultures, and languages can be celebrated in the writing we ask our students to complete. One way we can accomplish this for all our students is by moving the act of writing outside the classroom and *into the communities themselves*, providing our students with an opportunity to write about something that matters to them as well as make sense of themselves and the world around them.

Encouraging students to explore personally meaningful topics in this way can obviously increase the level of buy-in they bring to an assignment. Such validation of their ideas can also have a cumulative effect on the writing community you're fostering in your classroom. How often do students feel like their voices are truly respected in typical classroom settings? By listening to our students and trusting them to write about what matters to them, we implicitly send the message, as Shor (1996) argues, that "they count in the rhetorical setting" (p. 49). And when students feel they count, they immediately become "stakeholders in and creators of the learning process" (p. 49). Or, put another way: "By sharing authority . . . students take greater responsibility for their educations, which can translate into a more intense relationship between them and the learning process" (p. 199). Such a shift in student empowerment increases the likelihood that they will feel they have something worth writing about in the future, which can also translate into a greater willingness to write both inside and *outside* the school setting.

Shor's (1996) approach is starkly different from the traditional approach to writing, where it is almost exclusively the teacher who defines the terms and boundaries of each assignment. But, if we allow (or even encourage) students to have personal reactions to, or interpretations of, a variety of real-world settings, it is likely that their writing will be more purposeful than merely fulfilling certain assignment expectations to receive a particular grade.

Place-Based Writing Can Be Agentive

While we in no way would argue that students shouldn't be taught traditional written genres, one of the weaknesses of a traditional writing curriculum—especially one that adheres to strict formulas—is the lack of ownership it allows students to have. Put simply, writing authentically means making choices. These choices have to do with obvious things, like word use and sentence structure, but they also have to do with voice and style, and ensuring that the selected voice and style match the audience for which the author is writing. The success of the piece will often live and die by these choices. When students find themselves in a class where they are primarily writing a series of essays that no one but the teacher (or maybe one or two other students) sees, they're being deprived of the chance to view how writing works in the world outside the classroom. Because, let's face it, there isn't usually much decision-making in writing the traditional essay. The topic is usually tightly constrained and so is the form. The audience is nearly always the teacher, the purpose is, presumably, to get a good grade, and those two factors mean the voice and style are also predetermined.

Place-based writing, by contrast, can allow students to take ownership of their own writing. A necessary caveat to this trait (and all the traits, really) is that students have to be allowed a degree of flexibility in approaching their work. In the example we used earlier—generating imagery and writing a short, clearly defined paragraph using a specific number of words—students wouldn't have much ownership, even if the activity itself could still be characterized as place-based writing. But, if the students went outside, generated a list of sensory words, and were then asked to capture that experience in an original piece of writing with no limitation on form, they suddenly have ownership of their work. A descriptive narrative is acceptable, but so is a poem. Or a brief skit about two bickering gardeners. Or a letter to the editor arguing for the preservation of natural spaces. Or a reflective piece written from the perspective of a cloud. And *that* choice then engenders a range of other choices as the students write in their selected genres. There are certainly complicated issues to take into account here that you wouldn't have to consider when assigning the short paragraph, but the trade-off is that, with repeated opportunities of this sort, your students will more likely come to understand just how important it is to take ownership of their writing. That trait is essential if we want them to value writing even after they've moved beyond our classes.

Place-Based Writing Can Be Engaging

This isn't to say that traditional essays can't also be engaging. In one of her first college literature classes, Amanda was required to research the life of Toni Morrison and connect some aspect of her findings to her reading of *The Bluest Eye* (1970). The richness of Morrison's life and the complexity of that particular novel gave Amanda plenty of avenues from which to choose, and, as someone already interested in teaching, she was immediately drawn to the pervasive effect of internalized racism on young children. It was a traditional paper, but the latitude Amanda was granted by her instructor made all the difference. This underscores the point that, given the right topic, *any* kind of writing can be engaging.

The problem, of course, is that, for many of our students, the "right" writing never arrives because it's almost always constrained by the teacher. Even in a research paper about a controversial issue, that old standby in which students have a degree of freedom to research an issue of personal interest, the writing itself is rarely engaging because students are usually tied by the assignment sheet and rubric to a traditional written genre and set of arcane requirements that hijack any interest they might be able to muster about their topic. This isn't to say there isn't a time and place for teaching students about the fundamental aspects of different written genres. In many cases, we'd be negligent if we *didn't* teach them what makes a good newspaper article, book review, or haiku. But, if we're primarily after evidence that our students can do a certain kind of thinking or demonstrate a particular rhetorical skill, is it always necessary to default to the traditional essay when there are so many other engaging forms of writing available to them?

Place-based writing opens up the possibility for students to write descriptively, craft arguments, and conduct authentic research—among many other possible writing tasks—in a variety of real-world contexts. For instance, the compare–contrast essay is, like the traditional research paper, one of those hoary school genres with which all teachers (your authors included) have periodically engaged. What we're assessing with that assignment, however, isn't actually the students' ability to write an essay; we're assessing their ability to compare and contrast two things. So, if that's what we're truly interested in seeing—our students' ability to make connections and draw contrasts—aren't there genres other than the essay through which students can demonstrate it? And can't we create opportunities for students to write in those genres in real-world settings, where we compare and contrast things on a daily basis? In Chapter 2, as part of two case studies that have grown out of the work she has done with place-based writing in her own fourth-grade classroom, Amanda explains just such an assignment, in which her students were asked to contrast a single location from the perspective of two different time periods. For her students, this activity, through which they had an opportunity to actually explore the location about which they were writing, had more student engagement and buy-in than her previous attempts at more conventional compare-and-contrast writing. In our experience, an increased level of engagement can be the norm in a classroom where place-based writing is part of the teacher's repertoire.

Place-Based Writing Can Be Audience Oriented

By now, you probably see where we're going with this. Virtually all the characteristics of authentic writing we discussed earlier can also apply to place-based writing, and this is certainly true of its ability to provide students with the opportunity to write for an outside audience. Again, place-based writing isn't unique in this trait, but, because students are writing in the world outside the classroom, it makes sense that they would also have the opportunity to write for audiences outside the classroom. As we have mentioned already, much traditional school writing is completed for an audience of one: the teacher. The result, in our experience, for many students is the sense that there isn't much at stake in these assignments. Beyond simply writing for a grade, which isn't motivational for some students, the lack of an authentic audience means the piece of writing is often simply a recitation for someone who already knows all the answers. It's the literary analysis paper written in response to a prompt that hundreds of students have addressed previously, or the essay arguing for a change in school policy that never goes further than the teacher's desk. These are extreme examples, but they're a common type of writing that could be subverted in cases where the teacher actively looks to take students outside the classroom to write.

For example, writing logical arguments can readily be moved outside the classroom, and teachers can leverage students' interest even further by incorporating the use of written scenarios. Rather than simply asking students to argue against a school policy they would like to change (an exercise that often sees students simply reinforcing their own thinking rather than following a logical train of thought), we can present students with a scenario that requires students to "grapple with the kind of problems that resonate with them" and "immerse them in the process of drawing conclusions, supporting those conclusions for a skeptical audience, and assessing the merits of competing points of view" (McCann, 2010, p. 34). Of particular recent interest for many students in our classes was the founding of LeBron James's I Promise School, which guarantees, among other things, free college tuition for students who complete the school program and graduate from high school. Teachers could mimic this real-life situation by crafting a scenario in which a billionaire with an interest in the preservation of natural space (think Bill Gates or Warren Buffett) has announced a contest to build a new school adhering to certain environmentally friendly policies. The catch? The students, in collaborative teams, have to "pitch" the school design to the philanthropist, arguing for its sustainability in the hope that their plan would be the one selected. Teachers could use an open space near the school to situate the scenario and provide the students with a real location in which to ground their writing. To incorporate an authentic audience, the teacher could play the role of the philanthropist but could also ask community members (possibly someone with a science background or a local artist) to make up a panel that reviews all the proposals. There are even opportunities for an English teacher to team with a science teacher to talk about conservation, thereby ensuring the students have "access to the information that will help them to think about the problem" (McCann, 2010, p. 35). Such an activity would upend the traditional writing prompt and encourage students to think in new ways about what makes a good school—and, in the process, they would also learn something about the responsible stewardship of natural spaces (Jacobs, 2011).

Place-Based Writing Can Promote Change

We wanted to close out our list of criteria with the one that is the most aspirational and is therefore the most potentially transformative for students. Most school-based writing is inward looking. By that, we mean it is usually narrowly focused on objectives determined by the teacher or by some external circumstances (e.g., a district mandate to use a particular formula or a state standardized test), and it rarely asks students to meaningfully consider their place in the world and the changes they would like to make in it as they prepare for adulthood. But shouldn't we be looking for ways to help our students engage with the larger world? To recognize what's working but also diagnose its problems? And, having diagnosed those problems, to begin actively working to bring about positive change?

Traditional school writing rarely presents students with an opportunity for this kind of work, but place-based writing, implemented effectively, "helps students develop stronger ties to their community, enhances students' appreciation for the natural world, and creates a heightened commitment to serving as active, contributing citizens" (Sobel, 2004, p. 7). A place- and scenario-based writing activity such as the one we described above can help students think critically about school design, but it can also raise their awareness of what is gained and lost by building in natural spaces and what it takes to coexist in the environment without doing irreparable damage. Moving the act of writing outdoors can also cause students to take an active role in their local communities as they begin to look at their world with new eyes. Bomer (2007) refers to this process as "handover," whereby a student recognizes a problem and "without the prompting of authority . . . tries to do something about it" (p. 307). Smith and Sobel (2010) also acknowledge that, as the world becomes ever more complicated, "children now need to be educated to believe in their own ability to address local problems" (p. 40). Such a belief encourages students to see "the rich way local place creates and necessitates the meaning of individual and civic life" (Brooke, 2003, p. 10).

Teachers certainly have to look inward to address and account for the narrow objectives and mandates that are our professional responsibility. But how much more powerful would our instruction be if, in the process of looking inward, we managed to get our students to look outward and become actively and positively engaged with the world around them? As Brooke (2003) concludes:

> If education in general, and writing education in particular, is to become more relevant, to become a real force for improving the societies in which we live, then it must be more closely linked to the local, to the spheres of action and influence which most of us experience. (p. 5)

••••

Taken as a whole, then, what good is this discussion of the traits of place-based writing, other than providing you with a handy list of terminology? As we see it, knowing the traits can be useful in evaluating the place-based writing activities you create or use in your own classroom. It was initially tempting to borrow Kohnen's (2013) notion that authenticity exists on a continuum and simply graft place-based writing onto it. However, considering the number of potential moving parts we described above, it seems more helpful to think of place-based writing as a Venn diagram, with the writing activity or assignment at the center of between one and five overlapping circles. The more circles that overlap at the center, the more sophisticated a place-based writing activity it is.

As an example, consider Rob's story that opened this book. Using our framework, that activity, in which he and his tenth-grade classmates were assigned the task of silently observing the different areas of their high school and then writing an original story inspired by those observations, would look like Figure 1.1. For Rob, that particular assignment was decidedly personal and purposeful, agentive, and engaging. He took a personal interest in the story he was telling, he had ownership of what he chose to write about (and *how* he wrote about it), and, out of all the work he did as a tenth-grade English student, this was the only assignment engaging enough to remember (other than the play review, which was memorable for different, less positive reasons). His story, however, didn't have an authentic audience (it was going to be graded by Mr. Schaffer and seen by no one else), nor did it promote change. As a result, we'd consider that particular assignment to have three points of intersection. On the other hand, using the same criteria, the scenario activity we described above (wherein students propose an environmentally friendly school) would look like Figure 1.2. By incorporating an authentic audience (the review panel) and an emphasis on change (environmental sustainability), the scenario-based assignment adds the remaining two circles to the mix. This isn't to imply that activities with only two or three points of intersection are somehow not worth doing. They are. There is even a strong argument to be made for the place-based writing activity that consists of one lone circle. As an activity to start the year, for example, doing something engagingly place based that gets students excited about writing is hardly small potatoes. But, as you explore the rest of this book—and, more important, as you start to create new place-based writing opportunities of your own—you might consider these traits and the Venn diagram as a helpful way of evaluating the sophistication and authenticity of the work you're asking your students to do.

The final thing to mention about place-based writing before we turn our attention to the practical is that we recognize its use—especially its *regular* use—sounds daunting. And, in some ways, it probably does require you to reconsider some aspects of your writing instruction. After all, incorporating place-based writing isn't simply a matter of using a new formula to write about *this* when we used to use an old formula to write about *that*. It will mean creating new

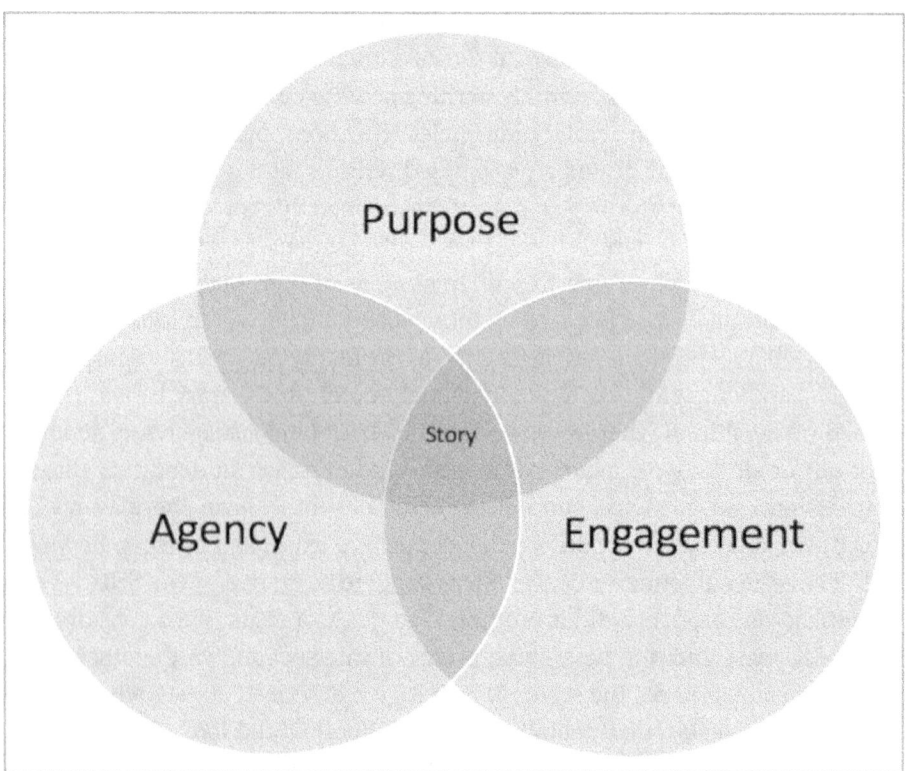

FIGURE 1.1. Venn diagram showing three benefits of place-based writing.

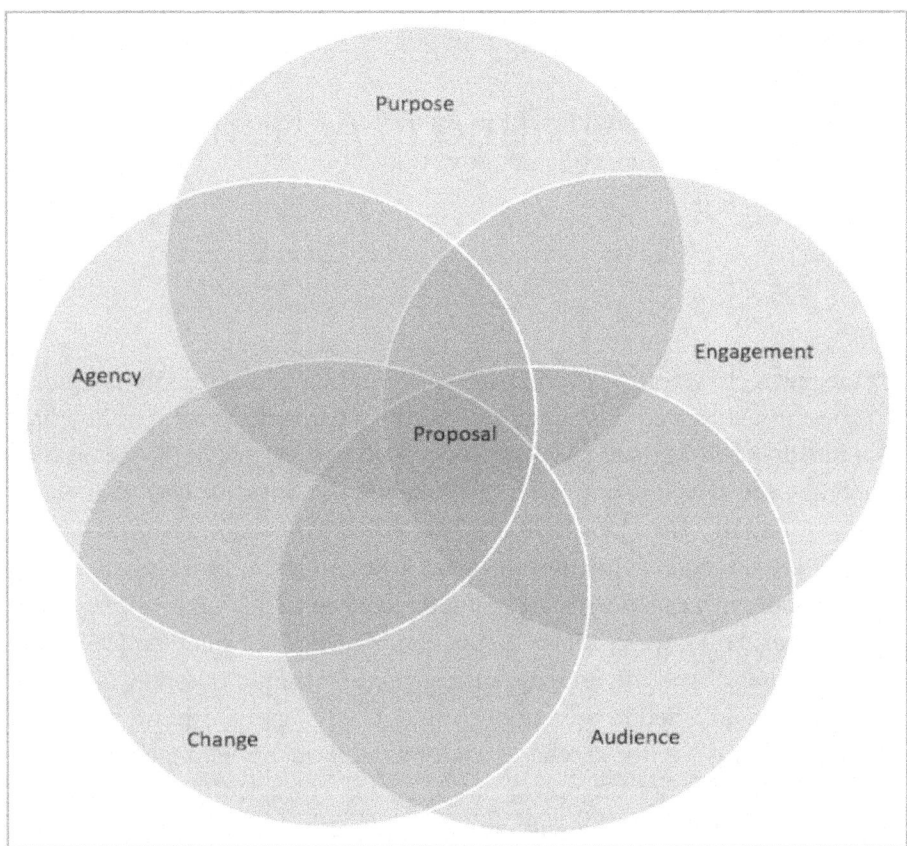

FIGURE 1.2. Venn diagram showing five benefits of place-based writing.

assignments, rethinking how and when you use peer feedback groups, evaluating your grading criteria, and so on. As Rob is fond of reminding his preservice students, "Everything you do in your classroom that's worth doing takes time." This certainly applies to place-based writing.

However, as teachers who have used, and who continue to use, a range of place-based writing activities with our students, we find the possibilities inherent in the form to be part of the fun: the consideration of what we're teaching, the goals we hope our students will meet, the possible locations we could take them. And, of course, the writing itself. Often messy, often raw, often requiring some significant wrangling and revision. But the life and energy we often see in our students and their writing when they are given an opportunity to engage with work that matters to them in a place that's real beats the relative ease of writing yet another essay. In the chapters that follow, we have tried to make assignment design as accessible as possible in the hope that you'll come to see place-based writing as a practice your classroom can no longer do without.

Place-Based Writing in Action

Imagine a classroom full of glazed-eyed children half-heartedly peering at you through tented lids as you model the day's writing activity. You hear more than a few groans as you finish explaining the goal for the lesson, and, as soon as you send them off to write, hands fly into the air with that oh-so-familiar question, "How long does this have to be?" This question is disheartening both in its predictability and for what it represents. A preoccupation with length usually means students are primarily concerned with meeting the (possibly arbitrary) rules we've set for them rather than engaging authentically with the writing task. And, on an existential level, this simple question can mean we've once again failed to present our students with an opportunity to see the value in writing—not just in school, but for what it can bring to their lives.

At the start of my (Amanda's) career, I often struggled to get all my students to consistently engage with and become excited about writing. I heard "How long does it have to be?" *a lot*. There were always those students willing to put effort into whatever I put in front of them (which isn't, it should be noted, the same thing as being enthusiastic about the work), but, more often than not, writing time was usually met with complaints and uninterested stares. Writing was a challenge for most of the students I taught, and even the most gifted writers struggled to see how the writing I assigned connected to their lives in that moment. My students weren't engaged, they had very little agency in the assignments I gave them, and I wrestled with ways to find an outside audience for whom they could write.

This all began to change when I sat down for a meeting with our Cobb County master gardener, Michelle. We had a new principal committed to building green spaces around our school to encourage student inquiry and STEM-based learning.[1] That summer, one of our school's community partners built us an outdoor classroom, sensory garden, and compost area. Intended as a stage for outdoor learning, the classroom is a large deck built among the trees with seating areas for students. Our sensory garden was built next to the classroom and contains three planter boxes, benches, and several areas with objects for students to touch and manipulate (see Figure 2.1). Based in Pagliano's (1998) research on the benefits of multisensory environments for, among other things, the "relaxation, therapeutic, and/or educational needs of the user" (p. 107), the sensory garden at our school provides our students who are struggling with various forms of trauma a place to go when the classroom environment becomes too overwhelming. Our ultimate goal, however, was to make this an additional space for outdoor learning as well as a space for students to explore nature in our school's urban environment. The compost area connects to our garden and provides an environmentally friendly way to supply our garden with soil and nutrients.

Our principal needed a classroom teacher to take the lead on creating a program to maintain these spaces. I immediately had visions of my students writing about the plants that grew in the garden and penning poems rich with description they experienced firsthand rather than pulled from artificial lists glued into their notebooks. I saw the potential for my students to get out of the classroom and experience learning in a more organic way, so I volunteered. Little did I realize, this was my first step toward a new way of teaching writing.

Michelle and I began to formulate a plan to get students involved in caring for our new garden and compost area. Our supplies weren't plentiful; we were limited to items donated by our parent organization and local businesses. We had a few native plants that had begun to grow: mint, rosemary, lemongrass, and lamb's ears. A crafty parent built us a wooden compost pile, and an old oil drum was fashioned into a rotating compost bin. We knew we wanted to start

FIGURE 2.1. Sensory garden.

with basic science lessons about plants, gardening, and compost, and, in the process, encourage our students to show us what they were most interested in learning. I hoped that, once my students were hooked by the natural world, they would be more willing to engage in writing about those experiences. I knew there would be a learning curve for me: I have terrible luck growing plants on my own, and the idea of getting close to a compost bin has never been at the top of my to-do list. But I knew taking the plunge myself was another step in the right direction.

The Plan: A Garden as Research Project

As a fourth-grade teacher, I find that some of the most difficult standards I am expected to teach center on reading and writing informational texts. According to the *Georgia Standards of Excellence* (Georgia Department of Education, 2015), my students must be able to demonstrate mastery of the following skills:

> ELAGSE4RI1: refer to details and examples in a text when explaining what the text says
> ELAGSE4RI3: explain events, procedures, ideas ... based on specific information in a text
> ELAGSE4RI9: integrate information from two texts on the same topic
> ELAGSE4W2: write an informational/explanatory text that includes multiple text features to aid comprehension (e.g., headings, charts, illustrations, and examples).[2]

I never felt truly successful in guiding my students to complete all of these tasks. While they could cite details and examples from a text or explain events they had read about, they struggled to understand why these skills mattered. I felt like each assignment missed opportunities for real-world application, and, subsequently, I saw these students fail to retain these skills as they moved into the upper grades.

At the same time I was struggling with these standards, I saw the obvious enthusiasm my students felt in studying science in our outdoor classroom. It was at that point I realized I could use the new outdoor setting as a springboard to involve students in real-world writing experiences, essentially combining my writing and science instruction in a way that would address those troublesome standards. By combining English and science, I could help my students see that writing is required by other subjects, and, if I introduced a research component, it would also help my students "understand how to ask those subtle underlying questions as a scientist would and how to make logical connections based on sound reasoning" (Bull & Dupuis, 2014, p. 75). With the garden as my source, I could also help my students see how writing could be engaging and personal as well as how they could take ownership of it by writing for a specific audience.

Before I describe the lessons themselves, I should first mention that, in the appendix of this book, you can find abbreviated lesson plans for the project as well as the scoring guide I used to assess my students' final products. Please remember that these plans were developed for my own student population; if you want to use these for your own classroom, some modification will be necessary to fit your individual goals and situation.

At the very beginning of this plan, I wanted to investigate what my students already knew about composting and gardening and to discover what they were most interested in learning. This project had to be personal so that students would feel an investment in the final product. I was surprised to learn, from our first trip to the garden, that many of my students had small gardens at home and enjoyed helping their families tend them. As we set off into the garden on our first day as Earth Ambassadors (the name we chose for this new program), I gave each student a sheet consisting of two columns labeled "What I Know" and "What I Wonder." Modeled on the K–W–L (i.e., **k**now, **w**ant to know, **l**earned) chart (Ogle, 1986), this instructional reading strategy commonly used to guide students through a text could also be used in this instance to gauge my students' prior knowledge of gardening and to focus their research by giving them an opportunity to explore what they wanted to learn next.

I was amazed to see my students knew far more than I previously thought they did. James[3] recognized that "some plants have a smell and some don't," while Diana was able to go one step further and identify plants based on their smell, recognizing one of them as mint. Some of my students' other observations included:

"I know that [plants] need good dirt to grow."
"I know that we eat some of the plants but others will make us sick."
"I know that lemon balm is used in tea."

As a class, we discussed this preexisting knowledge and created a list of these gardening facts to help with our subsequent research. My students were immediately engaged in the brainstorming because they could pull directly from the sights, sounds, and smells we had just encountered. Maybe more important, the fact that they were able to draw on their own knowledge and experience gave them a sense of expertise and empowerment that was new and exciting.

This discussion about what they already knew about gardening also revealed gaps in their knowledge. For instance, the class discovered that they knew very little about composting and, as a result, much of what they wondered centered around that aspect of the outdoor space. These questions ranged from Maria's simple query as to the purpose of the composting crates to the following pointed question from Zaccheus: "I wonder why there are more bugs in the bin then [sic] in the garden and if they will hurt me?" Once again, the class met together in a group and compiled their wonderings into a list of questions they thought were the most important to answer. To help my students make decisions about which questions were most important—as well as to teach some low-level argumentation in the process—I asked them to present their questions and explain why we should choose them for further exploration. After generating this prioritized list, we hung it in the classroom as a way to guide our research, and it eventually served as the basis for our final product's table of contents (see Figure 2.2).

Table of Contents

What is Composting?	1
Why is Composting Important?	3
What Goes Into Creating Compost?	4
What is Compost Used For?	6
Materials Needed to Start a School Compost Heap	8
Criteria for Becoming an Earth Ambassador	10
Steps in Cafeteria Composting	12
Tour of the Bins	14
Glossary	16
About Mrs. Montgomery's 4th Grade Class	17

FIGURE 2.2. Class-created questions eventually became the basis for our collaborative book's table of contents.

Promoting Engagement, Purpose, and Agency

Because I didn't want my students to see this project as simply something else a teacher was making them do, my next step was to distance myself from the process and allow them to take greater ownership of their learning. This was a scary leap. I was used to my students needing continual guidance in their writing, but now I told them, as they were Earth Ambassadors, it was up to them to decide what information needed to be researched, as well as how they would ultimately communicate it to other students in the school. Knowing that peer-to-peer presentation would be beneficial for my students' emergent public speaking skills, I had originally envisioned them going into classes to give a simple presentation about how to use the garden and compost area. But I also knew that this type of presentation was not always particularly engaging for either speaker or listener. In the end, I left it up to my students to decide what form the final product would take, because this was, after all, their audience, and they had a responsibility to teach them about our garden and composting area.

As nervous as I was about ceding ownership to my students, the potentially messy nature of this project actually encouraged my students to take on an inquiry stance. After all, as Ray (2006) reminds us:

> Outside of school, when faced with tasks that require composition, writers have to figure out how to write things. No one gives them a formula, and the struggle to organize and make everything work together is there anew every time. (p. 242)

Further, by giving my students more freedom to dictate the terms of the project, I was helping them consider "different alternatives for how to write something and then . . . let them do what writers really have to do—make decisions" (pp. 242–43).

My own anxiety led me to believe my students would be similarly terrified by the prospect of taking on such a big responsibility. I was wrong. The students decided that word of mouth, PowerPoint presentations, and posters weren't enough. During a classroom discussion about how to present their learning to the school, my students passionately argued against these types of projects they had completed multiple times throughout their school experience. They hungered for creativity and were motivated to make the experience enjoyable to their audience. As a group, they wanted to write a book about composting that we would put in our school's library. They were excited at the prospect of being "published" authors and were eager to begin the work.

The Research Begins

It became clear early on that, because the book was going to contain so much information, I needed to split students into groups to tackle the major topics in which they were interested. The topics for each group came from the "What I Wonder" list they created following our first outdoor visit. The class met together and we grouped similar topics and questions to form major sections of our book. For example, questions such as "I wonder what the crate is?" and "Why do we need gloves?" became a section discussing items needed in order to compost. Forming groups also allowed me to partner students who could support each other's varying learning abilities. Those students who were developing writers could become diagram artists or group photographers while students who had demonstrated a facility for grammar served as editors and proofreaders. The members had to contribute something to their sections, but they got to decide what that contribution would be (see Figure 2.3).

The next major step for the students was conducting traditional text-based research to fill in the gaps in their compositing knowledge. Students scoured our library and the online resources suggested by Michelle, the master gardener, to supply them with necessary background information. Even though each group

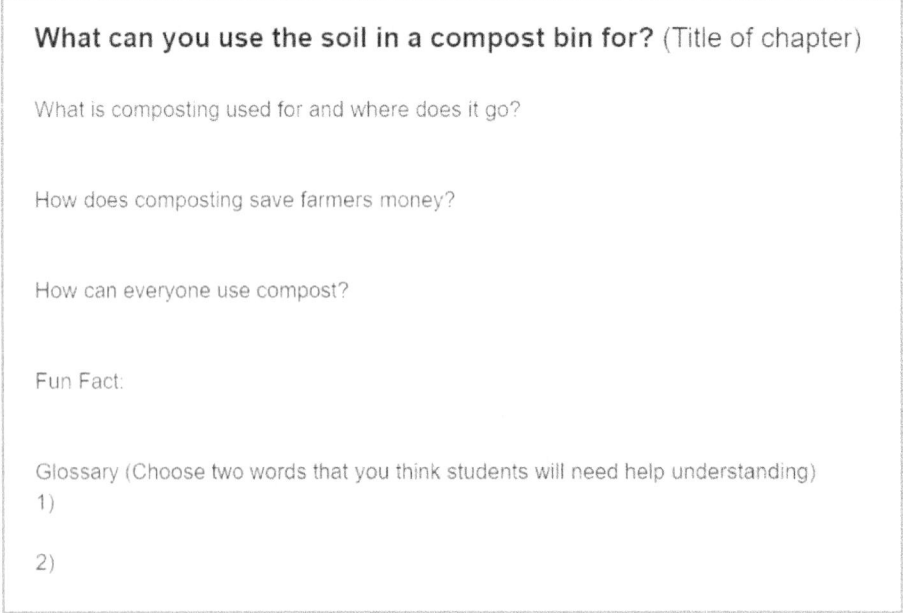

FIGURE 2.3. Example of group guiding questions put together by the teacher to help scaffold student research.

researched different questions, the garden and composting areas served as the common testing ground for all inquiry. The class went to the garden and composting bins several times throughout this project, for two key reasons: (1) to uncover new information their previous research failed to yield, and (2) to test their emerging understandings in a practical setting. For example, when one group found a source listing "good" bugs and "bad" bugs for a compost pile, they went outside to find some of those bugs in our bin. When they found a bug that wasn't originally on either list, they had to go back to their research to amend their information. Without knowing it, my students were also once again engaging in a form of argumentation, because they had to use evidence to show their answers and justify to their group why they needed to change what they had originally researched.

Students also got the opportunity to engage with experts when their initial research wasn't enough. One group struggled to understand exactly why some items went into a compost bin and others did not, so we reached out to our master gardener. She explained that, if something was once green and growing, it could go in the compost bin, but, if it had any components that were processed, it could not. She then showed students the contents of our bin and pulled decomposing materials out to show how they break down. Students were then asked to walk around the playground, examine any refuse they found, and determine if those items were decomposing. Students were able to notice that items like paper and apple cores decomposed naturally and easily, while plastics and Styrofoam didn't seem to be breaking down at all. Michelle then showed students a decomposing bug on the ground and taught them that animal waste could bring insects and bacteria into the compost bin that wouldn't be healthy. I was amazed to see my students taking an active and engaged role in their learning. They were coming to me with real struggles and embracing the need for solutions.

Putting It All Together

As the project neared completion, I asked each group to organize their information in preparation for writing their assigned chapter. I assisted each group by providing them with the guiding questions from the original class-created list. They collectively decided how those questions would be answered as well as how they would present their answers in the resulting chapter. Each member of the group had to write collaboratively to compile the research. I tracked this collaboration through daily group check-ins and individual writing conferences where I scaffolded the writing to fit the range of learners in the classroom.

With the information from each group beginning to come together, I decided to pause the writing and ask students to reflect again on what they wanted their final project to look like. We did this by taking a journey through the nonfiction texts in our library. Students spent two days perusing nonfiction texts, placing sticky notes on interesting and important features they thought would be beneficial to include in the finished book. At the end of this time, students shared with each other what they found and then decided as a class which features they most wanted to include. I simply sat back and provided them with sticky notes, research guidance, and the moral support they needed.

It was gratifying to see students illustrating diagrams of the composting cycle, taking pictures of items that could and couldn't go into a compost bin, and discussing the best way to answer their guiding questions. Underscoring Ray's (2006) contention that, by adopting an inquiry stance, "teachers let the writing itself shape and define what the content will be" (p. 243), I was surprised to discover the class had taken the initiative to create a glossary of terms for our book when they noticed other students struggling with vocabulary as they researched. The groups talked with one another about what words they were "doing" so that no words were repeated, all with very little guidance from me. This was a huge shift in my earlier attempts to get them to write about informational topics. Students often misused any text features they were asked to incorporate because they didn't see the purpose in them, but now students were engaged in their writing and understood that text features—a glossary of composting-related terms, in this case—were there to support their research and render it more accessible to their audience.

The final product was a book filled with complex information from multiple sources that included expertly used examples of various nonfiction text features (see Figure 2.4).

What Goes Into Creating Compost?

What items can you put in a compost bin?

Some items you can put in a compost bin are plain paper, cardboard, dead leaves, cabbage (not cooked), fruit peels, napkins, bell peppers, and dry grass clippings. Also these items must not contain chemicals or be processed

Items you cannot put in a compost bin?

Some items you can't put in a compost bin are onions, bread, cake, cheese, diseased plants, and yogurt. Any items with chemical or germs are bad for a compost bin. They can kill the good organisms that help to aid in the composting process.

FIGURE 2.4. Example from our *Earth Ambassadors* book.

Students were excited when we printed the books and added them to the school library. We had a book launch party in the classroom and celebrated each group's contribution to the finished product. The students also enjoyed going around to the first- and second-grade classes to share what they learned. They were able to create real change in our school by helping to educate younger students on a topic about which they previously knew little.

In the end, the biggest success I saw was how their views toward writing completely shifted. From that point forward, there were few days where writing time was greeted with a collective groan. It was far more common for me to hear my students ask, "Do we get to write outside again?"

Writing about the Past through Future Eyes

My next big place-based writing hurdle was to take students off school grounds and into the real world. Coming from a Title I school, finding the funding to go anywhere is no easy task. Applying for outside grants seemed to be one viable way of securing the necessary funding, and, in 2017, I was lucky enough to receive a small grant from the Georgia Council of Teachers of English. Now the question was, where to go?

I took a hard look at the standards and thought about the various places my community offered. I considered parks, wildlife areas, the town square, and even our local mall. It just so happens Marietta is located near Kennesaw Mountain National Battlefield Park, a sprawling wilderness area made famous by an American Civil War battle that occurred during Major General Sherman's "March to the Sea."[4] In addition to the undeniable historical value of the park, I also knew it provided us with access to local experts in the form of reenactors and park rangers. I decided this would be the ideal place to bring students for a little history and writing.

Getting Started

To start planning for these trips, I first visited the Kennesaw Mountain Battlefield on my own. I had been to the park several times before as a tourist, but looking through the lens of a teacher opened my eyes to its possibilities for writing. I knew any field trip would be conducted under tight time constraints, so I centered my research on the educational opportunities afforded by the park's visitor center. Exploring it now as a possible vehicle for place-based writing, I saw it as being an especially meaningful way for my students to reflect on the difference between firsthand and historical accounts of the Civil War.

At the same time, I didn't want to neglect the mountain itself. Critical to the South's advantage during the battle, I considered how actually viewing the battlefield could help students understand its impact on the eventual outcome of the skirmish. Reading the information available in the visitor center's museum, I was intrigued by what I learned about child soldiers and saw this as a way to help forge personal connections between my students and historical events that could seem too distant to be relevant to them. Finally, a ranger pointed me toward several paintings depicting key moments in the battle. Upon seeing many familiar details in each of them—details that students would recognize from their battlefield visit as well as from my classroom instruction—I realized these paintings could effectively serve as a bridge between the museum's written descriptions and the park's natural setting, in essence helping my students visualize the battle fought there over 150 years previously.

I took all the information I received from my solo trip and worked with a park ranger to put together some different writing prompts asking students to look at the paintings and reflect on what the soldiers in them might be feeling in the moment. I also asked students to pull details from one of the paintings to use in a narrative that described that moment in time.

The Trips

Thanks to the Georgia Council of Teachers of English grant, I could afford two trips to Kennesaw Mountain. During the first trip to the park, students participated in several hands-on activities with the park rangers. These lessons ranged from a demonstration of wartime transportation to a chance to try on Civil War–era clothing and imagine what it would have been like to be a soldier at that time. Students then went into the visitor center to view the paintings I identified during my previous trip. As the students viewed each painting, they responded to the questions created by the park ranger and me. Grounded in the writing of Chandler (2002), Elkins (2008), and Crovitz and Montgomery (2015), I wanted my students to "read" the paintings as visual texts, looking closely and carefully at each to extend their inquiry and reflect on the artworks' inclusion in the museum. This kind of work can help even younger students take tentative steps toward "articulat[ing] possible meanings, rhetorical impact, context, and implication" of visual texts (Crovitz & Montgomery, 2015, p. 15). Because students are bombarded with visual images each day, an ability to read those images can help them more critically navigate the world in which they live.

In addition to these activities, my students were allowed to answer any (or all) of the provided questions, and they were invited to write on a topic of their own choosing inspired by the paintings. They were also encouraged to take their writing (and a miniature reproduction of their chosen painting) outside so they could have the "real" mountain in front of them as they worked. All these activities were designed to help facilitate the students' engagement with and eventual ownership of the work they would complete after visiting the park a second time.

During the second trip to Kennesaw Mountain, my students again participated in hands-on lessons designed by the park rangers, this time focusing on child soldiers during the Civil War and what life as a child was like in the 1860s in the United States. Students read an excerpt from Katie Marsico's (2018) *Johnny Clem's Civil War Story*, an historical fiction book about a child soldier's experiences during the war. At a particularly suspenseful point in the story, my students were asked to predict what they thought would happen, based on their understanding of the life of a child soldier. They then read an informational piece on Johnny's life and compared their lives to his using the Venn diagram in Figure 2.5. The realization that children could be soldiers was an eye-opener for my students, and their imaginative story endings reflected the engagement they took in the topic.

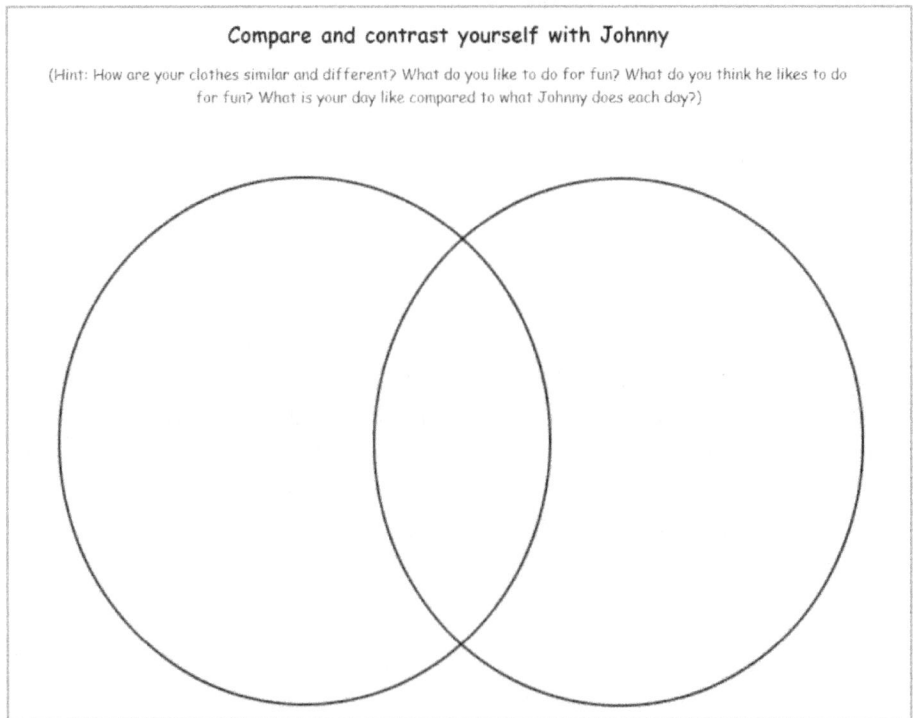

FIGURE 2.5. Venn diagram used to help students make connections between text and self.

After returning to school, students chose one piece of writing started at the battlefield to expand into a longer piece. Some students chose to write poems about one of the paintings they saw, while others wrote detailed narratives about what they would have experienced as a Civil War soldier. One student even researched what life was like as an African American soldier because he felt he didn't see enough information on that topic at the visitor center. Regardless of the individual approach, my students' work demonstrated key benefits of place-based writing. The firsthand experience they gained at the park lent their writing engagement and purpose, and, because they had agency over their final product, my students were able to take ownership of how they demonstrated their learning.

Conclusion and Next Steps

In the five years I've used place-based writing in my classroom, I've witnessed firsthand the degree to which it can transform the way students see their own writing. After completing a single place-based writing activity, students beg to go back outside to write. They begin to see that "good" writing considers audience and purpose, and they start to see how taking ownership of their writing can position them as agents of change in their own school—and, with practice (and a little luck), they can eventually effect similar change in their communities.

As we continue to mention throughout this book, not every place-based writing activity has to be a complicated, elaborate task. Simply taking my students to the cafeteria to brainstorm words we could use to describe our favorite foods has its benefits in the development of their writing lives. There can be something undeniably magical and inherently engaging about writing in a place you haven't written before. In the end, I learned that place-based writing was one solution I could use to help my students overcome the hurdles they often encountered in my writing classroom. These places allowed my students to have new experiences, make connections to their background knowledge, consider the audience for whom they were writing, and take ownership of their work. It showed them a purpose for writing and gave them hope for what their writing could be.

Writing in School Places

But First, a Note about the Flexibility of Place-Based Writing

Most of the rest of this book consists primarily of descriptions of practical lesson ideas, including the instructional context in which they can be used. One thing you will probably notice is that some of these ideas can, with little modification, be used in other places or with different genres of writing. For example, the series of lessons we describe in this chapter (an ethnographic thick description focused on various school cultures) could be modified to allow students to observe and describe other types of cultures in nonacademic public places (e.g., bowling alley culture, skate park culture, coffee shop culture, etc.). Similarly, instead of writing a thick description, which, as we explain below, involves a mix of description and interpretation, students could simply write a narrative that infuses details from their observation of a school culture (similar to the story about Rob's tenth-grade class that opened this book). As we mentioned earlier, place-based writing is malleable, and one of the things we find so exciting is that any of the ideas we share in the following chapters could be further modified to meet a range of instructional purposes.

Is there a "best way" to read the chapters that follow? Not really, except that you should do so with your own teaching context in mind. The first main section in each chapter—"Extended Lesson Idea"—presents a place-based writing activity that will, by necessity, involve multiple days of instruction. The activities described in the other, more genre-specific sections are relatively self-contained and can often be conducted in a day or two. But again, these descriptions shouldn't be taken as the definitive way to teach these lessons. Please adapt and modify as needed for your own students. On that point, it is also worth noting that in none of these descriptions do we prescribe *how* to teach anything. As you know, those individual instructional choices are a personal thing, often rooted in your own voice and personality as well as the classroom community you've created. To that end, we share with you some broad lesson ideas but leave it up to you to consider what daily implementation will look like.

The same is true of assessment. In some of these activities, a traditional written product will be a logical and natural means by which to gauge your students' learning. But, in many cases, we encourage you to consider products that involve writing but that aren't strictly *written products* in the conventional sense. Research projects are one place where this particular approach could be useful. Growing out of her work with immigrant mothers in Oakland, California, Dyrness (2011) describes participatory action research (PAR) as involving "the participation of nonexpert, less powerful people as researchers, and a focus on everyday life as the starting point for all research and action for change" (p. 204). That study, focusing on the mothers' efforts to create smaller schools for their children, culminated in research presentations for education stakeholders (including teachers and administrators) with the express purpose of effecting change in Oakland's schools. We hope you hear an echo of Chapter 1's place-based writing discussion in that description. That group's research was personal, organic, and local, and it manifested itself in a final product designed to be heard by an authentic audience. Isn't that what we would all ultimately like to see in our students' research?

If you find yourself nodding along but are worried about the likelihood of actually being able to teach a version of PAR, rest assured there's precedent for this kind of work with adolescents. Similar to PAR as it is described above, *youth participatory action research* (YPAR) "carves a space for community members to share experiential knowledge, conduct research on their own experiences, and act as agents of change in issues that impact them directly" (Bautista et al., 2013, p. 4). While YPAR often trains its focus on issues of educational injustice (Cammarota & Fine, 2008; Duncan-Andrade & Morrell, 2008), a more generalized approach can also serve a crucial purpose for our discussion of place-based writing, in the way YPAR encourages students to create nontraditional products "that are just as powerful, if not more effective, in soliciting dialogue and action within the community" (Bautista et al., 2013, p. 20).

Even in activities that may not be based in research, we believe students should have opportunities to situate their learning in real-world settings and create personally relevant products for authentic audiences. For that reason, you will see many instances where we recommend allowing students to create formal presentations, film and video products, pop-up museums, photo essays, grant proposals, and other work that has a real or implied audience other than the teacher. Shipka (2005) describes these kinds of products as being "at once *more and other than* writing" (p. 300, emphasis in the original). In the process of their creation:

> ...questions associated with materiality and the delivery, reception, and circulation of texts, objects, and events are no longer viewed as separate from or incidental to the means and methods of production, but as integral parts of invention and production processes. (p. 301)

In short, by adding layers of sophistication to the products students can create, we also ask them to make authentic, agentive decisions about what purpose the products serve, who gets to see them, and what form will be most effective for that audience and purpose. In all these possible products, "the possibilities for change come not from how research is conducted but from how it is used" (Dyrness, 2011, p. 203). We urge you to think carefully about the ways in which you can allow your students to use their writing for a purpose greater than receiving a grade.

At the end of each activity, we also explore how the lesson could be modified or adapted for different purposes. The first step is to identify which of our five intended benefits of place-based writing the lesson meets in its current description—that is, whether it is personal, agentive, engaging, audience oriented, or promotes change. We then offer, where applicable, ways to leverage other benefits. For example, with slight adjustments, some activities can be directed to an authentic audience and others can be used to promote change. Also, because we regret our own experiences with what Seale (2014) refers to as "teacher island years: those alienated years, surrounded by teachers in a variety of disciplines, going it alone" (p. 12), we also address ways that certain activities can incorporate interdisciplinary connections (just be sure to discuss it with your colleague first!). And, considering the variety of learning needs present in each classroom, at the end of each chapter we have also identified some modifications for students who need extra help or students who are learning English as a second language.

Finally, in Chapters 3 to 7, we begin each genre-specific section with a brief explanation describing how and why this type of place can be useful for meeting your curricular goals for that genre. This might help you clarify your own thinking about place-based writing, but it could also be helpful in crafting a rationale to convince an administrator that place-based writing is worth doing.

Writing in (or near) School Locations

In the last few years, we've shared our ideas on place-based writing with more than one hundred practicing and preservice teachers, in classrooms, at conferences, and as part of the Summer Institute of the Kennesaw Mountain Writing

Project. "This sounds awesome!" is what we hear initially—followed almost immediately with some qualifications like "But it's so expensive," "Our school doesn't do field trips," or "I'd never trust my kids to behave in public." The enthusiasm some teachers automatically feel for the idea of taking their students out of the classroom is immediately tempered by the challenges they fear.

This makes sense. Schools often place restrictions (sometimes unreasonably) on student travel—the cost may be prohibitive, or the hoops through which teachers have to jump are discouraging, or the slim availability of school buses narrows the scope of the off-site experience so much that it almost doesn't seem worth the effort. And, as much as we wish we didn't understand these teachers' third concern—that of trusting their students—we *do* know from experience that getting some students to fully engage in anything we want them to do is often a big ask. In that regard, place-based writing is potentially a huge belly flop into choppy waters.

To allay some of those concerns (especially since we're sure they're shared by many reading this book now), we want to start small, by thinking of the school building or campus as a productive location on its own terms. There are absolutely worthwhile activities that can be structured for students without ever leaving the school grounds, and these can even be viewed as possible trial balloons—either for yourself (evaluating the success of place-based writing for your own instruction) or for administration (who want to see what a version of place-based writing looks like in practice before they shell out for buses and subs).

Also, while there are obvious practical benefits to treating school as a place that can generate valuable writing, it's sometimes easy to miss the obvious: school *is* a place, and it's a place where students spend much of their time. Not only that, it's a place students are likely to have strong feelings about—whether positive or negative—and strong feelings, as we know, often lead to powerful writing. The tendency, however, often seems to be to disqualify school as a valid location. Because we view the classroom space as inauthentic for writing (for all the reasons we identified in Chapter 1), we often mistakenly extend this inauthenticity to the school site as a whole. But, if we take a step back and reflect on those non-classroom spaces—the gym, the cafeteria, the courtyard, the library, and so on—we can start to see each school as a collection of individual spaces that can be generative for writing. This can be true, too, of classrooms that fall outside the core subject areas. The band room, the art room, the theater—these often contain well-established cultures and norms that add to the richness of the school site as a whole. Additionally, students are deft at repurposing liminal spaces on the school grounds—hallways, stairwells, parking lots, doorways, and the like—into specific places with designated uses very different from what was originally intended. When Rob was a high school student, the hallway outside the band room was transformed into a traditional lunchtime meeting place, and there was a particularly isolated stairwell where more than one pair of amorous students was known to sneak in a little canoodling. All to say, the school should be considered a place rich with possibilities for authentic writing. Moving students out of the relative sterility of the classroom and into the vibrancy of the larger school community is a natural first step for teachers interested in trying place-based writing as well as for those teachers experienced with place-based writing who want to incorporate it in a comparatively simple way.

Extended Lesson Idea: Ethnographic Thick Description

The research paper assignment presents problems for many teachers. There's a legitimate belief that students need to know how to conduct and present research, but the complexity of the task is a pedagogical minefield, starting with the design of the assignment itself. Are students being allowed to research something that matters to them? Are they engaging in research in a way that resembles how it looks in life outside the classroom? Are they being supported in researching a specific line of inquiry instead of a general topic? Of course, there are also the myriad technical specifications of the paper: evaluating the validity of sources, paraphrasing versus summarizing, parenthetical citation, avoiding accidental (not to mention intentional) plagiarism, etc. And all this is in addition to simply getting the students to write a well-organized, well-developed representation of their research that, with any luck, will reveal something truly insightful about the question or topic at hand. It's no wonder the research paper is a perpetual challenge to teachers everywhere.

If, however, we return to one of the points we made in Chapter 1—that we ought to focus more on the skills and types of knowledge we're interested in seeing and less on adhering to traditional written genres at the expense of authenticity—we can start to see that there are alternatives to the research paper that would likely be more meaningful to students. One of these is the *ethnographic thick description*. As outlined in Geertz's (1973) seminal work *The Interpretation of Cultures*, the central goal of the thick description is, as the name implies, to describe the habits and routines of a culture *thickly*, in great detail. Crucially, what sets this task apart from a simple exercise in using imagery is the expectation that students also interpret what those habits and routines mean in the culture as a whole. Or, as Geertz (1973) puts it, "the ethnographer 'inscribes' social discourse; he writes it down [and,] in so doing, he turns it from a passing event, which exists in its own moment of occurrence, into an account" (p. 19) that can be read, analyzed, and interpreted. A simple example of this could come from observations of the school lunchroom culture. What conclusions can be drawn from the way different student groups sit together in that location? What are the noticeable behaviors that exemplify each group? When groups interact, what do you notice and what conclusions can you draw from those exchanges? Do any known groups seem to be missing from the culture, and, if so, what might that indicate?

As an assignment, then, the thick description is a blend of narrative and explanatory writing that checks some of the same boxes as the traditional research paper but ups the ante in other promising ways. In the process of completing a product that both describes a culture (using elements of narrative writing) and interprets its behavior (using elements of explanatory writing), students get to experiment with primary research: developing inquiry questions, taking field notes, and interviewing subjects, among other options. Additionally, Dean (2008) argues that ethnographic assignments require "students to use genres for authentic purposes" and allow them to "see [written] genres as actions more than forms" (p. 81). When students write their thick description, two genres will be required—the descriptive and interpretive components—while other genres will be options on a menu of possible choices as they conduct their research: observational field notes, interview protocols and transcripts, surveys and questionnaires, and so on. In the context of this assignment, each of these written genres serves a specific rhetorical purpose but can be taken up in a variety of ways (or excluded altogether) in the final product, depending on each student's research questions and methods. This act of tactical decision-making helps students recognize the importance of "choos[ing] among options to effectively accomplish their purposes in each particular situation" (p. 13).

In all these ways, the thick description assignment hits many of the same notes as the traditional research paper while adding other dimensions that the conventional paper usually doesn't begin to touch. And, when it is completed through the lens of place-based writing, the assignment also gives students an opportunity to research firsthand some aspect of school culture that matters to them.

The Assignment

In today's political climate, assignments that deal with culture are important but potentially divisive. If you teach in a school where parents are wary of teachers perceived to be pushing a political agenda, it makes sense for you to feel some hesitation about taking up issues of personal culture. For this assignment, we wanted to introduce the topic of culture in a nonthreatening way that would still allow for deeper cultural conversations later in the school year. One way to accomplish this is to consider culture as something rooted in place, and the kaleidoscope of place-based cultures found in every school site makes the building or campus itself a logical place to experiment with thick description. Whether these cultures are extracurricular (sports teams, band and chorus, theater, debate), geographical (the cafeteria, the courtyard, the front office), or academic (the art room, the foreign language class, the yearbook or journalism class), the school site presents a nonpolitical "way in" to thinking about (and understanding) the signifiers that make up individual cultures.

Understanding these signifiers can also be an effective way to build empathy between students and student groups. Using the gym or the football field as a practical example, think for a moment about the culture of the student athlete. Lipsyte (2016) rightfully points out the ways we are "bombarded with the symbols, attitudes, language, and rules of the athletic world" (p. xv), and this is underscored by Lewis and Rodesiler (2018), who point out that student athletes are often portrayed negatively in popular culture, "feed[ing] into a caricature of the adolescent-athlete that unfortunately is accepted as truth by the larger public" (p. 135). So how do these popular conceptions of athletes translate into the world of academics? In reality, the average student athlete is often more well disciplined, more hardworking, and more studious than the ways in which they are portrayed in movies, television, and literature (Shepard, 2018). At the same time, the stereotype of the student athlete as brash, pompous egotist is belied by Shepard's finding that student athletes "become so dependent on praise from coaches and teammates that, off the field . . . they often become withdrawn and resemble a person with no self-confidence" (p. 79). Such complexity will be true of any culture in your school, and the best way for students to recognize this is through the study of and interaction with members of that culture. As a result, students can find common ground with peers they may have unfairly stereotyped.

For students, the assignment then is to choose a place in the school that represents a particular culture (preferably one in which they do not claim membership, although this isn't necessarily a requirement); develop one or more research questions identifying something they want to learn about that culture; conduct observations of the place; interview members of the culture; and write a thick description that both vividly illustrates the culture in action and interprets the habits, routines, and behaviors of the people within it.

Logistical Considerations

Once students have selected their location and developed one or more research questions, you'll want to discuss when and how they will conduct their observations and interviews. Sometimes this requires students staying after school (if, for instance, they want to observe a football practice or theater rehearsal), but it also occasionally means making other adjustments for students who need to conduct an observation during class time (of, say, the yearbook class). This may mean putting limitations on the kind of locations they can observe, or specifying that they can only observe locations at lunch, between classes, or before and after school. When Rob conducted this assignment with high school seniors, he tried to be as flexible as possible, even if it meant allowing them to duck out of class for twenty minutes to conduct a brief observation. Again, the specifics will be up to you and what is possible in your own context.

Supplemental Lessons

Discussion of Culture

In our experience, it isn't unusual for students to default to broad conceptions of culture when the topic is addressed in class. Because of how they often hear it discussed on the news or at home, students may immediately call to mind notions of race, religion, gender, sexual orientation, and so on. However, we want to narrow the focus of what we mean by *culture*, mainly because we've found that doing so makes it more accessible for students. As an introductory activity (conducted prior to assigning the thick description), it may be helpful for students to identify the cultures to which they belong. Whether they're gamers, volleyball team players, comic book fans, or members of the marching band, they can start to think about questions like these:

- What makes a culture what it is?
- How do we know a culture when we see one?
- What are the habits and routines that are unique to your culture?
- What's the specific vocabulary you use when you talk to other members of your culture?
- What are the objects that are important to your culture? Why are they important?
- What places are important to your culture? Why?
- Why do cultures display certain behaviors or value certain places, objects, or language?

Asking students to do some informal writing and discussion about these issues helps clarify for them what we mean by *culture* and serves as important brainstorming prior to their even knowing what a thick description is.

Developing Research Questions

As we mentioned earlier, this is often a step left out of the traditional research paper process. When we talk to students about these assignments, they usually mention the "topic" they're researching: an author, a time period, a controversial issue. Generally speaking, though, real-world research is conducted to answer a question or solve a problem, one in relation to which the researcher feels some investment, curiosity, or interest. And, if one of our goals is to empower student writers, asking them to base their research in their own curiosities can "help them see that their questions matter and can lead to writing" (Dean, 2010, p. 124). An early lesson for the thick description assignment can involve helping students develop one or more lines of inquiry to help focus their observations and interviews.

As a first step, it would likely be helpful to discuss with your students the kind of questions that would be appropriate for this project. In Rob's experience, it was often a good starting point to have students conduct one observation without a specific question in mind but after completing the generative writing described in the previous section. Sometimes we don't know what we want to learn until we're faced with a particular situation, so the direction for this first observation was for the students to keep their initial writing in mind and simply notice things about their selected culture that revealed it to be a culture. As a result, a student who noticed the use of nonverbal communication between players at basketball practice might formulate a question asking, "How are verbal and nonverbal communications used between basketball players and their coach?" or, "In what ways are verbal and nonverbal communications essential to a successful team?" One year, Rob had a student study the school's "parking lot culture," eventually conducting observations and interviews to pursue the question "In what ways is student behavior in the parking lot different from behavior anywhere else on campus?" As you can see from these two brief examples, student questions can run the gamut from explorations of a culture-specific norm or ritual to broader questions getting at the heart of what makes a culture *a culture* in the first place. Your role will be to help them find something that interests or perplexes them about the culture they select and turn it into a researchable question.

Observations and Interviews

Of particular importance is the way in which the thick description provides opportunities to teach primary research. In our experience, the research paper as it is commonly taught consists almost entirely of secondary research. You probably know the drill: students consult a variety of published sources (usually found on the internet, unless stipulated otherwise) to find information they can plug into their own papers. The thick description, however, requires students to actually conduct original primary research of their own as they attempt to resolve their authentic lines of inquiry.

Because conducting primary research will likely be a new experience for many of your students, you'll want to consider how to support them in these specific methodologies, such as taking accurate field notes of the location they're observing and conducting effective interviews with members of the culture.[1] An easy foundational lesson is to present some rudiments of note-taking[2] (using abbreviations, capturing quotes, noting important details) and then give your students one or more opportunities to practice. A fun and productive activity Rob implemented was to stage an angry argument with one of his colleagues that his students had to observe and re-create in a descriptive paragraph using the field notes they took during the argument.

Similarly, practice is key with interviewing. We recommend a lesson wherein you share some guidelines for constructing interview questions[3] and then give your students time to practice interviewing each other. Considering the ubiquity of cell phones, it might be tempting to ask your students to record the interviews they conduct. However, before instituting such a requirement, it would be important for you to research your district's policies regarding consent and audio recordings. Even if you ultimately decide your students are permitted to record their interviews, they still need experience in taking notes *during the interview* so they don't lose important information or fail to capture telling visual cues that obviously wouldn't make it into an audio recording.

Descriptive Writing

The heart of the paper, once your students have observed their location and conducted their interviews, is the descriptive component, where they attempt to capture their subject in as much detail as possible. This part of the assignment can involve lessons on imagery, dialogue, direct and indirect characterization, narrative organization, or any other craft lessons we might typically find in a unit on narrative writing.

Interpretation

The trickiest part of the assignment, this is where students have to explain what their observations and interviews *mean*. What conclusions can be drawn from the way the soccer team members interact with their coach? From the way groups of students sit in the cafeteria? What specific jargon does the journalism class use, and what purpose does it serve? In Rob's experience, this section seems to present problems because it asks the students for a degree of speculation. They won't know with certainty why the members of a culture act and speak the way they do, yet the thick description asks them to draw those conclusions. What Rob finds helpful is to approach this section of the thick description in the same way we might ask our students to present their interpretation of a poem. Whereas each line of the poem represents textual evidence the student can use to defend an interpretive claim, in the thick description, we're using an observation or verbal exchange to defend an interpretive claim about a culture (e.g., "Despite the overall machismo of the football team, we can actually see that they're a tight-knit family in the way they hold hands on the sideline during tense or dramatic moments").

A helpful exercise for this part of the assignment is to show video clips from movies set in schools. By highlighting key interactions between members of a culture—for example, a locker-room scene from *Friday Night Lights* (Berg & Cohen, 2004) or a cafeteria scene from *Mean Girls* (Fey & Waters, 2004)—we can ask students to interpret the behavior of characters and explain how what we're seeing says something about the culture to which they belong. However, it is important to remind students that movies and television often present exaggerated, stylized behavior to provide narrative momentum. And, as we mentioned earlier, popular culture frequently depicts adolescents as caricatures of specific "types"[4] in the service of story and not necessarily to reflect reality. If you use such an activity to help students get a handle on the interpretive stance of the thick description assignment, be sure to caution them that the behavior they'll observe and make sense of in their school will almost certainly be more subtle, more nuanced than what they see in the video clips. They should resist making snap interpretations based on easy, usually inaccurate stereotypes reinforced by popular media (e.g., "This student is a jock, so he's acting like this" or "That behavior makes sense because she's in the Drama Club"). Even with this potential pitfall, using popular media texts seems to help many students get a handle on what we mean by "interpreting behavior," even if we initially do so in a tentative, superficial manner.

Summing Up

For obvious reasons, the thick description shouldn't be viewed as a comprehensive research project. While it incorporates many of the skills that we ask students to develop in the completion of a traditional research paper, it doesn't, for instance, ask them to conduct online or library research (although there are certainly ways such a facet could be added to it). This leaves a gap in their ability to cite sources parenthetically, summarize or paraphrase documents, or compile a bibliography. But what *does* it do? It asks students to think critically about the meaning of culture, develop primary research skills in observation and inquiry, and write for description and interpretation. And it does all this by moving the frequently sterile approach to research writing out of the classroom and asking them to engage with the larger, more dynamic school community in order to learn something about students with whom they might otherwise be unfamiliar.

Intended Benefits
- personal
- agentive
- engaging

Variations to Add an Authentic Audience
- Modeled after Humans of New York,[5] the assignment could be further expanded to *Cultures of [Your School] Night*. Conducted in the style of a pop-up museum,[6] each student could prepare an audio or visual representation of the culture under study (including, for example, photos of the members in action or excerpts from their interviews) and prepare a short talk for those in attendance.
- Alternately, condensed versions of the thick description—complete with photos and interview excerpts—could be compiled in an anthology, similar to but more detailed than the school's yearbook. In a high school setting, *A User's Guide to [Your School]* or *A [Your School] Survival Guide* could then be made available to incoming ninth-grade students at the start of the new year.

Writing about Literature and Other Texts

Literature is rooted in setting. Whether we're talking about Jane Austen's bucolic English countryside, the sweltering American South of *To Kill a Mockingbird* (Lee, 1960/2002), or *The Hunger Games*'s hardscrabble District 12 (Collins, 2008), quality literature draws on place to ground its story, provide its characters with history, and intensify its conflict. We can tell when a novel's setting feels lived-in: Joseph Conrad (1899/2012) makes Marlow's sweat practically slick our own palms as the sailor travels up the Congo in *Heart of Darkness*, and we find ourselves shivering alongside the Yukon-stranded protagonist in Jack London's (1908/1986) "To Build a Fire." Readers rely on vividly drawn places to provide the verisimilitude that will bring a story to life, and, for our students, it can be the difference between just reading words on a page and seeing a movie in their heads.

It makes sense, then, to consider how we can make connections between the places described in the texts our students read and the real places these same students inhabit. But we can also start to think about how place allows us to teach other literary aspects, from emulating an author's craft to deepening our students' understanding of the themes and issues we're exploring in a particular novel, story, or poem. Underlying all of this is the question we asked earlier: "Just how authentic are we allowing our students' experiences to be?" Because literary texts are written in real places about real places (or about places that we're supposed to *believe* are real, at least for a little while), it seems logical to embrace place as a way to help students engage in authentic, text-based writing.

Adopt an Author's Style

From the Romantic poets' meditations on nature, to William Golding's (1954) dense depiction of a tropical island in *Lord of the Flies*, to the ostentatious Jazz Age settings in F. Scott Fitzgerald's (1925) *The Great Gatsby*, vivid descriptions of place are often where we see an author's style in full flourish. After working with your students to identify the hallmarks of a particular author's craft, ask them to consider how that author would describe a contemporary setting. Task the students with spreading out and choosing a location around the school, and then give them fifteen minutes or so to observe that location. What do they see, hear, smell, and feel?[7]

Once they have a reservoir of sensory details at their disposal, ask them to write a description of that location in whatever style seems appropriate for their author. An Elizabethan sonnet about the virtues of the gymnasium? A Swiftian satire about the day's lunch menu? Virtually any school setting will work.[8] If you want to give your students more freedom, you can use this activity after reading and discussing the style or voice of a handful of different authors. Whichever approach you choose, it requires your students to have a grasp on an author's specific diction and syntax, as well as the ability to thoughtfully observe their surroundings and render those observations in believable detail.

Intended Benefits
- personal
- agentive
- engaging

Variation to Add an Authentic Audience
- Anthologies are often a simple way to bring audience authenticity to an assignment, and teachers could leverage students' familiarity with this type of text to create one here. The individual pieces could be collected and inexpensively bound, resulting in a class souvenir or even kept on hand to model choices in diction and syntax for subsequent classes.

Writing a Myth or Hero's Journey

Amanda's fourth-grade students are enamored with Rick Riordan's Percy Jackson and the Olympians series, and, once Rob's ninth graders had gotten past the antiquity of Homer's *Odyssey*, they thrilled to its tales of sirens and cyclopes. One popular way of assessing students' understanding of myths or the hero's journey is to ask them to write an original legend or hero's quest (which may or may not take poetic form, depending on how ambitious you feel).

An easy, place-based twist to this assignment is to ask students to base that writing in their school. Students can tour the school, making observations, taking notes, and considering the opportunities different locations offer for storytelling. What adventures can be had as their hero journeys all the way from the front office to the gym in search of a fabled artifact ("The Myth of the Lost Basketball")? For a visual addition, students can take photos of the different school areas making appearances in their epic and design a map of the journey.

Similarly, students can also create a school-based myth. Who's the equivalent of Zeus in the main office? What's the tragic story that explains the day's lunch menu? Either piece can tell you how well students understand the characteristics of myths or the hero's journey,[9] and doing so in this way allows them to base their story in a location they know well for creative or humorous effect.

Intended Benefits
- personal
- agentive
- engaging

Variations to Add an Authentic Audience

- Compile the students' myths in an anthology of school-based myths to be shared with younger grades.
- Collaborate with the drama teacher for an evening of oral storytelling.

Interdisciplinary/Cross-Curricular Connections

- Incorporate elements of World History class by discussing the oral storytelling tradition in ancient cultures.
- Collaborate with the art teacher to teach the students about mapmaking.

Cumulative Sentence Character Sketch

One of the most popular assignments among Rob's tenth-grade students was this descriptive piece, completed in the process of reading Richard Wright's (1945/1998) autobiography, *Black Boy*. Another type of mentor text activity (see the "Adopt an Author's Style" activity suggested earlier in the chapter for another example) and based on the grammar concept of the *cumulative sentence*,[10] this activity first requires students to experiment with sentence parts in order to create precise, memorable images. Wright uses the device throughout *Black Boy* to intensify detail, zooming in on a character or action with vivid imagery. Consider this passage, when Richard recalls meeting his father after a twenty-five-year absence:

> That day a quarter of a century later when I visited him on the plantation—he was standing against the sky, smiling toothlessly, his hair whitened, his body bent, his eyes glazed with dim recollection, his fearsome aspect of twenty-five years ago gone forever from him.... (Wright, 1945/1998, p. 34)

The repeated absolute phrases ("his hair whitened . . . his body bent . . . his eyes glazed") focus our attention on his father's appearance, an accumulation of detail that paints a rich picture. In this way, *Black Boy* acts as a mentor text to help students understand how cumulative sentences work as well as how knowing certain grammar concepts extend what is possible, descriptively speaking.

Once the students have a basic grasp of the cumulative sentence tactic, they choose someone at the school whom they consider to have a distinctive personality. For the next two days, they are to observe that person, taking notes on physical appearance, mannerisms, speaking habits, and so on. What sets the Character Sketch apart from the thick description activity described earlier—and the thing that makes it a place-based writing assignment—is that this activity is less about interpretation of behavior and more about describing how an individual interacts with their environment. By conducting the observations around the school, we're seeing one facet of an individual's personality as it is situated in a specific location. And, by only describing behavior (as opposed to interpreting or evaluating it), we're asking students to think like storytellers.

Before proceeding, it is worth mentioning that, as the teacher, you will need to decide how to frame these observations for your students. If you allow them to observe and write about other students, you might require that they disclose this to their subjects in order to avoid any stalkerish overtones. Similarly, you could confine the students' observations to one of their teachers, since part of being an educator is the assumption that we will be under students' gazes for the duration of the workday. There are certainly other ways you could handle these observations (e.g., Rob required that his students receive permission from their subjects, whether they were classmates or adults), but it is a practical consideration you will definitely want to take up with your students.

For the next step of the assignment, ask your students to bring their notes to class and, without telling anyone whom they observed, experiment with writing cumulative sentences that capture their subject's distinct personality. This can be a stand-alone exercise in writing cumulative sentences, or, as Rob adapted it for his classes, students can develop a formal piece of writing with a target number of cumulative sentences embedded.

Rob found the Character Sketch assignment to be an effective way to teach author's craft (specifically, the cumulative sentence with its various phrases), and the element of narrative playfulness made the activity an engaging experience for students. Perhaps most important, the experimentation involved in writing these sentences helped his students see that writers have choices, and it's through these deliberate actions that they can take control of their own writing.

Intended Benefits

- personal
- engaging

Variation to Add an Authentic Audience

- One stipulation of the assignment could be that your students are required to share their finished character sketches with their subjects. This would give them an authentic audience, but it could also help ensure that the students write a character sketch and not a character assassination.

Writing Arguments

Arguments don't exist in a vacuum. While some people argue as an intellectual exercise or simply to be contrarian, most arguments have real-world stakes. We argue *for a reason*, and it's usually a reason with personal import, otherwise we wouldn't bother in the first place. But Hillocks (2011) observed, through his extensive, career-long study of academic writing, that "although adolescents may intend to write an argument, they often see no need to present evidence or show why it is relevant; they merely express (usually vague) opinions" (p. 15). It makes sense, then, not only to ask our students to situate arguments in the real world, by moving them out of the classroom and into a more authentic context, but also to take the time to ensure they understand how to effectively construct these arguments using sound logic as their foundation.

Thinking about School Safety[11]

One weakness in traditional methods of teaching arguments can often be found in the assignments themselves. According to Hillocks (2011), when students are asked to make arguments of policy—for or against the death penalty, gun control, marijuana legalization, and so on—"their only problem is how to organize what they find in their secondary sources into a more or less coherent essay" (p. 68). However, when it comes to arguing these researchable problems:

> [It is important for students] to work with sets of readily available concrete data when investigating the nature of a problem and deciding what to do about it. Problems [that] come from students' immediate lives and surroundings, provide that available data. (p. 69)

Consequently, the school site immediately becomes a location ripe for writing authentic arguments.

After all, students are often more acutely aware of a school's nuances than are the faculty. As teachers, we make our way (with varying degrees of fatigue) from parking lot to workroom to classroom and back again, treading the same series of floor tiles day after day. Students, on the other hand, range (relatively) freely around the school, availing themselves of its classrooms, hallways, and stairwells, in the process gaining a familiarity with its affordances and constraints that we as teachers often don't possess simply because our knowledge isn't as comprehensive.

With that knowledge as our foundation, we can ask our students to tour the school and examine its different areas through the lens of school safety. This might relate to bomb threats or active shooter drills, but it could also extend to unmonitored stairwells, parking areas or driveways with poor visibility, or heavily trafficked hallways whose limited exits could easily become clogged in an emergency. After taking the tour and completing their observations, students can craft an argument advocating for a specific change to the physical school site that would increase the safety of students, faculty, and staff. The end result is an argument requiring students to make a claim, warrant that claim with evidence, and anticipate counterarguments, all in the service of making their school a safer place in which to learn.

To help students think through assignments like this one, we can look to Shor (1996, p. 162) for a simple heuristic that can help students plan their work:

1. *Description*. What is the problem? What does it look like and feel like? Who is being affected by it and how?
2. *Diagnosis*. How did it get like this? What caused it? What are its roots? Who set it up like this? Who benefits? Who loses?
3. *Solution*. What are some answers? Propose and explain three possible solutions to the problem you are analyzing.
4. *Implementation*. How would you go about implementing each of the three solutions? What do you need to get started?
5. *Evaluation*. How would you evaluate the success or failure of each solution? One year from now, what would you want to see changed? Five years from now?

While the students' final product likely won't include all the elements of Shor's (1996) heuristic, such a questionnaire will help them more fully consider the various facets of the problem and the practicality of their proposed solution(s).

Intended Benefits
- personal
- agentive
- engaging
- promotes change

Variation to Add a Research Component

- As part of their written argument, students could be required to conduct research into the severity of the problem in other schools or the efficacy of their solution. How widespread a problem is it? What would be the costs or timeline of their proposed change(s)?

Variation to Add an Authentic Audience

- The argument could be written as a letter to the principal or as a grant proposal—and, of course, if these were actually submitted to the intended audience, the assignment would become more authentic still.

Preserving or Developing the Community?

What happens when the community to which a school belongs undergoes a radical change? Amanda saw this recently when the construction of a new soccer complex resulted in the razing of an apartment building in which many of her school's students lived. Long-term development in the area (including the building of a new stadium for the Atlanta Braves baseball team) has also caused more shifts in the housing situation for her students. Should such developments be welcomed or shunned? What is lost in such changes? What's gained?[12]

In a scenario-based assignment, students can consider these issues for their own context. If you teach in a rural or suburban school surrounded by fields and trees, what would it mean if a large shopping or housing development were to be built in an adjacent area? If you teach in a more urban area, what would happen to the area around your school if the apartments and businesses were to be razed and replaced with a new office complex or medical building? Such a scenario can lead to students creating an argument either for or against such development, based on the lived reality of their school setting. To help formulate these arguments, a key component of this assignment should be to venture outside the school with your students, exploring the area to be affected so they know exactly what would be lost (or gained). Not only are students crafting a logical argument with this assignment, but they are also being asked to appreciate the value of their community and consider the relative gains and losses if that community were to be fundamentally altered.

This assignment can also reinforce the importance of compromise in such matters. If the scenario were structured so that the development were already a fait accompli, for which concessions would concerned voices want to argue? What elements of the existing environment or community could be preserved? Could other elements be added *around* the development, such as parks, courtyards, or other natural spaces? Modifying the activity in this way could help students understand that argument typically isn't a zero-sum game, and that compromise can often be reached so that both parties retain a degree of satisfaction.

Intended Benefits
- personal
- engaging
- promotes change

Variation to Add a Research Component
- In the process of crafting their argument, students could investigate such issues as population demographics or the cost of comparable developments.

Variation to Add an Authentic Audience
- An authentic audience could be simulated by asking the students to write their arguments in the form of a pitch to the school board or the development firm responsible for the new building.

Interdisciplinary/Cross-Curricular Connections
- If you teach in a rural school, consider partnering with a science teacher to discuss the environmental impact of such a development.

Making Room for Art

While some schools have been designed with aesthetics in mind (lots of open and green spaces, with good lighting and appealing decoration), the "school as prison" comparison still holds true in many places. An argument for students that could have actual local impact involves the adoption and placement of art in the school building. What would make the building more pleasing to the eye? What kind of art should be chosen? From where would it be sourced? Should it be commercial art or student created—or a combination of the two? In the case of the former, how much would it cost? For the latter, which students would create it? Could hallways be themed (e.g., pictures of authors near English classrooms, photos of nature near science classrooms, reproductions of famous paintings near the art room)?

The preceding questions are only some possibilities students could consider as they develop their arguments. You might wish to add additional complexity to the scenario by asking students to wrestle with some of the issues real-world locations encounter when undergoing a similar art selection process. For example, is there a mandate that all the art be inoffensive? Who gets to decide the line between "offensive" and "inoffensive" art? Is it truly art if it raises no questions or fails to challenge the viewer? In this way, the assignment can work on at least two levels: addressing the practical nature of selecting art for an academic setting and encouraging students to think about the nature of art and its role in the world.

The centerpiece of the assignment involves getting students out of the classroom and examining the impact of visual art in various school locations.[13] They could consider the placement of an external mural (as well as what it might look like), the exact nature and location of art in the school's hallways, and even if some locations would have paintings but others would display notable quotations.

Besides being an opportunity for students to write a logical argument in favor of improving a school's aesthetics, this assignment could, as we mentioned, actually effect change in the school if they were permitted to submit their arguments to administration. Such a piece of writing would allow them to consider tone and register, as well as the quality of their argument, and all of it would be grounded in the actual world of their school.

Intended Benefits
- personal
- agentive
- engaging
- audience oriented
- promotes change

Variation to Add a Research Component
- In order to add an extra dimension of reality to their argument, students could be required to research the estimated cost of the art they're proposing, including the time and labor required to install it.

Interdisciplinary/Cross-Curricular Connections
- A partnership with your art teacher would be a natural fit here. Students could learn broadly about the aesthetics of interior design, especially when it comes to selecting and placing art that blends harmoniously with its surroundings.

Writing Narratives, Poetry, and Scripts

"Write what you know." "Show, don't tell." These aphorisms have been the province of writing classrooms for decades, but it's unclear just how often we actually support our students in enacting such advice. If we want to think about place as the vehicle by which we teach elements of narrative writing, school is uniquely suited to help students understand the importance of writing from a position of knowledge as well as showing rather than telling. They know school as well as, and probably better than, any location other than their own home and immediate neighborhood. This knowledge base allows them to write with authority about a variety of school-based topics, from the numbing tedium of the classroom lecture to the electric surge of adrenaline when a fight is brewing in the hallway. And, rather than teach descriptive writing primarily from their memories or imaginations, why not utilize the location at hand to develop their abilities to use imagery, develop character, and capture believable dialogue? Teachers have society in microcosm right outside their classroom door, as long as they're willing to open it.

One additional note: While narrative might be the preferred genre for the activities described below (privileged as it is in the Common Core State Standards), it's worth noting that other genres could also be acceptable or even desirable. There's no reason to think students couldn't write effective poems or scripts that relay story, but your assessment criteria would obviously have to reflect any flexibility in the genres you allow.

School Map

A variation on the Life Map idea (Kirby & Crovitz, 2013), the School Map is a useful introductory activity for place-based narrative writing. The students draw (or are provided with) a map of the school. After a discussion of what makes a good story, the students label the map with the locations of places where they have stories to tell. As in previous examples, students are given the opportunity to go back to one of the locations they've identified (or a couple, if they're stuck between stories) and spend some time observing and taking notes, focusing on how they can bring that location to life in their story. And, even though the story may be fresh, visiting the source of it can help shake loose other details that they might not have recalled if they had simply been asked to write the story from memory in the classroom.

In the process of recalling stories and observing location, a variety of storytelling techniques can also be taught or reviewed, from effective openers to the incorporation of description to the use of believable dialogue. Such an activity also helps students understand what their stories actually mean. Why has this event stuck with them? What makes it worth telling? On an elemental level, the School Map activity can help students make sense of their own lives.

Intended Benefits
- personal
- engaging

Variation to Add Agency
- As with virtually all the activities we describe, there's no rule that says you can accept only one kind of product from your students. Maybe, after exploring the school and the events labeled on their map, it has more meaning for the student to write a poem or a short comic book. Would a song be acceptable? A reenacted script? There are no immediate reasons to prohibit any of these ideas, so, if you want students to take absolute ownership of their work, you might consider a degree of flexibility to the finished product.

Variations to Add an Authentic Audience
- Consider a time to share these stories aloud, especially if you allow for flexibility in their final products.
- If such an option exists, you could display the stories in the actual physical places they are located so that they can be read by other students and faculty.

Interdisciplinary/Cross-Curricular Connections
- If you wanted to further bring these stories to life, you could partner with the drama teacher to turn the stories into short plays to be reenacted for the class or even for parents.

Writing Marathon

While the Writing Marathon does not have to include written narratives, it's worth introducing here as a general place-based writing strategy that *can* include narrative and that could also easily be incorporated in the locations we explore in our subsequent chapters. Additionally, the Writing Marathon can be useful in encouraging students to draft several different pieces in a variety of genres.

To conduct a writing marathon, you will need to select several locations around your school that can inspire student writing. In short, the idea is that students will be led from location to location and given a period of time to write in each. The exact amount of time you provide will be up to you, based on the kind of writing you want your students to do as well as how long you can reasonably expect your students to focus. Rob found ten minutes per location to be manageable for high school students, but this was only after building them up to it over several weeks with short in-class writing activities.

Similarly, the kind of writing you ask students to do in each location can potentially be anything you want to read and assess. In a true narrative writing unit, you might work with the students in class beforehand to develop a protagonist and antagonist and then have them develop their story during the Writing Marathon. Each location at which you stop could be designated as another setting for their story, and, for ten minutes, they could quick-write how that location could be used as a setting in their developing narrative. But you could also ask students to write a haiku in each stop, practice descriptive writing by using specific literary devices to detail each place, reflect on the associations they have of each location and connect it to their sense of identity as a student, or any range of other possible ideas. You can also, of course, simply ask that your students write about anything they wish. This can increase the students' levels of purpose, agency, and engagement, but, if you use this approach, we've found it necessary to include one or two optional prompts in each location for those students stuck for something to write about.

Intended Benefits
- personal
- agentive
- engaging

Interdisciplinary/Cross-Curricular Connections
- Because the direction you take the Writing Marathon can vary widely from teacher to teacher, there are nearly as many interdisciplinary connections to make. For example, do you want your students to observe and take notes with a scientist's eye? Consider asking a science teacher to talk to your class about field observations. The kind of connection you make with other subjects will depend on the kind of marathon you're facilitating.

Writing for Research and Inquiry

As we mentioned in our introduction to the thick description activity, the research paper is an easy assignment to do inauthentically. Because we tend to focus more on the technical hoops required by the paper (research skills, source validity, summarizing vs. paraphrasing, parenthetical citation, etc.), we lose sight of why people actually conduct research in the first place. Whether it's a scientist toiling away at a data set in a lab or a movie fan poring over a newly discovered director's Internet Movie Database page, we research because we want information. *We research because we have questions about the world.* This means admitting we have gaps in our understanding, and that can be an uncomfortable proposition for teenagers who often see ignorance as weakness instead of opportunity. But it is in this "subtle unsteadying of our confidence" that "the quest for learning occurs" (Fecho, 2004, p. 154). By shifting the traditional research paper's focus outward—to encourage students to think about the genuine questions they have about their world, especially on a local level—it becomes a logical next step to consider how place can play an integral role in the inquiry process.

On the Chopping Block

As English teachers who are also minor-league science nerds, we'd be the last people to argue against the importance of the core subjects students are required to take. But we also recognize the importance (we might even go so far as to say "the essential nature") of extracurricular courses. Drama and music classes got both of us through high school with our sanity intact, and we'd be willing to bet most students have that one noncore class that they look forward to each day, and that might even be their one reason for coming to school at all. Art, music, drama, physical education, home economics, and many others: these classes make a difference. Yet we also know it's these classes that are the first to be cut when austerity measures take over.

No one is better positioned to advocate for these classes than the students who love them, a fact that can be positioned as a project for both research and argument. In it, students are asked to select an extracurricular class they enjoy (or *think* they'd enjoy, if they haven't taken it yet), research its benefits, and write a product (paper or otherwise; see variations below) that argues for the class's importance. What do students gain by taking an art class? Journalism? Choir or band? This would involve an element of traditional academic research, such as finding print or online sources dealing with the value of noncore classes. In addition, to ensure the class's value is represented with sufficient detail, students would also be required to observe the class in question (either as an outside observer or as a participant) and interview other students and the teacher.

While the students' research questions are likely to be relatively narrow (mostly variations on "What are the benefits of this class for students?"), the specificity of focus might actually make this assignment a valuable initial research experience. They are invited to research a class that interests them, conduct participatory research (which, in our own students' experience, tends to be more engaging than the usual "go look something up online" variety), and frame their research as an argument in favor of something about which they're passionate. The constrained nature of the topic, however, makes this less intimidating for students wary of the name "research paper." The value of the On the Chopping Block project is that it teaches students important research skills, demonstrates real-world research purposes, and gets the students actively involved in their school community in order to make a positive difference.

Intended Benefits
- personal
- agentive
- engaging
- promotes change

Variations for Added Authenticity
- Similar to some of the other argument-based activities we describe, this one could also be framed for rhetorical authenticity, such as we described earlier in the context of Dyrness's (2011) work with PAR. Because these classes are often at very real risk of being defunded or declared unimportant, there are absolutely ways to get students thinking about who is in a position to hear (and be convinced by) their arguments. A presentation to the school board? A letter to a philanthropic organization to fund the school's arts program? There are numerous possibilities; it would be up to the students to decide which would be most appropriate for their own work.
- Schools are often more apt to listen to parents or the business community than the students they serve. This already-valuable project could be parlayed into an evening during which students present their research to parents and other community members. Even in districts where money is flush, such an event could make a compelling argument for the vitality of extracurricular classes.

Interdisciplinary/Cross-Curricular Connections

- Because the project will presumably require (or at least encourage) students to connect with the adult who teaches the class they're researching, the interdisciplinary connection is baked in. For the students to write about the value of their coursework, it's unavoidable that they'll have to speak knowledgeably about a school subject other than English.

Writing for Change

In Chapter 1, we discussed five benefits of place-based writing. The fifth—"place-based writing can promote change"—is arguably the benefit that lends this kind of writing its greatest degree of authenticity. Not only are students writing for real purposes and to real audiences, but, when that writing effects change, even incrementally, it tells the students that their voices have been heard, that their voices *matter*. There can be varying degrees of overlap with some of the other kinds of writing we discuss in each chapter—there will almost invariably be elements of argument or research in writing for community purposes—but the focus of this section will rest on activities that are specifically designed to promote change.

Making the School More Environmentally Friendly

As with many of the activities in this chapter, making improvements to the school site is one way to start small with place-based writing. Although the ideal lesson for teaching environmental consciousness might be to have students explore their home communities to find larger eco-friendly solutions, it's important to consider where we begin that broader conversation. One way—similar to the school safety assignment we described earlier—is to ask students how they might make changes around the school to ensure the building and its community are more environmentally conscious. Even a small-scale project can encourage students to think about how their actions impact their environment. The benefit of such thinking, as Shrake (2000) reminds us, is that, "if we can induce in our children a sense of connectedness to the earth, we can almost ensure its survival" (p. 74). Fostering a sense of environmental stewardship becomes even more pressing when one considers the special report from the Intergovernmental Panel on Climate Change (2018) that forecasts a range of climate-related catastrophes by the year 2040. If students explore this topic on a local level, it might help them see firsthand how they can help counteract such dire predictions.

While teaching about climate change and environmental advocacy may not seem like an obvious fit for the English classroom, a movement to legitimize this area of study has been gaining steam. In early 2019, the National Council of Teachers of English published its "Resolution on Literacy Teaching on Climate Change," which recommended that students "need to imagine consequences and possibilities [of climate change], and take action individually, locally, and nationally" (para. 2). Additionally, Beach et al. (2017) remind us of our classrooms' potential to be "places of moral and ethical reflection about new ideas and complicated human realities" (p. 6). This dovetails with Bruce's (2011) belief that, as English teachers, "our expertise in addressing the aesthetic, ethical, and sociopolitical implications of the most pressing human concerns of our time enable us also to reach toward embrace of environmental problems" (p. 14). Buttressing this advocacy is the rich nature of the English language arts curriculum itself. We have a variety of ways to approach teaching the climate crisis, from studying informational texts pertaining to it, to evaluating arguments made by those critical of its impact, to exploring possible solutions at home and abroad.

Writing also provides us with an avenue to explore the topic in specific, locally relevant terms. As you would expect, a key component of this assignment is not to have students merely speculate about ways to make their school more environmentally friendly, but to actually have them explore the school site to see what they notice. Just how much waste do they see being produced by the cafeteria? Are there areas on the school grounds where more trees could be planted? To what recycling program (if any) does the school belong? What about pollution from school buses or single-driver student and faculty automobiles? There are a range of issues that students might notice as they explore the school, and the chance to return to the classroom and discuss their observations can yield even more discoveries. In a written argument, the students can discuss the problems they identified and propose one or more viable alternatives to solve it.[14]

The written product that results from these observations and conversations will be most authentic if they are directed to an audience in a position to make a difference. It could be a letter to the district office, a formal presentation to be delivered at a school board meeting, or even a grant proposal to secure funding for schoolwide eco-friendly light bulbs.[15] It's certainly important that an assignment like this one can help students learn how to construct a logical argument, but, in terms of an impact with more longevity, it also allows students to see how their writing—grounded in a location they might not previously have considered in such a way—can promote responsible behavior and bring about positive change.

Intended Benefits
- personal
- agentive
- engaging
- audience oriented
- promotes change

Variation to Add a Research Component
- It would make sense to ask students to conduct research into both the issue they have identified and their proposed solution(s). Used effectively, these factual details will add authority to the argument they devise.

Variation to Add an Authentic Audience
- As mentioned above, it would make sense for the students to actually submit their final product to someone outside the classroom. This could also be part of the research component noted above: who is in a position to see their solutions come to fruition?

Variation to Add Agency
- Depending on the audience selected as part of the above, the students' final products may differ in appearance. As discussed earlier, it could be a letter to the principal, but it could also be a grant proposal or a formal presentation. Understanding audience expectations in different genres, and how that can be leveraged to achieve a specific purpose, will only add to the agency with which the students approach this project.

Interdisciplinary/Cross-Curricular Connections
- A collaboration with a science teacher would be relevant to this project in order for students to adequately understand the factors that contribute to environmental impact, as well as the range of possible solutions available for different problems.

Further Considerations

As mentioned earlier, we conclude each chapter by describing a few possible modifications for students with special needs and those learning English as a second language. These suggestions are by no means comprehensive, and some of the considerations we share in one chapter could easily be used to adapt activities in other chapters.

Considerations for Students with Special Needs

- A menu of questions compiled through a discussion with students before they conduct an interview may help scaffold what information is most important to collect. Also, explicit practice and modeling in how to conduct an interview could help a student understand the norms of an interview and allow for a real-world connection to future job searches.

- A map of the school that labels its major areas (e.g., cafeteria, classrooms, gym, etc.) could be provided to help ground the students' writing in real places and remind them of their options when brainstorming their stories. Allowing students to take ownership of this map by labeling some areas themselves or by providing pictures might also help aid in vocabulary use and memory recall.

- The School Safety assignment could be modified slightly to become a self-advocacy project. Students could examine the school environment in search of opportunities to improve access for students of all abilities. They can investigate items such as wheelchair-friendly playground equipment or signage that is inclusive of all. The central purpose of the assignment remains the same, but the focus shifts slightly to consider access as well as safety.

Considerations for English Language Learners

- Students can conduct interviews in their home language with other speakers of that language and then translate those interviews into English. This translation practice is an important skill in which they will need instruction and guidance as they begin to navigate the use of multiple languages. You should consider that this practice will require the student to do twice the work (interviewing and then translating), so the overall workload will need to be modified to reflect that.

- Consider breaking down any mentor texts or cumulative sentences into a series of sentence frames that would allow a student to access the author's craft while not overwhelming them with language. This would also allow a more structured environment in which to discuss elements of English grammar, syntax, and word choice.

- Remember that students new to the school may not have many local experiences in which to ground their writing. Asking students to observe and reflect on the patterns and norms of their new school may help to address misconceptions and anxieties. We have to remember that some students are learning not only a new language but a new culture as well. Allowing students the space for this type of reflection will allow you to get to know them as they get to know you and ease their transition into a new space.

4

Writing in Museums

Go ahead: think of a museum. We'll wait.

Got one? What did you come up with? The Smithsonian? The Louvre? London's Tate Modern? New York's Metropolitan Museum of Art? Or was it something closer to home? Chicagoans might have thought of the Field Museum of Natural History. If you live in Cincinnati, maybe you envisioned the Museum Center at Union Terminal, while, if you hail from Louisiana, the New Orleans Jazz Museum might have been the first thing to spring to mind. Every major city has a handful of museums like these, the centers that represent collections of learning in art, science, and history.

It makes sense to immediately think either of museums that have earned national (or even worldwide) reputations for excellence, or of those that serve as tourist destinations in or near our own communities. We, Rob and Amanda, are no different. Ask us about Atlanta museums and we could quickly rattle off the High Museum of Art, the King Center, the Center for Civil and Human Rights, the Fernbank Museum of Natural History, the Georgia Aquarium, the Atlanta History Center, the Margaret Mitchell House, the Center for Puppetry Arts, and, yes, even the World of Coca-Cola. These are certainly productive places in which to engage your students in writing, and many museums of this caliber likely have an education department that can aid in planning and facilitating writing activities.

Just as important and just as productive, though, are the museums in smaller communities, the ones that fly under the tourist radar and that might actually have more relevance to your students and your curriculum. For instance, venture just half an hour north of Atlanta and we also have the Tellus Science Museum, the Booth Western Art Museum, the Autrey Mill Nature Preserve and Heritage Center, the Etowah Indian Mounds, and the Kennesaw Mountain National Battlefield Park (which Amanda detailed in Chapter 2). This list just scratches the surface of other museums and learning centers in the area, a list that can also include restored homes with historic connections. Your community is likely no different, possessing some larger museums that dominate the conversation but also benefiting from a network of smaller museums that unfortunately often exist on the periphery.

It is also important to remember these smaller museums when planning place-based writing activities because, as we mentioned in Chapter 3, these experiences needn't be expensive or inaccessible. For instance, if we want to take our students to a museum featuring exhibits on local Native American history as part of a unit centered on Sherman Alexie's novel *The Absolutely True Diary of a Part-Time Indian*, it might be unrealistic to bus them to the Atlanta History Center in the middle of the city. But, for schools north of Atlanta, the Funk Heritage Center, which features exhibits on Native American history and is designated as a Trail of Tears interpretive center, is just up the road and might provide a practical and equally valuable alternative.

But why museums at all? If the goal is to get students writing authentically about their surroundings, why take them to a location that in some ways seems to contradict this objective? After all, for many people, the stereotypical image of a museum likely includes exhibits under glass or paintings cordoned off by ropes. Watchful docents. Warnings prohibiting flash photography and food and drink. If we want students to engage in the vibrant, messy nature of the world outside the classroom, why take them someplace so seemingly sterile and artificial?

There are a couple answers to that question. The first lies in the very preservationist nature of the museums themselves. If we want students to write about local history, for example, it makes sense to take them to a place where that history has been preserved for them to experience. That preservation necessarily requires a controlled environment. The goal of this kind of writing is inherently different from asking students to compose a poem about a natural space or observe the ways in which people interact in a public place. *The value is in the sterility*, because we need collections of artifacts to tell their stories without fearing they'll be contaminated by greasy fingerprints or spilled soda. This is true of virtually any museum you'll visit with your students, regardless of whether the goal is to write about history, science, art, or anything else. And, while some museums incorporate certain "living history" aspects whereby patrons might be encouraged to interact with exhibits, the pieces under protection serve as the heart of most museums. This is, after all, why we visit museums in the first place: to see those things we are unlikely to experience in our everyday lives. We need a degree of artificiality to ensure these experiences are preserved.

Another reason why museums can be productive locations in which to write exists in their own status as places. Think back to Agnew's (1987) three characteristics of locations. One of them is *locale*—or all the things that, taken as a whole, contribute to something being a place. For museums, we've got obvious areas that cater to the business aspect of the museum (e.g., lobby and ticketing area, café, gift shop), but we also have a range of different educational areas. A museum might have one or more atriums, exhibit spaces (some of which may be open or exposed and others behind closed doors), outdoor artifacts (e.g., sculpture gardens or horticulture exhibits), or a movie theater. And the exhibit spaces themselves may take wildly different shapes depending on the kind of museum you're visiting. The National Museum of the United States Air Force near Dayton, Ohio, is housed in a mammoth hangar with lots of open space, while St. Louis's City Museum in Missouri is a labyrinthine fever dream of repurposed industrial materials. The specific character of each museum *as an individual place* opens up additional place-based possibilities for writing.

Taken in tandem, these two responses to the question "Why museums?"—they represent collected and protected knowledge and they exist as individual places themselves—should start to provide you with a justification for writing in museums or learning centers. In short, museums can provide your students with an opportunity to experience and write about exhibits and artifacts to which they would otherwise not have access. At the same time, the museum space itself can be viewed as a productive environment in which to write for a range of audiences and purposes.

Finally, before we begin describing some of the place-based writing activities specific to museums, we call your attention to something we mentioned in the introduction: It's our goal to describe these activities broadly enough so they can be more or less universally applicable. That is, an art museum activity we describe should be usable in *any* art museum, regardless of whether you live in Seattle or Tallahassee (or anywhere in between). Geography shouldn't be seen as an impediment to place-based writing, but as an opportunity for you to tailor these activities to your specific curriculum and the museums in your local community.

Extended Lesson Idea: Exploring Local History

As we discussed in the previous chapter, the research paper has long been a vexing issue for teachers: it's boring; it's inauthentic; it's too long (and it takes too long); the formal and technical demands of quoting, paraphrasing, and citing information frequently ride roughshod over the quality of the paper's writing; and so on. In a possible case of the obvious answer eluding us, some of the problem may be baked in from the very beginning. If authenticity is the goal—and we firmly believe it is possible for even a traditional research paper to possess a degree of authenticity—we have to start with the writing task itself. We know students are more willing to write about topics that matter to them, so it seems to make sense to ask students to connect their developing sense of identity with the history of their local community. This small-scale research can also help "young people see what is valuable and worth preserving in their home communities" (Smith & Sobel, 2010, p. 44).

But how many students actually know much about the place where they grew up, let alone what makes it worth preserving? Rob's hometown of Greenville, Ohio, possesses an authentic stone-grinding flour mill built in 1849 that is on the National Register of Historic Places, was the birthplace of sharpshooter Annie Oakley, and, in 1795, saw the signing of the treaty that opened up the Northwest Territory to settlement. However, these aspects of Greenville's history (among others) went largely unknown to him until he was an adult. The same can probably be said of many students: unless they have a good reason to learn about their community's history, they don't.

Even so, "home" is a concept with power, and many students already feel strong positive connections to the place where they have grown up. Gruchow (1995) reminds us that home "is the place in the present where one's past and one's future come together" (p. 87), and we both have seen this familiar point of convergence lead students to write convincingly and powerfully about their associations with home, both as an idea and as a concrete place. In terms of student engagement, there is also something to be said for asking them to write about something they already know, even if they don't yet possess certain information on a deep level. Importantly, this kind of writing may also stand in stark contrast to the work students are typically asked to complete. After all, how many times have we seen students tasked to write about "a predetermined list of topics that might be of interest to students but aren't necessarily grounded in their personal experiences" (Esposito, 2012, p. 71)? For all these reasons, the local history museum can be a place where students learn more about the community in which they live while simultaneously making the kind of personal connections likely to increase their engagement with the research project.

The Assignment

Local history museums can provide the deep dive into a town's past that the students often lack. If you haven't visited one of these learning centers in your own community, they often contain exhibits on the settlement and evolution of the area itself (that often include information about transportation and industry), notable personalities that contributed to that process, significant cultural figures (such as musicians, visual artists, or authors), and even information about local flora and fauna. As an example from our own area that illustrates the breadth of information available in these museums, the Augusta Museum of History features exhibits about the growth of the city, Southern history, the city's popular radio station, the specific importance of the railroad and medical industries to the city's history, and two special exhibits: one focused on "godfather of soul" James Brown, who grew up in Augusta, and the other on the history of the Augusta Masters golf tournament. A good local history museum—even in communities that don't, on the surface, seem as culturally or historically diverse as Augusta—will contain a wealth of information about the area. If students thoughtfully consider how their own interests connect to noteworthy people or events from the town's past, they will surely be able to develop one or more research questions focusing on a topic that matters to them.

Once you have identified a local museum to visit, students should be given enough time to explore it. A guided tour can certainly be helpful, if one is available, but we also think it's crucial for students to spread out and visit the museum at their own pace so they can home in on areas that are of specific interest to them. As they explore, the students should keep a record of their questions and curiosities, in the process narrowing their interests to a single topic about which they can begin to formulate one or more lines of inquiry. How much latitude you allow the students in topic selection is up to you. If a music fan visits the Augusta Museum and wants to research the history of soul music and James Brown's contribution to it, as opposed to simply researching the life of James Brown, would that be okay? Our answer would be an unqualified "yes." The purpose of using the museum as a catalyst for research is to provide students with a deeper understanding of their community, but it's also to allow them to learn more about something specific that interests them. A similar scenario could present itself with the exhibit on the Augusta National Golf Club. If a student showed little interest in researching the sport of golf but wanted instead to pursue the history of racism and anti-Semitism that has perpetually dogged golf clubs like Augusta's, we would be hard pressed to deny the student the freedom to research that important topic. Again, the key in starting this project at a local history museum is to encourage research about a topic with both local relevance and personal meaning. In the process, we can both deepen the students' connections with their community as well as check many of the boxes traditionally associated with the traditional research paper.

To that end, what form does the finished product take? As with the breadth of your students' topics, this can also be determined by your individual aims for the project. A traditional research paper would certainly be a logical expectation, but, for the sake of authenticity, you might also consider products written for outside audiences and purposes. For example, the students could create a promotional brochure for the museum incorporating elements of their research. If you were to take a multigenre approach, students could be asked to write a fictional narrative about their selected topic that nonetheless incorporates elements of the research they conducted.[1] These narratives could then be submitted to the museum, demonstrating its impact on local students (and, in the process, providing an authentic audience for the students' writing). By more fully taking up the notion that the museum is a specific place itself, you could ask the students to write the script for an educational film to be shown at the museum. If you wanted to be even more ambitious, the students could create a version of that film by making a PowerPoint or Prezi presentation and recording their script as an accompanying voiceover. To further leverage the conventions of museum as learning space, students could record an audio tour that extends what they learned in their research (and, in the process, consider such elements as clarity, tone, and audience). They could even record a podcast, such as the "crossing boundaries" podcast assignment described by Hurst (2015), in which students develop research questions, interview participants and analyze the resulting data, storyboard their findings, and record their audio. It is certainly important to ensure our students are comfortable writing in traditional genres, but, as we have mentioned elsewhere, place-based writing also gives us the opportunity to consider how we can teach traditional skills in the service of real-world purposes.

Logistical Considerations

Outside of identifying the final product for this research project, the biggest initial consideration is thinking through the selection of a museum and anticipating all the details that go into facilitating the field trip. This will vary widely from reader to reader, and, for that reason, we can't offer much help except to encourage you to make arrangements early to head off the annoying obstacles that invariably arise. Bus transportation falls through? Three students forget to return their permission forms? No parents want to help you chaperone? As anyone who's led a field trip can tell you, planning ahead might not eliminate issues like these, but it will at least better prepare you to deal with them.

With the practical details taken care of, you will also want to consider the kind of research you're asking your students to complete. Will it be based primarily in the museum? If so, you'll need to provide plenty of time for them to note the information required to write an effective paper (or script, or brochure, or whichever product you've chosen). However, we recommend asking the students to continue their research after leaving the museum. This can take the form of traditional internet or library research, but you might also consider allowing your students to interview members of the community who have been involved with their selected topics. To continue using examples from the Augusta Museum of History, a student researching the history of radio in popular music might be able to interview a current or former disc jockey, and another student learning more about Georgia's rail system could interview someone employed at Augusta's railyard. Museums can often put your students into contact with these local figures or provide them with resources to identify them on their own. Taking this extra step will certainly deepen your students' research, but it will also reinforce its authenticity by rooting local history in the context of real people, as opposed to a book on a shelf or the result of a Google search.

There is one other important issue to anticipate. Amanda's student population is highly transient, and it isn't unusual for her to have students move in and out of her classroom several times during the year. If you are teaching in a similar community, you may very well have students who don't have much of a connection to, or any built-in knowledge of, their new home. For those students, this project needs a slightly different frame. Rather than approaching it from the standpoint of deepening the students' ties to home, you can use it as a way to familiarize new students with the area. Keep in mind that most of your students—regardless of how long they've been residents of the community—will be coming to its local history as blank slates. For that reason, the nature of the research itself won't be affected, but the way you introduce the project might.

Supplemental Lessons

The Rudiments of Genre

Similar to our discussion of the thick description assignment in the previous chapter, this Rudiments of Genre project will require you to teach some initial lessons in research paper basics. In that earlier discussion, we focused specifically on the importance of developing genuine research questions, but, if this project requires your students to write a traditional paper, you'll also likely need to find time for lessons in summarizing and paraphrasing research, incorporating and parenthetically citing direct quotations, compiling a bibliography, and so on. If you're going to encourage your students to conduct interviews as part of your research, you'll want to provide them with some guidelines and time to practice.[2] In other words, what are the elements of research you're most interested in assessing in your students' work? Be sure you teach them so your students will have a reasonable expectation of success.

Similarly, if you're going to allow your students to write in a nontraditional genre, you'll want to feel confident they can be reasonably successful at that task. For instance, what are the components of a promotional brochure? How do they decide what information to include and what to omit? How might research be incorporated in such a document? How do photos and other graphics complement the text? Just as with the traditional paper, you'll want to be sure to address the characteristics of any unconventional genres you're allowing.

What Is Home?

Be ready for blank stares (and at least one groan from *that* kid) if you introduce this project by telling your students they're going to research local history. Taking this approach plays into every stereotype of the research paper that so often makes the assignment a challenge. Instead, because the Exploring Local History project will eventually encourage students to consider their personal links to the community in order to identify meaningful research questions, try starting with some informal writing about home and community:

- What does the word *home* mean to you?
- How would you describe your home to help someone else see it the way you do?
- Other than your house, where else in your community do you feel at home? Why?
- If you could pack a bag with all the items that make you feel at home, what would you pack?[3]
- What activities make you feel at home? Why?
- Which people make you feel at home? Where can these people be found?

Phrasing these questions in this particular way encourages students to think of home as not just a physical place. It can also be an emotional reaction to something that makes us feel comfortable. Rather than simply asking students to create a list of hobbies, these questions ask them to take up the concept of home as something specific to their sense of self. One year, one of Rob's students, Pilar (a pseudonym), wrote about how one of the places she felt most at home was cooking with her mother. Although Pilar had never considered cooking to be a hobby central to her identity, and nor had she ever envisioned learning more about Mexican cuisine, she ended up researching and writing about the influence of Aztec culture on contemporary Mexican food. By asking students to think about home in the context of who they are and where they are most comfortable, students often come to see value in places, activities, and people where they had never previously looked. This isn't to say one of their more obvious interests can't make for a viable research project, but this approach can expand the horizon of possible topics and encourage students to think more deeply about the things they value. If one of your goals for this project is to ground your students' research in something personally meaningful, this writing activity can help them start to make connections between self and place.

Reflecting on the Process

In the final stages of any major project, we often ask our students to write a short reflective piece discussing their process and what they learned *about themselves as writers and learners* from completing the assignment. It's certainly wonderful if they're able to acknowledge what they learned about research, but we should be able to determine that from their finished projects. Instead, we're more interested in our students' developing metacognitive awareness—their capacity for noticing "areas of difficulty and pride in their work" (Kirby & Crovitz, 2013, p. 234). An important step in becoming a confident writer is the ability to recognize what works in our writing (so we can tactically deploy those skills in the future) as well as acknowledging those areas of struggle or weakness (so we can troubleshoot them as they arise). If students monitor their development in this area throughout the course of a school year, we've found they have a much stronger sense of who they are as writers and are better equipped for success in the future.

Getting at this kind of thinking can be remarkably simple through asking questions like these:

- What was the easiest part of this project?
- What is your favorite part of your finished product?
- What do you deserve a high five for?
- What did you find most challenging about the project?
- When you struggled, what strategies did you use to get "unstuck"?
- What recommendations do you have for students completing this project in the future?

Some general questions can help students unpack their own writing strengths and weaknesses. Additionally, if you use the writing prompts about *home* listed earlier, it can also be illuminating for your students to write specifically about the ways in which that initial writing enabled them to approach their research with a greater degree of personal interest. Similarly, you might also include some reflective prompts about the value of the museum trip and how this project influenced the way they think about the community and their connection to it.

Concluding the project with this kind of reflection can both develop your students' metacognitive abilities as well as provide you with some valuable insight into your students' growth as writers and the success of the project as a whole.

Summing Up

At first glance, this project may seem unusually broad. But, if you recall the varying definitions of *authenticity* we presented in Chapter 1, you'll likely remember that many of them shared the conviction that one of the integral traits of authentic writing is the personal investment students find in it. As soon as we box in students' possible research interests, we start to lose that investment. This has long been one of the problems of the traditional research paper. By specifying that the paper has to present a controversial issue, or that it must be an author study or written about a particular literary movement, we're already contracting the students' realm of research possibilities. Grounding this project in an element of local history that interests them and about which they have genuine questions (even if they don't yet realize they have those questions) provides an opportunity for students to take an authentic interest in their selected topic. And because history is multifaceted, allowing the students a certain degree of latitude to explore the topic in a way that *increases* their engagement will, for many students, only increase the seriousness with which they take the assignment.

Is this a more complex proposition than the traditional research paper? Absolutely. But ask yourself: How satisfied have you been with the traditional research papers your students have completed? In our own practice, we usually find that, when something habitually fails to work well, the problem isn't with our students, it's with what we're asking them to do. If we want our students to understand the real-world value of research, it's incumbent on us to provide them with experiences that mirror how they might use research in their own lives. And how do we often use it in our own lives outside an academic setting? By learning more about things in which we take a personal interest. We read, we watch videos, maybe we talk to relevant people, all of which this particular project is geared to accomplish.

Intended Benefits
- personal
- agentive
- engaging

Variation to Add an Authentic Audience

- It's always worth remembering that research can be presented in a variety of genres. As we mentioned above, some of those genres—such as advertising material or the script for an educational film—will necessarily involve an audience other than the teacher as assessor.

Interdisciplinary/Cross-Curricular Connections

- The historical nature of the project obviously lends itself to teaming with a social studies teacher well versed in local history. There would also be opportunities—depending on the students' research interests—to connect with other disciplines as well. Students focusing on visual art or music could find support from those teachers, just as students researching some aspect of the natural environment could find value in connecting with someone from your science department.

Writing about Literature and Other Texts

Despite first reading Harper Lee's (1960/2002) *To Kill a Mockingbird* as a high school student in 1988 and teaching it half a dozen times throughout the 1990s and early 2000s, Rob didn't fully understand the following line about Maycomb, Alabama, until he moved to Georgia in 2009: "In rainy weather the streets turned to red slop" (p. 5). Anyone growing up in the Southeast would immediately latch onto that detail—the way the red clay soil turns into a crimson slurry that sucks at your shoes whenever it's exposed to water. However, as a child in Ohio and a young adult in California, that detail meant little to Rob. Similarly, just a few lines later, Lee (1960/2002) writes about "men's stiff collars wilt[ing] by nine in the morning" (p. 6). Ohio humidity isn't Southern humidity, and the implied oppression in that description can't be fully appreciated until you step outside your Georgia home at 8:00 a.m. on a July morning and feel humidity so thick you could practically suck the moisture out of the air with a straw.

It's true that these are minor details, and Rob's failure to completely grasp them didn't affect his ability to read and understand Lee's book. But they *are* important when it comes to setting the scene, and, in some texts, that *can* influence a reader's textual comprehension. This becomes especially important to remember when we're asking our students to read literature or other texts set in locations with which they may not be completely familiar. In these instances, getting the students out of the classroom and into environments found in (or related to) the text they're reading can be a valuable experience on multiple levels. Museums, learning centers, and historic homes can help replicate the settings you encounter in classroom texts for a variety of writing purposes.

Grounding Literature in the Real World

Using the previous paragraph as a springboard, this activity is specifically designed to better familiarize your students with literary environments. The first thing to say about it is that, while it is entirely dependent on your local resources, you shouldn't consider yourself bound by the actual geography of the text you're reading. If you want your students to get a clearer sense of the Grangerfords' home from *The Adventures of Huckleberry Finn* or Jay Gatsby's house from *The Great Gatsby*, you don't have to travel to Kentucky or Long Island. It could be just as valuable to take your students to a historic home in your own community that replicates what a house of those time periods could have looked like. Once there, you can stage a mini-writing marathon (described in Chapter 3) in the different rooms on display. This could consist of a range of different prompts, such as considering how a visit to this location helps them "see" the setting of the novel, describing what a character from the novel might look like in this specific house, making connections between their own house and the historic house, or any number of other prompts specific to the text you're reading. Such a trip can help your students come to a fuller understanding of the time period in which a text is set, but it can also encourage them to think more broadly about the ways in which a novel's setting enriches its action.

Museums can be connected to texts in thematic or historic ways, too. Many novels—canonical and contemporary alike—shine a light on issues of injustice, and many communities have at least one museum that focuses on civil or human rights. During the course of reading books like Lee's (1960/2002) *To Kill a Mockingbird* or Elie Wiesel's (1960) Holocaust memoir *Night*, or even current texts such as Angie Thomas's (2017) young adult novel *The Hate U Give* or the late US Representative John Lewis's graphic novel series March (Lewis & Aydin, 2013, 2015, 2016), you could arrange a visit to a local civil rights museum to give students a more thorough picture of what the struggle for human rights looked like (and continues to look like) in this country and elsewhere. Notably, some museums have resources that will speak directly to your students' experience. In our community, the Kennesaw State University Museum of History and Holocaust Education features an exhibit focusing on the lives of teenagers during the Holocaust, and this could connect directly to a reading of *Night*—or other texts, like Livia Bitton-Jackson's (1997) *I Have Lived for a Thousand Years*—deepening your students' understanding of the text. But such an experience can also be used to help students think about issues such as justice and empathy, and, depending on which exhibits are on display at your local museum, you can ask your students to write about the connections they see between themselves, the text, and the world.

The place-based writing experience described here can obviously be used with novels and memoirs, but it also has utility in relation to other genres. Reading an informational text such as Martin Luther King Jr.'s (1963) "Letter from a Birmingham Jail" would be strengthened by visiting a museum with an exhibit about King or the American civil rights movement, as would a genre study of Harlem Renaissance poets. Museums and learning centers can be used to enrich the reading of a range of texts by content, theme, or history, and, in all those cases, the inclusion of writing can help students articulate their learning.

Intended Benefits
- personal
- engaging

Interdisciplinary/Cross-Curricular Connections
- Because the historical angle is such an obvious choice, teaming with a social studies teacher to present a thorough account of the time period in question would be a natural fit.

Edgar Allan Poe and Building Suspense

Edgar Allan Poe never seems to go out of fashion. "The Cask of Amontillado" (1846), "The Tell-Tale Heart" (1843), "The Masque of the Red Death" (1842), "The Black Cat" (1843): if these short stories aren't included in your classroom anthology, you or a colleague probably drag them out around Halloween. And, despite their challenging diction and labyrinthine syntax, students still understandably enjoy Poe's macabre world. It seems, however, that we could do more with his work to help students develop a stronger sense of style and narrative structure in their own writing.

With your students, read one or more of Poe's stories for the purpose of identifying his techniques that create suspense.[4] What is it about his stories that makes us anxious? Certainly, some of it involves the extreme measures his characters take (entombing people alive, burying old men under the floorboards, and the like), but there's more to it than that. We could point to things like his use of first-person narration, strategic repetition, foreshadowing, and a range of other flourishes that create suspense. With this as a foundation, you could then visit a historic home similar to those we described in the previous Grounding Literature in the Real World activity. If you live in an older community, it isn't unusual for there to be restored nineteenth- or early twentieth-century homes that are open to the public, often with guided tours. During the tour, your students will obviously learn more about the home and the time period in which it was built, but they should also take notes that they will later incorporate in a suspenseful story of their own creation. How would they describe the way the house looks? What sounds might contribute to a suspenseful atmosphere? Do any rooms smell stale or musty, and how might they use those details to create an original story?

Through this activity, Poe's prose serves as a mentor text to help students develop their own narratives.[5] Going one step further and situating these original tales in a real place not too far removed from the setting of some of Poe's own work can help add a degree of verisimilitude that might otherwise be lacking in the students' writing.

Intended Benefits
- personal
- agentive
- engaging

Variation to Add an Authentic Audience
- Inviting parents to an evening of eerie storytelling would be one way to broaden the audience for the students' stories. If you conducted this activity around Halloween for maximum suspense, so much the better.

Writing Arguments

As we mentioned in Chapter 3, the real-world necessity of crafting logical arguments means we should actively look for ways to help our students couch those arguments in real-world settings. While museums themselves are not strictly real world (for all the reasons we described at the start of this chapter), their collected artifacts and the accumulated knowledge they represent nevertheless provide us with opportunities to help our students develop their facilities for argumentation.

Argue the Innovation

This first activity is the simpler of the two we share in this section and represents a more traditional approach to place-based writing (which may be desirable, especially if you're also looking for an experience that results in a traditional final product). Any museum exhibit will include a constellation of different displays that relate to a similar theme. An exhibit on World War II (or any war, really) will provide patrons with information about different generals, battles, strategies, wartime innovations, and so on. An art museum exhibit on Surrealist painting will certainly share the works of a variety of different artists working in that style. Similarly, science and natural history museums represent a particular body of knowledge about different types of scientific disciplines (astronomy, paleontology, geology, etc.).

We can leverage the accessibility of these collections by asking our students to tour a museum, identify an exhibit that appeals to them, and craft a paper arguing for someone (or some*thing*'s) importance. For example, in touring an American Civil War museum, students could argue for which was the most pivotal battle in the war or which of the Northern generals was most crucial to the army's success.[6] After touring a science and industry museum, each student could argue for the innovation or discovery they deemed most significant. Who was the "best" Impressionist painter? Which figure in the civil rights movement contributed most to the cause? The possibilities for this activity are only limited by the breadth of the museum.[7]

The resulting paper can be used to teach a concept we've consistently found to be one of the trickiest in argument writing: warranting a claim with evidence. Our students are usually adept (often scarily so) at making bold claims. Stating opinions isn't the problem. Where they often struggle is in presenting evidence and then explaining, or warranting, *how* the evidence supports the claim they're making. This is the crux of constructing a logical argument, and it's often one of the components we sidestep precisely because it's a challenge. But Hillocks (2011) reminds us that the warrant is a component of argument writing we ignore at our peril: "The easiest way to attack claims of judgment is to attack the warrant and the definition underlying it" (p. 109).

To provide a specific explanation, then, students have to have a working definition of what they're arguing. In order to claim *The Lion King* is the best animated Disney movie, the arguer has to have a clear sense of the criteria that constitute a good animated Disney movie, and then they have to provide evidence showing how *The Lion King* meets that criteria better than any other animated Disney movie. *Showing* is the key word. It may be true that *The Lion King* has an exciting conflict, but, in order to warrant the claim (thereby closing the circuit in their argument), the arguer would have to explain what it is about the conflict that makes it so much more exciting than any other animated Disney movie. That makes the definition an essential step of the process, because, in many ways, the argument hinges on its clarity.[8]

In legal terms, Hillocks (2011) uses the example of court cases involving first-degree murder. In order to convict a defendant of that crime, the prosecution has to prove premeditation. In a definition of *first-degree murder*, that's the key component. If the prosecution can't show compelling evidence of premeditation, the defendant can't be convicted, because the crime no longer fits the definition. This underscores the definition's importance. The arguer has to have a clear conception of what is being argued so the provided evidence will adequately show it to be true. By asking students in this assignment to argue that something is definitively best, most influential, or most important, we're asking them to engage in the kind of logic building that is essential to crafting an effective argument.

Intended Benefits
- personal
- engaging

Variations to Add an Authentic Audience
- The traditional nature of this activity means a limited audience is somewhat hardwired into it. However, you could certainly experiment with ways to broaden things slightly beyond the "teacher-as-assessor" model. For example, students could present their arguments in a debate format or create posters or videos representing their findings.

Interdisciplinary/Cross-Curricular Connections
- As with many of the activities in this chapter, it would be a natural fit for you to team with a colleague from another department (e.g., science, history, or art, depending on the type of museum you visit) who could supplement your students' museum experience.

Defend Your Curation

This second activity is a slight variation on the first, and it focuses on the notion of curation itself. If you're assembling an exhibit of collected works centered on a particular topic, what are your criteria for what makes the cut? This activity asks your students to consider the relative value of different works of art and then construct an argument in a scenario-based piece of writing.

Imagine that a wealthy philanthropist (maybe the same one we discussed in Chapter 3?) is going to supply your school with five paintings to brighten the surroundings. They will arrange to have them transported from your local art museum to the school. Price is no object. The catch? The student who writes the most convincing argument will see their paintings selected for display.

At a local art museum, your students' task is to select the five paintings they want to see at their school and develop the argument that will win over the philanthropist. This will obviously involve your students exploring the art museum, making evaluative judgments of the art on display, and taking notes they can use to justify this mini-exhibit they're curating. In order to make their selection and write their argument, the students will have to consider the questions we posed above (e.g., "Out of all the paintings on display, why these five?"), but they'll also have to go beyond mere personal preference to write a convincing argument. What's the historical significance of each work? How much diversity is represented in their selections? How do the paintings visually complement each other? Is there any thematic significance to their selections?

In keeping with the scenario-based nature of the activity, the finished product will be a proposal written to the philanthropist wherein the student explains their choice of paintings and the rationale for each. This also presents you with an opportunity to teach the proposal as a type of written genre as well as how to employ the kind of voice appropriate for it. Where the first activity in this section asks students to argue for the import of a specific person or thing in its original context, this activity requires students to think about what it means to curate a collection, and how to thoughtfully engage in that process.

Intended Benefits
- personal
- agentive
- engaging
- audience oriented

Interdisciplinary/Cross-Curricular Connections
- One possibility is to team with museum staff or a knowledgeable art teacher to talk about how museums acquire paintings and the kind of deliberations that take place when planning new exhibits.

Writing Narratives, Poetry, and Scripts

At first blush, museums may not seem to be the most logical place to generate ideas for storytelling or poetry. This is especially true if we lean too heavily into the stereotype we discussed earlier of the museum as an antiseptic, impersonal place. After all, the stories that move us pulse with energy and vitality. They often get messy as they plumb those weighty moral and ethical issues that make them resonate across the years. They're about living, breathing people, and museums are often preoccupied with those no longer with us. How can we bring stories to life in a location that wants to capture things under glass or hang them on a wall?

The answer, simply, is that the best museums tell stories of their own. Historical figures, artists (and the art they create), scientific innovations—the paradoxical nature of museums is that they help us see the life in these things by capturing them in stasis for us to examine. When we visit an American civil rights museum, we're reminded of the centuries-long history of oppression and the figures who have risen up to thwart it. We don't study Martin Luther King Jr. as a lone figure who existed in a single moment—good museums rightfully position him as a pivotal figure who had historical antecedents and whose good work continues to resonate long after his death.

Museums often tell powerful stories. As teachers, we can help our students find inspiration in them to tell stories of their own.

Ekphrasis: Writing Poetry (and Prose) about Art

What do W. H. Auden's "Musée des Beaux Arts" (1939), Anne Sexton's "The Starry Night" (1981), and Allen Ginsberg's "Cézanne's Ports" (1961) have in common? They're poems written about paintings using a device called *ekphrasis*.[9] Showing these poems and the artwork that inspired them can help our students begin to see how "real" authors look to other artists for inspiration. There's a fallacious belief among some students (especially less-confident writers not yet sold on their own storytelling abilities) that writing always springs from the ether or comes fully formed to the author in a dream. Such beliefs are disempowering. After all, if you don't have those dreams or your access to that mystical wellspring of brilliant ideas is closed off, where do you get your ideas?[10] Introducing students to ekphrasis can help them understand that they're surrounded by potential stories and poems, and, with this idea as our foundation, we can look to local art museums as sources of inspiration for students to craft stories or poems about existing works of art. Furthermore, by tapping into "the higher level skills of applying, analyzing, evaluating, and creating" (Moynihan, 2016, p. 68), ekphrastic writing is likely to see students produce work of greater sophistication than the standard essays they are used to producing.

There *is* one catch: in our experience, students have had little exposure to paintings or sculpture, and, even if they have, they tend to look at them passively, without thinking about them as something just as ripe for interpretation as literature. Students, however, *are* often quite skilled at articulating the meaning they find in photographs or other still images, which means the leap to viewing and finding meaning in other works of visual art should be a small one. You may find, though, that you first need to show your students one or more paintings in class, to walk them through the process of interpreting this art.[11] Rob frequently uses Renoir's painting *Bal du moulin au Galette* to introduce this concept. The party scene in the painting is easily recognizable but also broad enough to allow for multiple interpretations. Students take turns sharing their interpretations of what they see in the painting, and, crucially, also indicate the specific features in the painting that led them to this interpretation (in much the same way we would ask students to cite lines of a poem to support their meaning-making).

For the place-based writing activity itself, take your students to a local art museum and give them some time to explore on their own. During this time, they should find a work of art[12] that inspires them (or resonates with them or perplexes them) enough that they would want to write a poem or story about what they see happening in the art. It's vital that students have time to explore *and* time to write. This is especially important if the museum prohibits photography. Your students will need time with the painting so they aren't having to craft their ekphrastic piece solely from memory and note-taking.

Intended Benefits

- personal
- agentive
- engaging

Variation to Add an Authentic Audience

- It wouldn't be a bad idea to find time for the students to share their writing. At a minimum, you could do this sharing in class. But you might consider reaching out to the museum you visited to see if there are opportunities to display the students' work in the museum itself or to stage a reading for patrons.

Interdisciplinary/Cross-Curricular Connections

- It would obviously make sense to involve your school's art teacher in this activity, especially if you feel uncomfortable with the idea of teaching art to your students. They could supplement the activity by helping students start to see painting techniques (use of light and shadow, focus, weight, etc.) and their effect in specific paintings.

Thinking about Perspective

As we mentioned in the introduction to this section, museums often help students contextualize the roles played by historical figures. When we merely read about politicians, civil rights leaders, scientists, or soldiers, it's often difficult to see them as real people, even if the text describing them is effective. A museum, on the other hand, can help bring these figures to life for your students. By using photography, film, audio recordings, and other creative methods of presentation, students can begin to understand these figures in a way they may find difficult when confined to words on a page (especially if your students, like ours, are often reluctant readers).

What does this have to do with writing narratives? We find museums particularly helpful in developing our students' abilities to write believably from perspectives other than their own. Locate a museum in your community that features historical figures. Broadly speaking, any type of museum that deals with history will suffice. It can be local, national, or world, focused on civil rights, literature, or the military (or, really, anything else). The important thing is that it represents a range of personalities, and the more diverse the better. As in many of the other activities we describe, it's good to provide your students with some time to explore the museum for the purpose of finding one or more figures whose story interests them (which is why you'll want to ensure that a range of personalities is represented). Once they have identified those figures, they should take some time in the museum to learn as much as they can about them, including looking at photos, viewing film, or listening to available audio. The resulting product from this experience will be a short piece of historical fiction relating a story from that figure's life, told from that figure's point of view, and incorporating accurate historical detail.

An alternate product (especially if your class is currently reading a play) would be to ask your students to learn about *at least two* figures. Instead of writing a narrative, you could ask them to write a script capturing a conversation between the different characters. This variation would still meet your needs for teaching your students perspective, but it would also help them learn the fundamentals of playwriting (which can obviously include lessons in voice, word choice, punctuation, and a host of other elements commonly found in English language arts curricula).

The intent in either version of this activity is similar to the ekphrastic exercise above—helping your students find inspiration for creative writing in something they learned at the museum—but it can also help distant history spring to life as students wrestle with and take ownership of the past in a piece of original fiction.

Intended Benefits

- personal
- engaging

Variation to Add an Authentic Audience

- As we advocate in various places throughout this book, students should be encouraged to share their work with each other. This could be especially effective if you used the scriptwriting variation of this activity. Your students could actually dramatize their scripts by performing them for the class.

Interdisciplinary/Cross-Curricular Connections

- The scriptwriting activity could be developed even further by presenting the scripts in conjunction with the drama class. This would give your students the valuable opportunity to see their work performed by others. Further, if your class is currently reading a play, it will strengthen any of your additional lessons on blocking and stagecraft.

Stories Set in Museums

E. L. Konigsburg's *From the Mixed-Up Files of Mrs. Basil E. Frankweiler* (1967) is a perennial children's literature favorite for good reason. The story of runaway Claudia Kincaid's adventures in New York's Metropolitan Museum of Art treats the museum as an exciting, mysterious location ideal for storytelling. More recently, the Night at the Museum (2006, 2009, 2014) movie series also illustrates the narrative possibilities of museum as story setting. In the introduction to this chapter, we pointed out the ways in which museums are unique in their collection of public spaces. With exhibits, gift shops, cafés, atriums, outdoor areas, and more as narrative possibilities, students could use their visit to the museum as an opportunity to explore the grounds and make detailed observations that could be used to craft a story, poem, or script. Whether these original works end up rooted in reality or fantasy, using the actual museum space as inspiration for writing can help your students see the exciting possibilities in venturing into the real world.

Intended Benefits

- personal
- agentive
- engaging

Variation to Add an Authentic Audience

- As we've mentioned elsewhere, the relatively minor variation of asking your students to share their stories with each other in class can make a sizable difference in its degree of authenticity. When they know someone other than the teacher will hear the finished product, they tend to take it more seriously.

Writing for Research and Inquiry

As we hope we illustrated in this chapter's extended series of lessons, it makes sense to treat a visit to the museum as inspiration to engage in authentic inquiry. The visit itself is, in essence, a form of research. As in that earlier activity focused on local history, it's doubtful the visit will be the sum total of research the students conduct, but it can be an initial point of contact that generates ideas and helps them formulate one or more questions to pursue. This process starts at the museum but continues in your own classroom and beyond.

Most museum-inspired research activities (including the one we describe next) will be more focused versions of the Exploring Local History research project explained at the beginning of this chapter. The specific nature of any research project you teach will ultimately depend on the resources in your area.

Missing Voices

No art museum is comprehensive. That might be a sentence so obvious it hardly bears mentioning, but, for our students, many of whom aren't conversant in visual art, what they see may very well represent to them the totality of a particular movement or time period. However, keeping in mind that an art museum exhibit represents only one way of looking at a particular topic—say, one version of the Impressionist story or of the nineteenth-century American story—it's worth encouraging our students to conduct further research on the voices missing from an exhibit that particularly appeals to them.

Such a research activity doesn't require you to have an extensive knowledge of visual art yourself. The goal is for the students to tour the museum and identify a movement or time period that resonates with them in some way. They should make note of the artists represented in the exhibit and conduct subsequent research to identify artistic voices from the same time period or movement that don't appear in the exhibit. For example, many Expressionist exhibits display the usual white male suspects: Wassily Kandinsky, Marc Chagall, Paul

Klee, Egon Schiele, and so on. Usually omitted from these exhibits, though, are equally noteworthy female Expressionists like Elaine de Kooning and Mary Abbott. This project can give your students a more thorough grasp of visual art, but it can also help them start to see the ways in which curated exhibits often (and sometimes unintentionally) erase already marginalized voices.[13]

Taking such an angle likely requires a final product more audience oriented than a traditional research paper (which would likely amount to little more than a summary of artists and works). Instead, consider having your students write a letter to the museum arguing for the significance of a particular artist and suggesting possible works that could be included in the museum. Even though it doesn't take the form of a traditional research paper, a compelling letter would have to include elements of the student's research (including the artist's history, influence, and important works), and its inclusion of an authentic audience would raise the stakes for the assignment. Finally, the museum letter would also provide you with the opportunity to discuss professional voice with your students. If the letter is to be convincing, it can't come off like an angry screed. The art of written tact is something your students will certainly need throughout their lives.

Intended Benefits
- personal
- engaging
- audience oriented
- promotes change

Interdisciplinary/Cross-Curricular Connections
- Teaming with your art teacher to present supplemental information would be a natural connection for you to make (especially if you feel like your own knowledge is lacking).

Writing for Change

A recurring theme of this chapter has been the tricky problem presented by the very nature of museums. As useful as they can be in other ways, their artificiality requires us to devise different inroads to place-based writing. This is certainly true when it comes to writing for change. Museums typically deal with established knowledge—some (or even much) of which happened in far-off locations and eras—so how can information that might be dramatically removed from our own experience be used to promote change in our communities? Our proposed workaround for this challenge is to stay local. And that brings us back where we started: the local history museum and the possibilities it presents your students to make their voices heard.

What's Missing in Your Community?

As we discussed in the previous activity, any curated exhibit will, to one degree or another, represent an accepted body of knowledge about a particular topic. This is both a strength and a weakness of museums. By visiting a particular exhibit, we're treated to knowledge or exposed to art that we might not have otherwise experienced. But, if we're unfamiliar with the subject and something isn't included in the exhibit, we *don't know* it's not there. That omission means we're getting an inaccurate impression of the exhibit in question, and, if we don't conduct additional research on our own, we'll never know what's missing. The lack of inclusion isn't necessarily malicious. In fact, it's usually a matter of practicality and finance. What museum (outside of landmark institutions like the Smithsonian, the Louvre, or the British Museum) can present a comprehensive view of *anything*?

But the question of what's omitted in museums and individual exhibits—and what we could reasonably argue should be included—is an interesting one, especially on a local level. Our students' knowledge of their own communities is often specialized or specific, and that knowledge will likely revolve around their lived experience. It probably wouldn't have appeared in Rob's local history museum in an exhibit focused on midwestern life, but he could make the argument that the local Little League fields were vital to what it meant to be a child in the early 1980s. He spent countless hours in practice and games, and summer nights often revolved around the entire experience of commuting to the field, playing the game, buying candy at the concession stand afterward, and conking out in the car on the ride home. If those fields were omitted from any museum about the life of the town, it would be an incomplete picture.

So, after visiting a local history museum, what do your students think is missing from it? What part of the community (or what activity) is unrepresented? What should be included, to give museum visitors (especially those from other communities) a fuller picture of life in their town? Such an activity validates your students' experiences—actually arguing why their experiences matter to others. It also functions as an effective way of teaching argument writing. To craft a compelling argument, students will have to make a claim, establish criteria for what makes an exhibit necessary, and present evidence that their location or activity meets that criteria.

Crucially, if this activity is truly to promote change, these arguments have to find their way to the local history museum. This could take the form of individual letters, but you might consider other, more innovative ways for students to present their arguments. They could create posters or videos making their cases, which would subsequently be presented to the museum. It might be even more effective, however, to take a page from the playbook of YPAR (discussed in Chapter 3) and have your students actually create a pop-up museum consisting of exhibits detailing these "missing" places. Parents and museum staff could be invited, and the students would have the opportunity to share their arguments in person.

Whichever form the finished products take, what truly elevates this particular activity is its emphasis on your students' own lives and experiences. It tells them their voices matter, and this can be a crucial first step in encouraging them to take on even bigger community service projects in the future.

Intended Benefits

- personal
- agentive
- engaging
- audience oriented
- promotes change

Considerations for Students with Special Needs

- To increase engagement with activities set in art museums, we might consider ways of helping students make personal connections with artists. It would be beneficial for them to hear about the contributions of artists or historical figures who also had special needs (e.g., Michelangelo possessed limited use of his hands due to an undetermined medical condition, Van Gogh was bipolar and suffered from epilepsy, and Matisse was wheelchair bound after surgery for cancer).

- One way to better contextualize how students can advocate for their own local knowledge may be for you to start by having them write about their own personal life experiences. A timeline of events, experiences, likes, and dislikes should be enough for them to begin thinking about what might be important to add to a local history museum. They can compare their life story to the exhibits on display and choose one major event or location on which to focus.

- Regardless of the activity (and if the museum allows it), give students the option of taking photos of the pieces, exhibits, or events they will be responding to, so they will have relevant support once they are back in the classroom. While picture and vocabulary scaffolds are a common and somewhat obvious support to suggest, we find it critical to remind you of it for this type of place-based writing.

Considerations for English Language Learners

- Visiting an art museum provides an important opportunity for students to engage in cultural connections. Students can become experts in artists in the museum that share their cultural heritage. If the museum does not have an artist that fits the bill, students can take ownership of researching and presenting an artist that would. This provides students the chance to connect to a topic that is even more relevant to them and gives them an opportunity to not only argue from experience but also do research on artists with whom they may be able to share similar life experiences. In sharing what they learned about this artist with their peers, students are not only provided validation for the importance of their own culture but we are also fostering a classroom of students who understand that their own culture is not the only one that matters.

- Because it may take some students more time to process the visual and written information provided in a museum while also trying to make connections to literature, it may be beneficial to provide your students with excerpts from the text you're studying. Amanda used this technique with two intensive English learners when she brought them to the Cobb County Youth Museum. At key points, as students moved through the different rooms, she provided them with passages from the book they were currently reading (Ann McGovern's [1975] *The Secret Soldier: The Story of Deborah Sampson*). In doing so, students were able to make connections between the vocabulary and events in the book and the real-life stories that helped inspire it.

5

Writing in Public Places

A cursory glance at our table of contents may seem as though we're splitting hairs. Why do "public places" get their own chapter? After all, didn't we just spend an entire chapter dealing with a type of public place—the museum? And how does the very next chapter's focus on natural places differ from this one? Are these just arbitrary distinctions? To answer just that last question, "Yes—and no." It's true that museums are public places, and it's also true that the areas on which we focus in Chapter 6 are also types of public places. But, as we thought about how best to delineate the different kinds of places that could be fruitful for student writing, it seemed as though there has to be a middle ground between places like museums (that are public but often restricted by admission fees) and the natural places we address in the next chapter (that are public but also undeveloped).

Our solution? We're using the name "public place" as a sort of catchall, and we intend for that title to encompass a range of spaces that have two distinct characteristics in common: they have all been planned or developed (and therefore serve a social function), and the public has reasonable, free access to them. For the sake of clarity, here's a not-at-all-exhaustive list of the kind of places we're classifying as "public":

- town squares
- shopping areas (malls as well as open-air shopping districts)
- monuments and historic landmarks
- public art displays (including murals and statuary)
- running/biking/walking trails
- cemeteries
- parks and playgrounds (including dog parks and skate parks)
- preserved historic areas
- public buildings (such as libraries or community centers)

Even if this list isn't complete (it isn't),[1] it should give you enough of an idea to begin creating an inventory of the public places in your own community. All of the listed spaces are accessible and, crucially, serve a variety of public purposes. They can be used for recreation or commerce, they can be used to beautify an existing area, they can be educational, or they can commemorate a spot (or a person) worth remembering. Aesthetic or utilitarian, these are places we encounter every day, and they may even be places with which we're so familiar we don't even notice them. We recognize that, even if you're willing to get on board with this classification, you may still have some hesitation. After all, if these locations are so commonplace, why write about them at all? If you're going to invest the time and energy in planning a place-based writing experience for your students, is your town square or a mixed-used shopping area going to give you the most bang for your pedagogical buck? We think so.

For one thing, consider these places *as places*. The town square, the park, the shopping center, the art installation, the monument: all of these have been designed for aesthetic or functional purposes (and sometimes both). Cresswell (2015) writes of the idea of "genius loci," which originally referred to "a Roman belief that places had a particular spirit that watched over them" (p. 129). As the term has evolved, however, it now usually refers to "the assemblage of physical and symbolic values in the environment," which include "both 'natural' aspects of a place . . . and the human landscape" (Cresswell, 2015, p. 130). In short, when you visit the town square, or the shopping mall, or the landmark, how does each harmonize with its surroundings? How has the architect or planner accounted for these surroundings, and how does that help or hinder the way we view (or use) this public place? And, crucially for an English class, how does this contribute to a place's *character*? What makes this place distinct from other places? Such thinking can unlock powerful narrative, argument, and research writing possibilities.

Running parallel to that notion—"What makes a place the place it is?"—is the idea that some public places, like shopping malls or supermarkets, are, as Augé (1995) terms them, "non-places." These "spaces where people coexist or cohabit without living together" (Augé, 1995, p. 100) exist in contrast to places like town squares, landmarks, or historic neighborhoods that draw on a very distinct sense of history. Non-places, on the other hand, are transient, where "particular histories and traditions are not . . . relevant" and are usually "marked by mobility and travel" (Cresswell, 2015, p. 78). Does this impermanence render these non-places any less authentic than, say, a building preserved for its historic significance? How is its character different?

Complicating matters even further is the public place whose character has undergone seismic change over time. In Chapter 3, we mentioned the upheaval that has occurred in Amanda's school since several apartment blocks were razed to build a state-of-the-art soccer complex. Gentrification of this kind is increasingly commonplace, especially in urban settings. The superficial view of such development is that it's altruistic (or at the very least benign), bringing to a community new opportunities for housing and commerce that didn't exist before. But what such a view ignores is the classist and racist displacement that is a result of these new "opportunities." Christensen (2015) points out the intentionality of gentrification, that it is a process whose acts "rest on a platform of racism, privilege, and decisions made by people in power" (p. 16). For those being gentrified, these intentional decisions mean "homelessness, displacement, expensive and inaccessible housing, and a challenge to the cultural diversity, practices, and tolerance that have been a mark of their neighbourhood" (Reid & Smith, 1993, p. 199).

Importantly, students who live in gentrified neighborhoods are not ignorant of their changing environments. Kinloch (2010) tells the story of Phillip and Khaleeq, two teen boys who live in a rapidly gentrifying Harlem. As her interviews with the teens reveal, gentrification raises all manner of troubling questions for those who live in these communities. At one point, Phillip posits that, while the changing nature of the community has made it safer, "'Why we have to have gentrification give us things we should already have based on the fact that we're human, we're people?'" (p. 8). The process of gentrification can be bewilderingly tense, especially for adolescents who are still in the process of figuring out how they belong in the world. For Phillip, it means feeling "'in the middle'" (p. 40), neither grateful for, nor resentful of, gentrification. He sees its benefits—a new Rite Aid, revitalized buildings—but he also recognizes this means higher rent that the community's longtime residents can no longer afford. It also means an influx of new white neighbors who fail to recognize "'the community that's already here before they decided to move on in'" (p. 40). Because these students are savvy to the changes in their own community, Kinloch argues that it is no solution to sidestep the issue. Instead, as teachers, we have an obligation to make central in our classrooms "the lives, literacies, and languages of our youth in the out-of-school communities that they call home" (p. 57). This means tackling the complicated issue of gentrification head on. In the process, by privileging their experiences and empowering their voices, we can help position our students as fierce advocates for themselves and their communities.

But this isn't valuable work just for students who have seen gentrification firsthand. For those students whose communities haven't been gentrified, it can also be powerful to contemplate what has been erased in the name of "progress" and to consider how their writing can be used to help those who have been marginalized by such development. The notion of adopting multiple perspectives to better understand our neighbors and their world is a common theme in the English language arts classroom. But, as Kinloch (2010) reminds us, "One cannot insist on the value of multiple perspectives without modeling it and believing in its worth" (p. 54). Using place-based writing to actually get students into these changing communities can help them better understand the price of gentrification and build their capacity for empathy. The result for all these students, directly affected by gentrification or not, can be to help them "envision their civic roles and duties within a larger, democratic society" (Kinloch, 2010, p. 54). Christensen (2015) echoes Kinloch's belief, stating that, as teachers "we have an obligation to create opportunities for our students to use our classrooms to work toward justice by combating the injustices of the past and present in the hope of a better future" (p. 21).

At the same time, please remember that the writing activities you facilitate in public places don't have to take up such heavy, heady, ideological topics. As vital as that work is, we recognize it may not be possible for a variety of reasons in your current context. Rest assured there are just as many opportunities for observation, description, and reflection of other sorts. For instance, we can look at a public art installation as a very specific kind of public place. When we encounter sculpture in an otherwise nonartistic location, such as a city street or outside an office building, we have an opportunity to reckon with it not just as a work of art but as a work of art existing in a potentially contradictory context. How are we supposed to interpret it? What story does it tell (especially as it relates to its physical location)? What might the artist's intent be in designing such a piece, or why might this particular sculpture have been selected for this specific block of an otherwise busy street? Similarly, if we add statues or monuments with a historic commemorative purpose to the mix, we can also consider the intersection of appearance, purpose, and location. How does the monument show respect for its subject and in what way does its location reinforce or subvert that intention? And, of course, public places are rife with opportunities for observation and storytelling, from the businesspeople hurriedly scarfing down a meal in the mall food court to the canine characters romping in the dog park. Whatever your objective for writing, you can probably find a public place to meet it.

Also not to be overlooked is the fact that public places are highly accessible. Where museums and many parks will likely involve admission fees in addition to the transportation and coverage costs you incur by missing part of the school day, some public places may very well lie within walking distance of your school. As we noted in Chapter 3 with regard to writing in school places, it can be powerful for your students to recognize that inspiration for writing can be found just around the corner. In that same vein, while public places as we're defining them may not seem to present obvious opportunities for writing about the environment, we can still encourage students to think critically about the role of nature in their daily habitats. Green spaces, public gardens, urban waterways, and more: nature can still be found even in the most developed areas. Writing about the environment in a local context can encourage your students to see how advocacy works in their own backyard.

In the sections that follow, we discuss specific writing activities that take up some of these ideas. However, to return to a common refrain, by establishing the complexity of spaces that many of us have taken for granted, we hope you'll be able to develop writing activities unique to the public places found in your own communities.

Extended Lesson Idea: Rooting Narrative in Place

For years, narrative writing has been seen as the less serious sibling of argument and research. If the latter two modes are the diligent, conscientious students all the teachers love, narrative writing is the class clown whom few people take seriously. It was the same when we were students, and it's a trend that persists today. Narrative writing is, for whatever reason, seen by many as frivolous and less worthy of our time (Romano, 1995).

There is, of course, little truth to this. Writing a good story—one in which the characters are believable, and the dialogue crackles, and the plot is absorbing—is no easy feat. Completed novels and short stories don't just fall from the sky waiting to be published. Writing a quality narrative is every bit as labor intensive as writing the well-reasoned argument or the exhaustively researched report. Authors have to weigh word choice and sentence length. Narrative structure. Character descriptions. Dialogue that isn't just plausible but entertaining. Creating an engaging conflict and resolving it in a way that isn't trite. The assumption made by many critics of "creative writing," as Romano (1995) reminds us, is that it "equals no discipline, no rigor, no craft, no skills, no thinking. Just spewing, gushing, spilling" (p. 3). The truth is, though, as anyone who's tried to write creatively knows, *it's hard*.

This criticism of creative writing is even more dubious when you consider the flip side. How many truly *bad*[2] argumentative essays have you read from your students? Ones in which the claim is dubious, the organization confounding, and the evidence nonexistent? Between us, we have thirty years in the classroom, and we've read quite a few of these. We're sure you have, too. But the way argument and explanatory writing have been privileged seems to automatically take as gospel the notion that *all* our students' arguments and explanations are meaningful. That just the act of writing them—no matter how disappointing the final product—amounts to something important. However, if you recall the brief history of writing instruction we explored in Chapter 1, we know that much of what passes for academic writing has been flawed for a long time. And much of that academic writing has been—you guessed it—arguments and explanations. If you're willing to buy into the credible notion that well-written narratives are just as intellectually demanding for students as other types of well-written essays, it makes logical sense to start looking for ways to give them more prominence in the classroom.

The Assignment

One way to meaningfully emphasize narrative writing is to structure an extended assignment around a place-based writing experience (in the same way we often plan a lengthy research project). Public places are uniquely suited for such an assignment, considering they represent both a range of opportunities for practice as well as various possibilities for narrative inspiration. From using imagery to establish setting, to developing and describing compelling characters, to capturing believable dialogue, public places represent a real-world laboratory in which to practice these techniques. For more ambitious or advanced writers, we can even begin to discuss "the ways that the social and cultural features of a certain setting, along with its environmental features, affect, and are affected by, the characters" (Case, 2017, p. 7). Migrating their writing from the classroom to a public location can help students develop their own skills in various components of narrative craft, which they will ultimately turn into an original piece of storytelling that uses the public place as its setting.

First things first. Even though the story will be rooted in a version of the place your class visits, the students don't have to have specific geographic fidelity. If Amanda takes her fourth graders to visit a dog park, they don't have to write about a dog park *in Marietta, Georgia*, or even about a dog park at all. The location is simply grist for the narrative mill. Nor do we argue that the entire story be set in a single location, although that might be a sensible approach, especially for less skilled or confident writers. However, if students want to tell a story on a larger canvas that uses the public place as only one of their settings, we'd at least be willing to entertain that possibility. Essentially, the intent of the assignment is for the students to use their observations of place to inform an original narrative, regardless of where it's ultimately set.

The parameters for the story itself are flexible. How long should it be? What's the minimum number of characters (if any)? Are the students responsible for including a certain number of literary devices? Is dialogue required? There's no "right" answer for any of these questions. Or maybe it's more accurate to say the right answer will depend on what you plan to assess. If you want to gauge how well your students use believable dialogue (however you're defining that), you'd better require it in their stories. Similarly, if a goal of the narrative assignment is to ensure your students can create and effectively employ literary devices such as metaphor or personification, it would be unusual for those things *not* to show up in your grading criteria. But we don't want to set those expectations here, mainly because, just as the assignment will conform to your own specific objectives, individual stories require a variety of stylistic flourishes. What happens if you require dialogue for the assignment but one student wants to write a story as a first-person internal monologue? What if you ask students to write a story between six and ten pages in length, but several students find they can write theirs effectively in four? These considerations aren't meant to discourage you from the assignment. Instead, we mention them here as a reminder of something we advocated in Chapter 1: intentionality and thoughtfulness in your assignment design.

As for the place-based visit itself, we recommend doing it at least twice, if at all possible. One reason for this is that it gives your students an opportunity to consider the character of the place under different conditions. Even though the structure of the school day means they'll likely be visiting the site at the same time of day (and probably the same time of year, unless you're making it a *very long* project), it should go without saying that no two days are the same. Your students will unavoidably notice different things in each visit. But making multiple visits also allows you to focus on different elements of craft each time. In one visit, you could focus on the physical description of the place itself; in a second trip, you could ask your students to spend their time capturing important details of the people who inhabit the place. Taking only a single visit for the purpose of observation and first-draft writing means the students have to cover a lot of ground in that one trip. This isn't to say you shouldn't make a single visit if that's all that's viable. Just be sure to focus your students' work in that time (and temper your expectations for what they can reasonably accomplish).

Logistical Considerations

Given the emphasis on setting that's central to this long-term assignment, the public place you visit will be of paramount importance. What are the public places within reasonable distance of your school (which may include walking distance, in certain cases) that would provide your students with a chance to observe, experiment with language, and find inspiration for a story? You can use the list we provided as a starting point, but there are certainly other places that could be fruitful. In general, we prefer places where there's a lot to observe: manufactured and natural objects, people interacting in different ways with each other and their environment, animals, even vehicular traffic. Public parks can be especially bountiful in this regard, and, if it's a park with several different areas,[3] it will give your students a lot to observe.

A word of warning about these observations. Any time children are involved, you obviously want to exercise even more caution. For this reason, it isn't a bad idea to discuss with your students the pitfalls of observing playgrounds (or even make playgrounds off limits altogether). Even if your students have the best academic intentions, parents can become rightfully suspicious of anyone who seems predatory. Sitting on a bench with an open notebook and taking avid notes of small children would justify such suspicion.

Finally, the only other variable you'll need to consider prior to starting this project are your areas of instruction. What specific craft lessons do you want to teach (and assess) as part of this narrative unit? We discuss several below, and our hope is that you consider ways you can coordinate teaching them with one or more visits to the location you've identified. In this way, your students will have an opportunity to practice them in a real-world setting central to their stories.

Supplemental Lessons

Using Imagery

Teaching imagery is a tricky thing because, to one degree or another, our students are at the mercy of their vocabularies. To employ descriptive language effectively, a writer has to have enough command of the language to do so. This presents obvious problems for our students who are English language learners, but many of our native speakers aren't in a position that's any more enviable, especially in the younger grades. You don't know what you don't know, and it's a fool's errand to tell a student with a limited vocabulary that they need to write more descriptively without actively supporting them in how to do that.

For this reason, we advise against starting with an activity that already assumes they know how to write descriptively (unless you know for certain they can). We've fallen prey to this ourselves, asking students to write descriptions of striking photographic images or describing the tactile sensation of reaching into a box and touching an unknown object. If your students already have a capacity for descriptive language, these can be effective activities. But, again, remember that you may need to meet your students where they are and start small.

One way to start small is to think about the very act of embellishment and elaboration. When we read a sentence lacking in description, where do we need more detail? If you share a sentence like "My teacher dresses weird," your students immediately recognize what needs description. And, in this case, many students will quickly leap to fill in the gaps. They each have an idea of what "weird" looks like, and providing that imagery will be second nature. It might not be especially sophisticated, but it's a starting point. To further develop this skill, you might consider using a mentor text—for example, sharing a passage from a young adult novel that describes someone looking weird (or dressing unconventionally), or even writing one yourself. Following up the initial activity in this way can help your students start to see the range of possibilities for their own writing.

Additionally, you may find you need to do some grammar instruction. It might be necessary to teach specific concepts, from building blocks such as descriptive adjectives to more sophisticated tools like absolute phrases. These concepts—what Noden (2011) calls *brush strokes*[4]—help emerging writers adhere to the old adage to "show, not tell," and in Noden's estimation, increase their ability to visualize "specific details that create a literary virtual reality" (p. 3). This can actually be a powerful way to teach grammar, moving instruction away from isolated drills and worksheets in order to emphasize the ways in which we use grammar in our everyday speaking and writing to make sense of the world.

Once your students demonstrate some facility for using descriptive language, you can move on to other activities, such as describing photos or objects, to further develop this skill. And, of course, it probably goes without saying that this would be a good time to schedule an initial visit to your selected public place, so your students can begin to experiment with some first-draft descriptive writing.

Two additional notes on this topic. First, we recommend starting with imagery, as the lessons in characterization described below depend in part on your students' ability to write descriptively. Finally, if you want to do more work with imagery, you can refer to some of the school-based activities we described in Chapter 3.

Creating Characters

As we consider teaching our students to write quality narratives, characterization is an aspect that is both essential and accessible. In fact, this is one of those topics in relation to which we can especially leverage our students' existing knowledge. Thanks to movies, television, video games, and graphic novels (not to mention popular book series like Harry Potter or The Olympians series with Percy Jackson), most of our students will come to us with a hardwired understanding of character, even if they're not avid readers of the texts we assign. As an introductory lesson on characterization, students can begin by identifying characters from pop culture that resonate with them. What draws them to those characters? How would they describe them? What makes them believable or relatable? How does their physical appearance support or subvert their behavior? Such a conversation sets the stage for some original writing and also serves as an implicit introduction to direct and indirect characterization.

Before doing some first-draft writing in the public place you selected, it's important to take at least one more lesson to make sure the basics of characterization are in place. Building on the earlier conversation about characters in pop culture, you can flesh out the definitions of direct and indirect characterization as well as help students develop an emerging understanding of the common techniques authors use to populate their fictional worlds (e.g., physical description, dialogue, internal monologue, action, etc.). An activity we've tried with some success is asking students to describe themselves as fictional characters. This requires them to take a step back and think about how they would capture their appearance and personality for a reader. And, as with the introductory lesson on characterization in pop culture, they're describing a character they know well.

With some basics in place, you can travel to your public place and give the students an opportunity to conduct some observations of the individuals who people it. How would they describe those people—not just the way they look, but the ways in which they interact with their environment? In the process, would any of these character "types" be useful to them in a story? In what way could they mine these observations to develop a story? Some students may argue that this is backward—that they need the plot first. This will likely be a matter of personal preference for you as the teacher, but one thing we find is that compelling stories are often *grounded in character*. Create believable characters first, and a story worth reading will emerge from them. However, if a student comes up with a story to tell before they've fully thought through their means of characterization, we'd be hard-pressed to tell them not to write it. But we also think starting with character is a powerful strategy that will serve them better in the long run.

Crafting Believable Dialogue

This is arguably one of the trickiest things to do. Even otherwise skilled writers can present a reader with dialogue that rings false. And therein lies the problem with dialogue: it has to *feel* true in the context of character, even if it may not reflect the way people actually talk. Very few people (if any) speak with the clever, biting snap of Elmore Leonard's tough guys, but we believe it because it feels right for the characters. So, when giving students opportunities to practice writing dialogue, it helps to have models.

As with our introductory lesson on characterization, we can turn to pop culture to help with this. The best writers for movies and television have turned dialogue into an art form, and one of the most skilled is William Goldman (screenwriter of *Butch Cassidy and the Sundance Kid*, *All the President's Men*, *Misery*, *Marathon Man*, and many others). In *The Princess Bride* (1987) (which, like *Marathon Man*, Goldman adapted from his novel of the same name), the negotiation between hero Westley and evil genius Vizzini for Buttercup's freedom is a masterclass in entertaining dialogue that also reveals character. You can watch this scene (or others) with your students and ask them to analyze the dialogue. What makes it entertaining? What makes each character's method of speaking distinct? What do we learn about the characters from the things they say? There's no shortage of films[5] you can use to introduce your students to dialogue.

With a few models in mind, we again recommend providing students with some time to experiment in class. One activity Rob used with his high school students was to provide them with some general two-person scenarios they would script solely through dialogue. Here's one example he used with tenth graders:

> *It's the end of the school day, and Connor is excited to get home. He jumps in his car, hurriedly reverses out of his parking space, and speeds toward the parking lot exit. Distracted by his ringing phone, he looks down and fails to notice the stopped cars ahead. He quickly slams on his brakes, but it's too late. With a crunch of metal, he rear-ends Keri's brand-new Audi. Furious, she leaps out of the driver's seat to confront Connor.*
>
> *Script a scene that sees Connor deescalate the situation without resorting to violence.*

Working with a partner, the students are given time to think through the basic "plot" of this scene, figure out how they will resolve the conflict, and then collaborate on the resulting dialogue. In a subsequent class—or later in the same class, if time allows—the students can read their scenes aloud. This allows them to actually *hear* their dialogue and consider its plausibility and effectiveness, but you can also use this time as an opportunity for your students to give each other feedback on their work.

Moving this activity into your selected public place for practice isn't essential, but it can help. One thing you can ask your students to do—maybe in tandem with the place-based characterization activity described above—is to have your students make note of any memorable turns of phrase or exchanges they overhear during their observations. If it turns out there's a place for them, those bits of conversation could eventually be incorporated into their emerging narratives.

Sketching the Structure

We're always of two minds about teaching narrative structure. Too much emphasis can create the impression that there's one "right" way to tell a story, but to avoid it completely ignores the fact that many narratives nevertheless adhere to Freytag's (1894/1968) by-now-familiar pyramid: exposition–rising action–climax–falling action–dénouement. To resolve this tension in our own practice, we find it helpful to present Freytag's model as a common, but not exclusive, approach. If nothing else, it can help students think through their individual narratives and make some tactical storytelling decisions. What information initially needs to be shared for your reader to make sense of the story? When does the conflict emerge? What are the complications that lead to the climax, and how is the conflict resolved?

Sketching out these items on a graphic organizer of the pyramid can help students think through their narrative details before they do much drafting. Using mentor texts here can be helpful, too. Analyzing stories that follow the pyramid can help them see the inherent logic to this structure. On the other hand, examining stories that *don't* follow one or more aspects of the pyramid can open up narrative possibilities your students likely hadn't considered. For instance, Poe's (1843/2017) "The Tell-Tale Heart" essentially ends at the climax with no resolution (or maybe it's more accurate to say the climax and resolution occur simultaneously), while Ernest Hemingway's (1927/1997) "Hills Like White Elephants" involves such an unconventional conflict that students may be challenged to identify the rising action and climax. In both cases, an analysis of existing stories can encourage structure-bending experimentation in your students' own writing.

Summing Up

The flexibility of this project can be intimidating. We believe one reason narratives have been de-emphasized in the classroom is the fact that they can be just about anything. Even if we don't adhere to a specific formula, we know arguments are going to contain specific features (e.g., a claim, evidence, counterarguments, etc.). Similar things can be said of the compare–contrast essay, the short story analysis, the poetic explication—the content is generally going to be constrained by the genre. Even the research paper, at least as it's traditionally taught, consists essentially of two parts: the presentation of a topic and a summary of information about that topic. When it comes to teaching all these essay types, we cling to what we expect to read.

A narrative doesn't give us the same kind of security. Even if a majority of your students follow Freytag's pyramid, you still have to contend with the variety of ways characters can be developed, settings can be established, conflicts can be heightened, and so on. But there's just no denying the power of story to engage and entertain writers and readers alike. Generally speaking, our students have been most engaged when writing narratives, and the stories themselves often fizz and pop with the kind of energy absent from other kinds of writing. The narrative project is certainly an undertaking, but, in our experience, the results are worth it.

Intended Benefits
- personal
- agentive
- engaging

Variations to Add an Authentic Audience
- The time and effort spent on this assignment practically demands publication of some sort. The resulting narratives could be shared aloud in class or in an evening of storytelling (with parents and other family members invited to attend), or they could be collected in an electronic or print anthology as a testament to the class's work.

Writing about Literature and Other Texts

Unless you happen to live in an area where a novel has actually been set, it can be tricky to envision ways to leverage public places for writing *about* literature. What does the local dog park say to us about *The Scarlet Letter*? Not much. But there *are* connections to be made, especially if we broaden our scope and look for indirect connections that transcend single texts. There are certain traits that most prose texts share, and exploring these outside the typical classroom setting can allow us to look at them from different angles. In this section, we describe two different ways of thinking about characterization—and the same principle can be applied to different aspects of literary study.

Honoring Character through Epitaphs

Identifying what we know about literary characters, explaining how we know it, and exploring what it means is important but well-traveled ground in the English classroom. This often culminates in a set of character analysis essays, most of which probably sound similar. But are there other ways of capturing character that might be more engaging and accessible to students, especially approaches that exist in the real world? The social media profile is one method: a constructed version of reality that allows creators to present themselves exactly as they wish to be seen. However, since the traditional mode of character analysis involves the examination of one (fictional) person by another (real) person, is there anywhere in the real world where we see something similar happening—one individual's life summarized by another?

Not as morbid as it might sound at first, for this particular activity, you'll take your class to a local cemetery to look at gravestone epitaphs.[6] This can be a self-guided exploration, but, if your school is near a large enough cemetery (especially if it's one where notable figures are buried), there may even be guided tours you could take. Either way, you'll want your students to focus on those short eulogistic engravings and consider some fundamental questions:

- What sentiments are typically expressed in epitaphs?
- What kind of information is usually included?
- How would you describe the language used in them?
- What *isn't* included?
- Did you see any epitaphs that stood out as unusual? If so, what made them distinctive?

In an ensuing discussion, you'll see that this is a lesson that's as much about summary as characterization. When it comes to encapsulating a person's life in just a few words, what should be the focus? What gets left out? When it comes to what's included, how do you phrase it for maximum effect in minimal length? Is it possible to have a distinctive voice with such brevity?

The product for this activity (which can be created in addition to something more traditional) is to have your students write epitaphs for the characters in a book they're reading—either a common classroom text or something they're reading individually or in small groups. Although there's no reason to mandate that the characters actually have to meet their demise in the text, there are certain Shakespearean plays that seem tailor-made for such an activity. In *Romeo and Juliet* alone, students could create epitaphs for the title characters as well as for Mercutio, Tybalt, Count Paris, and Lady Montague. In the process, they will demonstrate proficiency in summary and character analysis through a real-world genre of writing.

Intended Benefits
- agentive
- engaging

Interdisciplinary/Cross-Curricular Connections
- In conjunction with the art teacher, students could design literary tombstones featuring their characters' epitaphs. This could even be a project ideal for Halloween.

The Character of a Place

As we mentioned in the introduction to this chapter, the term *genius loci* has come to refer to the general sense of place possessed by a particular location (Cresswell, 2015). By considering "sense of place" in a real location, we can actually address several areas relevant to a range of literature: characterization, mood, personification, and metaphor. For this activity, we recommend taking your students to two separate locations:[7] one we might classify as *authentic*, in the way it's rooted in a sense of community or history (e.g., a town square or a historic neighborhood), and a second we would consider to be one of those *inauthentic* "non-places" (Augé, 1995) we mentioned at the beginning of this chapter, such as a supermarket or shopping mall.

Your students should explore each location with a focus on sense of place. In short, how does the location "feel," and what are the features that contribute to its feeling? The general assumption is that these locations are either all authentic or inauthentic—the town square is comfortable and welcoming, the mall is impersonal and efficient—but it's entirely possible your students could find variations within one specific place. Observing the space through this lens gets them thinking about mood and how mood is established.

Then, to take it one step further, how would your students *characterize* each place? When Rob conducted a similar activity with his students, he asked them to think metaphorically by using their observations about place to personify the location. In other words, if the mall were a person, how would it dress? Who would its friends be? What kind of books would it read or which TV shows would it watch? What would its favorite sayings be? The resulting character sketch asks students to consider both sense of place and methods of characterization, but it also requires them to engage in some metaphoric thinking—translating their understanding of the location into a different context.

Once back in the classroom, you could also use this activity to make an even tighter connection to the literature you're currently teaching. For instance, if you're reading Fitzgerald's (1925/2013) *The Great Gatsby*, how might students characterize the "valley of ashes," East Egg, and West Egg? What do those differences in characterization say about the people who live there, or about what we might interpret Fitzgerald's attitudes toward them to be? This kind of comparison could be made in any number of texts. Here are a few:

- Lee's (1960/2002) *To Kill a Mockingbird* (the Radleys' house, the Finches' house, the Ewells' house)
- Golding's (1954/1988) *Lord of the Flies* (the bower, Castle Rock, the platform)
- Thomas's (2017) *The Hate U Give* (Garden Heights, Williamson Prep)

By characterizing distinct locations in a text, students can come to a deeper understanding of how authors use place not just to serve as a story's foundation, but also to heighten tension, establish mood, and do some of the book's symbolic heavy lifting.

Intended Benefits
- personal
- agentive
- engaging

Variation to Add an Authentic Audience
- The character sketches could be written instead as dramatic monologues to be performed in class or in conjunction with a drama class.

Writing Arguments

This chapter is the first to focus on activities in which students are actually outdoors, not confined by classrooms or exhibits. The lack of structure means, for the first time, we can start to think about arguments embedded in places students encounter as part of their day-to-day lives—arguments that arise from current events or even happenstance. We wouldn't classify these arguments as more important than the ones described in previous chapters, but it's also true that the two activities described next are the first in the book to consider the broader social function of arguments. One is rooted in politics, the other in the workplace.

Monuments and Context

The current political landscape in the United States has made it particularly fascinating to explore the nature of historic monuments. Why do we commemorate historical figures with statues or other displays? Should those monuments remain standing in perpetuity, or is there a specific time frame in which they should be honored? If we're setting aside valuable property for *this* person, who else are we leaving out? The debate over what to do with statues honoring Confederate generals from the Civil War has recently brought this particular topic to a boiling point.

If you have one or more historic monuments in your town—even if they aren't particularly controversial—give your students some time to visit them and do some reflective writing. They might address the following or similar topics:

- Who is this individual (or group of people)?
- Based solely on the monument, what did they do?
- How is the subject of the monument depicted?
- What does the monument make you feel or think of?
- Does this monument have contemporary relevance?
- Based on your knowledge of your community, is there anyone else worth honoring in this way?

With this reflection as a starting point, your students will eventually choose a monument—local or global, in their own backyard or in another country—and argue for or against its preservation. In order to increase their engagement with this argument, we recommend giving your students the freedom to write about a monument that resonates with them in any way they see fit. That is, it doesn't have to be for historical reasons. If their argument against demolishing a monument uses purely aesthetic criteria, we'd still let them make it. As an argument, it might be trickier to construct, but since when should we discourage our students from a challenge?

In writing these arguments, they'll have to consider the justification for the subject's commemoration as well as the figure's personal history,[8] not to mention any changes in political or social circumstances that have occurred since the monument was built. At the end of the activity students will likely have a deeper understanding of this issue's complexity as well as a keener sense of how historic context matters when judging an individual's importance.

Intended Benefits
- personal
- agentive
- engaging

Variation to Add an Authentic Audience
- If you want to narrow the scope of the assignment, you could ask students to focus on a local landmark and address their arguments to your mayor or town council.

Variation to Add Research
- This may be something you want to do anyway, but this activity has an obvious research component (see Hillocks's [2011] comments about "researchable problems" in Chapter 3). Your students will certainly come to possess a more thorough grasp of their monument and its subject if they research both.

Interdisciplinary/Cross-Curricular Connections
- Because many monuments are historical in nature, you could team up with a history teacher to provide your students with more information about local monuments or even the evolution of monuments throughout history.

Travel Blogging

One opportunity afforded by place-based writing that we haven't adequately addressed is its facility to incorporate real-world genres. If the goal of place-based writing is to get students out of the classroom, it makes sense to explore ways writing exists in the world. This is especially true in light of the current emphasis on college and career readiness. In our experience, much is done for the former but less for the latter.

When we ask students to think about the real-world application of argument writing, reviews are often an overlooked genre. But reviews of all types—movie, restaurant, book, and so on—are commonly read forms of arguments. After all, the author is making a claim (this movie or restaurant is worth your time) followed by evidence supporting that claim (the characters are finely drawn, the lasagna is to die for). Also working in their favor, reviews are so common that they can easily be used as mentor texts, not to mention the fact that our students are already comfortable rendering their opinions (solicited or not) on any number of things. With all this in mind, we can look to the review genre as an accessible way of developing our students' abilities to argue effectively.

There is obviously a variety of ways you could facilitate this lesson. One simple introductory activity we could have mentioned in Chapter 3 is to provide students with examples of restaurant reviews and then ask them to review that day's cafeteria lunch. But, to get them more fully out of the classroom and into the world, we recommend taking them to a commercial center in your town—a mall, an open-air shopping district, a street that features a range of shops and restaurants—and ask them to explore the area as if they were a travel blogger:

- Does the area offer a variety of places to shop and eat?
- How would you characterize the restaurants (e.g., is there a mix of casual and fine dining, or is it all fast food)?
- If someone were in the mood to shop, what kind of businesses would they find?
- How attractive is the signage or window displays?
- What other aesthetic considerations have been taken into the area's design?
- If prices are displayed, how reasonable do they seem?

With these and other considerations in mind, your students will write a review of the area, making one or more recommendations for out-of-town visitors and providing evidence that supports their claim(s).[9] Through this activity, students can be taught how to write effective arguments in the context of a common, accessible form of real-world writing.

Intended Benefits
- personal
- agentive
- engaging
- audience oriented

Variation to Add an (Even More) Authentic Audience
- A WordPress blog is quick and easy (and free) to set up, and this could provide an authentic venue for students to display their reviews. This could be especially effective if you ask them to write multiple reviews

throughout the year. The blog could be set up in such a way that you feature specific review categories (movie reviews, food reviews, book reviews, etc.), with your students' work featured in each.

Variation to Promote Change
- If your students find the area they visit is especially limited in terms of its available businesses, you could submit their reviews to your town's Chamber of Commerce. This obviously provides them with an authentic audience, but it also draws attention to a facet of the town that adults may not have apprehended.

Writing Narratives, Poetry, and Scripts

As we've discussed elsewhere in this chapter (including the Rooting Narrative in Place extended lesson at the beginning), stories depend on an author's ability to create verisimilitude, and public places can be especially good locations for students to practice that skill. Setting, character, dialogue—even if these elements are stylized,[10] they need to seem real *in the context of the world the author has created*. Readers will willingly suspend their disbelief if the effort seems worth it. But, for the effort to seem worth it, characters have to move plausibly through recognizable worlds. And that requires a skillful use of detail that, for most writers, only comes through practice.

For developing writers such as those we teach, taking a lesson that deals with narrative craft and moving it into a public place can help students ground their writing in the kind of detail that may be challenging for them to invent on their own. And these lessons (such as ones dealing with imagery or believable dialogue) can also transfer to playwriting or poetry. Writing in public places can be helpful with a range of classroom concerns.

Voice and Point of View

For this activity, try taking your students someplace "busy" with inanimate objects—somewhere like a public park or a shopping area. The more natural as well as manufactured objects there are, the better. For example, in a public park, you've got shrubbery, lampposts, bike racks, playground equipment, benches and picnic tables, trash cans, and more. Ask your students to choose an inanimate object that would have a unique view of the place—and, for that reason, a story to tell. No matter how silly it feels (and it may feel *very* silly), students should sit with that object for a while and take some notes. What does it "see"? What does it "hear"? How is it treated—that is, what value does it have in the place? How does it feel about all of this?

With these observations as the foundation, the students will write a piece—a descriptive reflection or a monologue would be two natural genres—from the perspective of their chosen object. While this may sound like a frivolous exercise, it can actually be used to teach a range of different techniques. One is obviously description, as the students endeavor to accurately capture the object's experience. But, in this activity, there's also room to develop point of view and, more challenging still, a believable voice. By wholly removing themselves from the equation and adopting the perspective of an object that's completely foreign, students actually have to think critically about what's needed to give their object a believable voice. Asking students to "think like a trash can" sounds ridiculous,[11] but, in our experience, some of the most powerful lessons are the ones in which the learning is camouflaged as something unapologetically fun.

Intended Benefits
- personal
- engaging

Variation to Add an Authentic Audience
- Many activities dealing with point of view can be adapted for the stage. If you ask your students to write a monologue from the perspective of the object, these could easily be performed for the class (or another audience).

Interdisciplinary/Cross-Curricular Connections
- Involving the drama teacher in an exercise dramatizing the object (e.g., "How does one embody the character of a bike rack?") could be an entertaining and meaningful way of further extending the activity.

Writing Poetry from a New Angle

Similar in approach to the activity in ekphrasis we described in Chapter 4, this activity asks students to find inspiration in their surroundings. But, whereas that earlier activity used art as a catalyst for writing, this activity is rooted in the commonplace. Too often when we write, we overlook everyday objects or settings that seem otherwise mundane. But, as an exercise in writing descriptively—not to mention as a general life lesson in appreciating what we have—it can be beneficial to write about things that at first seem uninspiring.

Any of the places we listed at the beginning of the chapter (among others specific to your own community) would work for this activity. First, ask your students to write about their general observations of the place. This is basic scene setting that may (but doesn't have to) contribute to the eventual product. Where are they? What does it look like? Sound like? Is it crowded? If so, what do those people look like?

With these initial impressions out of the way, your students should take a variety of photos with a smartphone or digital camera.[12] These photos can be wide angle or close up, but ask your students to try taking them from a perspective they might not normally consider. For example, instead of just taking a photo of a fire hydrant, what angle would let us see the fire hydrant in a new way? If you're at a historic monument, ask students to identify a feature that people typically ignore (e.g., the base, the border of its descriptive plaque, the backside, etc.) and to take one or more photos of it.

Back in the classroom, ask the students to scroll through their photos and identify one that could be the inspiration for a poem. Taken in tandem with the scene-setting details they noted at the site itself, the poem can be a description of the object, a piece inspired by the photo, or a broader depiction of the actual place and the object's role within it. There are no particular constraints on the completed poem as long as it helps your students see how inspiration can be found in the conventionally uninspiring.

Intended Benefits
- personal
- agentive
- engaging

Variation to Add an Authentic Audience
- If the students' photos were to be printed out, the combination of photo and poem would be an appealing display in the entrance to the school building.

Writing for Research and Inquiry

Appearances to the contrary, public places can be powerful locations to inspire inquiry, and their public nature can also present us with opportunities for primary research. In two of the activities described next, we draw on our earlier discussion about the nature of public places, especially the process by which these places evolve and, in some cases, disappear. For the third activity, we bridge the gap between personal and public, asking students to consider how something as seemingly mundane as the food they eat can result in compelling authentic research. In each of these instances, our underlying argument is that public places are freighted with potential for research, especially if one of our goals is to encourage students to tangle with the complex, frequently messy world outside the classroom.

The Aesthetics of Place

Public places are never accidental. If you consider the different types of public places we've described in this chapter, they all require a significant degree of planning and likely involved a lengthy process on the road to their development. This activity starts by asking your students to consider a public place in their community. You could take them to a park, a town square, a public art display, or any of the other locations we've mentioned throughout this chapter (or any place we haven't mentioned that fits our definition of a public place). Once there, students should consider its obvious design elements and conduct some exploratory writing. For example, if you visit a public park, they might consider some of these issues:

- What facilities are available (e.g., playing fields, picnic areas, trails, etc.)?
- How have these facilities been laid out? Is there an obvious flow?
- How aesthetically pleasing is it? What choices can you tell the planners made to make the place pleasing to the eye?
- In what ways has access for people with disabilities been considered?
- How about parking and traffic flow in and out of the place?
- How does the place harmonize (or not) with its surrounding environment?

These considerations will vary depending on the public place you visit, but they'll simply be variations on a theme—that is, what are the design choices that have made this a place worth visiting?

After discussing all of this with your students post-visit, ask them to research a well-known public place—in the United States or elsewhere—and to explore both the history and the development of the place through the lens of those design elements they identified in their own community. They can include information about how the place was created and how it is used currently, but their research could also reveal how the place has evolved over time as well as any controversial aspects of its creation (such as the multiple controversies that surrounded the development of the Martin Luther King Jr. monument in Washington, DC).

We recommend providing a list that includes some noteworthy public places as a starting point, mainly because a Google search of "public place" will be too vast to navigate, but also because the list you curate can include public places representing a range of countries and cultures. Your students may gravitate to places they recognize from movies or television—New York's Times Square or the French Quarter in New Orleans—but, as you will know from your own reading and travel, there's a nearly limitless abundance of public places for your students to explore.

What does this have to do with an English class? To rationalize this activity for yourself as well as your administration, keep in mind that it is, first and foremost, a vehicle for teaching research skills, not just a fun day at the park. Importantly, though, it's also a vehicle that maps onto particular career paths and real-world considerations. The combination of activities in this larger project can introduce students to the kind of work done by city planners and architects, but it can also show them how to be more thoughtful citizens by introducing them to some of the variables to consider when faced with the development of new public places in their own communities.

Intended Benefits
- personal
- agentive
- engaging

The Cost of Change

This activity directly takes up Gruenewald's (2003) endorsement of merging place-based education with critical pedagogy as well as Kinloch's (2010) desire to privilege students' experiences in their home communities. Therefore, it won't be for everyone, especially if you teach in an area where directly addressing social justice causes might be frowned upon. We believe, however, that it could be one of the most illuminating pieces of writing your students complete. In short, this activity involves taking a look at how public places change over time, especially as a result of gentrification. As we mentioned earlier in this chapter, there's often a perception that progress is a net good. Whether or not you agree with that sentiment, there's no doubt that, when a public place sees change, it often involves the loss of what (or who) was originally there. This project gives your students an opportunity to explore this important issue. Locating a relevant neighborhood may be difficult if you teach deep in suburbia. However, if you teach in an area with some roots—like our proximity to both Marietta and Atlanta in Georgia—you'll find a variety of paths to make this work.

An initial visit to a place in your community[13] can focus on the here and now. What's the place? Whom does it serve? What is its current value to the community? What would be lost if it were to disappear tomorrow? Once your students have considered questions like these, share with them the history of the place. Use photographs, if possible. This will be most powerful if you actually conduct this discussion in the place itself, so your students can immediately see what was left behind. This can be followed by more writing: What was lost as a result of change? Whom did the changes most affect? In your estimation, were the changes worth it—in other words, were the changes a net positive or a net negative? If your students have personal connections with the neighborhood in question, it's critical that they be allowed (or even encouraged) to write personally about their own experiences with change, to become, as Kinloch (2010) calls them, "soul singers," or those "who [sing] back to exclusionary measures brought about by the gentrification of historic Black spaces" (p. 48).

The combination of community visit and reflective/personal writing sets the stage for your students to conduct some original research of their own, focusing on the issue of community change and loss. To maximize the students' interest and agency, we recommend encouraging them to research an area that matters to them, especially if it's their own. Equally, this can also be an especially important accommodation for transient students or students new to the area. They may not feel any particular connection to a place in their current community, but there may be a place in their previous town that resonates with them. Similarly, other students may want to research something in another community entirely, one they've encountered through pop culture. For example, the movie *Blindspotting* (Casal et al., 2018) focuses on the gentrification of predominantly African American neighborhoods in Oakland, California, and numerous movies and TV shows feature blithe, jokey observations about how neighborhoods in New York City have become less "gritty" (pop culture shorthand for "ethnic") with the advent of coffee shops and art galleries (pop culture shorthand for "white gentrifiers"). Such research can take up the question of how a potentially debilitating issue like gentrification is handled by popular media as well as the degree to which these depictions may actually contribute to further community change.

In any event, we believe students should be permitted to conduct this research on a public place in a community that interests them, whether that happens to be their own or someone else's. Regardless of location, the emphasis should remain on the nature of change: what's changing, who's responsible, and what's lost in the process. From this project, students can gain a more informed perspective on their own community's history. Arguably more important, however, is reaching an understanding of how cultural identity is often rooted in place—and how the loss of place can lead to the loss of a community's identity. And, critically for those students wrestling with gentrification in their own neighborhoods, it gives them an opportunity to "have ownership of the spaces and places they called home" (Kinloch, 2010, p. 46).

Intended Benefits
- personal
- agentive
- engaging

Variations to Add an Authentic Audience
- If you teach in a community large and diverse enough to focus your students' research on their current community, the resulting research could be turned into a visual presentation. These presentations could be displayed in an evening dealing with the theme of "Lost [Your Town]," during which your students share what they've learned about the history of their community.

- Embedded in this project are opportunities for other types of written products, such as a multigenre research paper or, as Christensen (2015) recommends, a piece of historical fiction. Either of these could be shared in a broader setting than merely submitting them to the teacher for a grade.

Interdisciplinary/Cross-Curricular Connections
- The historical nature of this project makes it a natural fit for you to collaborate with one or more members of your social studies department, perhaps to provide a general overview on the history of your community (or even to help your students locate relevant historical records for your town). Another valuable resource could be securing a speaker from your community's historic preservation society (or a local history museum), who could offer students a more thorough depiction of the town's changing demographics.

Local Foodways and Food Traditions

The proliferation of farmers markets in communities large, small, and in between gives us a public place seemingly tailor-made for authentic research. After all, if one of our goals is to help students make personal connections between themselves and the lines of inquiry they pursue, the food they eat may be one of the most authentic general topics they could explore. And, fortunately, we now live in a time when a quality farmers market will likely be only a short drive away.[14]

If students are given the opportunity to explore a local farmers market, they could identify a foodstuff they personally enjoy and research its origins and culinary application. Where was it first grown? If it isn't an indigenous product, how did it come to be used in the local area? How is it grown now? In which recipes can it be used? What significance does it have to the local food culture?[15] Answers to some of these questions can obviously be found in a variety of online sources, but a more meaningful strategy would be to encourage your students to engage in some primary research by interviewing the people actually working at the market. The locals selling the ingredients are often the very ones responsible for the growth and harvest of their wares, so an informal interview could yield firsthand information that is both more personal and more honest (and maybe even more accurate) than the usual online sources. Another potential venue for primary research could be to interview family members who regularly use the ingredient in their cooking. Many of us are familiar with the evocative nature of certain foods and their ability to bring to mind family traditions and holidays with friends and loved ones. This interview would also allow students to incorporate a welcome narrative element to their research, honoring those important customs at the same time it yields valuable primary research.

A more traditional variation of this same project could be used to introduce your students to some of the complex and rapidly changing issues surrounding food production and consumption, including challenges involving socioeconomic inequality (both locally and globally), race, gender, and environmental activism (Williams-Forson & Counihan, 2012). A visit to the farmers market and some accompanying low-stakes writing could be a vital first step in an eventual research project that tackles one of these pressing issues involving the food we eat.

Intended Benefits
- personal
- agentive
- engaging

Variation to Add a Narrative Element

- Instead of a traditional research paper, students can be asked to incorporate their research into a food-centric narrative that could be either fictitious or autobiographical.

Variations to Add an Authentic Audience

- Because food-related issues affect all of us, this is a project that practically demands an authentic audience. A class blog in which students present their food-related research could be one publication venue for the second idea described above. And for the first? We can't imagine a more authentic or delicious option than a culinary celebration that sees your students prepare visual displays of their ingredient-related research accompanied by one or more representative dishes they've prepared themselves.

Interdisciplinary/Cross-Curricular Connections

- This activity's emphasis on foodstuffs, cooking, farming, and food origins might fall outside your wheelhouse. In that case, a natural connection could be forged with health, nutrition, or home economics colleagues. If your school doesn't have such resources, you could also turn to a community partner or nonprofit organization to supplement any lessons in nutrition education.

Writing for Change

One thing that particularly commends the use of place-based writing in public locations is the way it can encourage your students to get involved with their own communities. Because these locations are often central to the character of your town, students' thoughtful engagement with them can reinforce the notion that civic engagement matters—that the well-being of the community *rests with the community*, and not solely with the local government or the residents who have the most money. It's vital for our students to understand the importance of their voices, especially in the place they call home.

Community Means Everyone

Many communities have one location people would agree is its heart. This might be a town square, city building, community building, or shopping district. In our town north of Atlanta, it's the main street, which features a range of shops and restaurants and has an active rail line running parallel to it. It's a hub of activity in the evening, with couples and families shopping and dining out. There's a wedding venue and a community park, and the area is occasionally blocked off for events ranging from car shows to culinary experiences. No matter what town you call home, this central area is probably responsible for your community's personality or sense of self. It's a place that matters. But no place is perfect. It's important to consider who isn't represented in the location widely considered to be the town's heart. How do we make it more inclusive, more harmonious? What can we add without fundamentally altering its genius loci?

You can begin this activity by discussing with your students where *they* think the town's heart is. This could reveal important differences about the ways in which your students view their community, especially if differences break down along lines of race or class. If you're able to work on a tight time frame, you could choose one of these student-generated locations for your visit, or you might choose one place in advance to help you plan. Whichever you choose, your students' observations during the visit will focus on the things that make this place the emotional center of your community. What can people do there? Who do they see? In what specific ways does it create a sense of community?

For the purpose of this assignment, they will eventually want to move to the flip side of those initial questions. Who *isn't* represented? Who might not find this location a positive representation of the community? What could be added (or removed) to make it more diverse and inclusive for all the town's residents, including those who have been marginalized (such as homeless populations)? As another local example, one of our neighboring communities features a quaint downtown area with a range of shops, restaurants, museums, and a children's playground. It initially feels like a comfortable place for all families to visit. But look closer and you'll see a small park in the center of downtown flying the Confederate flag. Considering its symbolic meaning, that flag seems paradoxically uninviting despite the rest of the area's family-friendly nature.

All this formative writing should lead your students to the following question: If this location plays a pivotal role in the town and who its people are, in what ways can we make it more welcoming for everyone? Based on their observations and any reflective writing you've asked them to conduct, your students will devise a list of changes or additions that would increase the sense of community in this central location. The final product will be a proposal written to the town council wherein they describe their desired changes. They're essentially writing an argument that includes a claim (their proposed additions), evidence (an explanation of why the additions are desirable), and anticipated counterarguments (why the council or others might object to their proposed additions). As in some of the other activities we've described, the actual genre of this proposal can vary. It could be a letter, but your students could also compose the script of a speech to be delivered to the mayor or a pitch to the city council. There are also opportunities to create videos or other visual displays that could be shared in an evening centered on the theme of community.

A sense of community includes (or *should* include) everyone, including your students. This particular activity encourages them to have a voice in the place they call home and speak up on behalf of those who have been marginalized or unrepresented altogether.

Intended Benefits
- personal
- agentive
- engaging
- audience oriented
- promotes change

Considerations for Students with Special Needs
- If possible, allow students to video record parts of places you are visiting in order to reference them later in their writing. While having a simple picture of each location could help students write, this would provide only one-dimensional support. Video footage could make it easier for them to reflect on things like sound (and volume), activity level, and their own personal point of view in that place.
- When asking students to review a business, they are uniquely positioned as possible experts for how best to represent their individual needs. They might reflect on how physically accessible the business is or how it supports patrons who are developing readers. For your students with sensory needs, what considerations might that business make to better support them?

Considerations for English Language Learners
- Many Latinx countries have holidays celebrating deceased friends and family members (such as Mexico's Día de Muertos). When asking Latinx students to complete the character epitaph activity, you might consider modifying it to better connect it to those celebrations. Instead of an epitaph, students can create an altar celebrating a particular character and reflect on how their analysis of that character contributes to the

altar's construction. And this isn't only the domain of your Latinx students. You can discuss with your non-Latinx English language learners which holidays or celebrations surrounding the deceased their culture celebrates. Taking advantage of opportunities to celebrate and explore your students' many cultures can help to boost their agency in, and engagement with, the activity.

- You may consider allowing your speakers of other languages to write their reviews in a language other than English as a way to encourage businesses to represent multilingual patrons. They might also be allowed to look more closely at the business's online presence and provide feedback on how that information could be presented to multilingual patrons.

- Many cultures hold food as a central component of their representation and history. Students could turn the Local Foodways and Food Traditions activity into an opportunity to leverage the wealth of knowledge possessed by their own families. Students could interview family members about important food items, spices, or cooking methods and present them to their peers. This would not only provide an opportunity for students to celebrate their own families as experts but also offer a space for the sharing of cultures and cultural practices.

Writing in Natural Places

A red-tailed hawk wheels overhead, unfurled wings etched into the cerulean scrim of the midday sky. The tall grass sighs. Where we sit in the meadow, a whispered breeze ruffles our hair and tugs softly at the corners of our notepaper. Almost out of earshot, right at the edge of sound, comes the faintly cicada-like scritching of a dozen pens on paper. Heads canted over notebooks, clenched fists moving furiously, the students engrave their thoughts in blue and black ink. Some of their lips move, as though speaking directly to the paper, the pen an unwanted intermediary. Occasionally, they look up, brows clenched, the image they need just out of reach. Then, they smile and dip their heads back under the surface of the written word. We're in El Capitan Meadow. These students have just discovered place-based writing.

For a few years in the late 1990s, Rob chaperoned a trip to Yosemite National Park with his school's Environmental Science Club. The dozen students and three chaperones met a park ranger in Tuolumne Meadows, the vast high country that makes up the park's upper reaches. After a few days' exposure to that ecosystem, they descended to Yosemite Valley to conclude the trip. Although the purpose of this outing was ostensibly to study the geology and ecology of the park, Rob was asked by the club's sponsor to facilitate some writing activities as the students experienced the park's various regions. They wrote reflective pieces contemplating a range of topics—from the importance of preserving the park to the shift in perspective that came from sitting at the base of El Capitan's massive granite face—as well as writing more traditional scientific expository writing. And, even though these were students with a penchant for science—stereotypically the kind of kids who would resist "creative" writing—they eagerly wrote poetry and short narratives based on their observations and field notes. The students found it impossible not to be inspired by their natural surroundings, and, like John Muir and many other writers before them, writing became a natural way for the students to process their experiences in the immensity of nature.

A weeklong trip to Yosemite National Park probably isn't in the cards for many of our readers (although, if you find it is—do it!). But, as we've emphasized in previous chapters, place-based writing opportunities needn't be extravagant. Even if you teach in an urban environment, where it might seem like the natural world is hard to find, it's important to remember how green spaces have been preserved in many city centers. There are dozens of city parks within Atlanta's city limits (including flagship parks such as Centennial Olympic Park, Piedmont Park, and Central Park), and many of them are connected by the Beltline, a running-biking-walking trail that winds through the city's neighborhoods. As we mentioned in Chapter 5, we want you to remember that, while these urban green spaces might not be "nature" in the same sense as unspoiled wilderness, they can still give your students a taste of the natural world. You might need to get creative, but we want to disabuse you of the notion that writing in natural places means a lengthy and expensive trip.

And the reason why it's important to stress this yet again is our belief that writing in natural places can arguably be more valuable—inspiring, engaging, meaningful, and authentic—than any other general location we describe in this book. Why is this? On a basic level, we find the simple act of writing in nature engages students in a way that, for many of them, borders on the elemental. In our experience, there's just something about putting pen to paper in the great outdoors that students connect with. This isn't to say every student takes the work seriously. Every class always has at least one student more interested in digging in the dirt or flinging sticks at passing cars, and, of course, we have to consider how we tackle that particular issue. But we've found that even our students who are most resistant to writing in the classroom view writing outdoors as markedly different from what they're used to. Whether it's the sheer novelty of the practice or something fundamental to the act itself that resonates with them on a deeper level, writing in natural places encourages students to become more engaged with their work.

It's also more urgent than ever that students of all ages understand the importance of environmental conservation and stewardship. We mentioned the recent report from the Intergovernmental Panel on Climate Change (2018) in Chapter 3, but one of its most alarming conclusions bears repeating here: unless we take drastic steps to reverse our contribution to global climate change, we can expect to see a range of environmental catastrophes by the year 2040. Even if you're predisposed to doubt climate change as a consequence of humanity's habits, surely we can at least agree that taking care of our environment and resources is a practice to be encouraged. And if we can agree on *that*, it's only logical to look to place-based writing as one way we can help our students begin taking that kind of responsibility as they witness their connection to nature firsthand. Does it belong in an English class? Absolutely. If one of our goals is to help our students become more sophisticated users of language and understand the importance of written communication in real-world settings, why *wouldn't* we facilitate activities that help them become more responsible citizens?

As we mentioned in Chapter 1, environmental activism is the one facet of place-based writing where considerable work has already been done. Smith and Sobel (2010) write compellingly of their belief that the "best education is an education that sees schools as integrated with rather than segregated from the lives of the human and other-than-human beings that surround them" (p. 115). We can see this philosophy implicitly guiding the work of other educators. Jacobs's (2011) students explore their identities in relation to a natural place, in the process writing from positions of authority, bearing witness to their own experiences, and recognizing their connections to nature. By asking her students to examine aspects of the natural world and write poetry about it, Pearce (2000) sees them become more aware of their relation to the environment. Cortez-Riggio's (2011) fifth-grade students "became more aware of their existence in a larger world" and reached a greater understanding of "their future life purposes" (p. 43) by advocating for a variety of environmental issues in a service-learning project. By partnering with a science teacher to help her students explore their rural Nebraska community, Bishop (2003) found her students better able to "be members of a participatory democracy" (p. 81), precisely because their place-based experience revealed how local issues often have global implications. In short, finding opportunities for students to write in natural places can put their increased sense of ownership and engagement in the service of writing to make a difference in the world.

For the purpose of the activities we describe in this chapter—as well as thinking through the natural places in your own school community—we're loosely defining *natural places* as locations that have largely gone undeveloped. This can include woodlands, grasslands and meadows, desert areas, or rivers and streams. City, state, and national parks are also fair game (especially if you live and teach in an urban community), even though we technically classified them as public places in Chapter 5. The general idea is that you're asking students to write in a location where the emphasis is on the natural world and, as part of that process, to consider their individual relationships with the environment.

At this point in the book, we want to remind you that many of the activities described in earlier chapters can be translated with few adjustments to different types of places. For example, all the narrative activities described for public places in Chapter 5 would work just as well with natural places in this chapter.

This is why you don't see an activity in this section that involves writing a short story based on general observations of a natural place. We invite you to return to earlier chapters and consider ways in which some of their activities also have a place in the great outdoors.

Extended Lesson Idea: Protecting Our Wild Places

When students see images of advocacy in the media—if they see them at all—it's usually advocacy writ large: the protest march on television, the White House petition on Facebook, images of celebrities promoting social causes on Instagram. This actually makes a lot of sense. For an advocacy project to gain widespread traction, it needs to be big enough—or feature someone popular enough—to appeal to a wide audience. Those who still watch the evening news may see an occasional small-town human interest story, but it's not likely our students see too many examples of *local* advocacy, of people being actively mindful of their own communities, no matter how small.

The fact that small-scale advocacy lacks much of a media presence is unfortunate, but it also presents us with an opportunity. Using place-based writing to effect change on a local level can develop in our students an interest in becoming engaged citizens aware of how their actions impact others. And, as we mentioned in the introduction to this chapter and elsewhere, if our students see how their actions can promote positive change on a small scale, it increases the likelihood they'll continue to seek out opportunities for civic engagement on a larger scale as they grow into adulthood.

In previous chapters we explored ways that place-based writing can accomplish this kind of advocacy,[1] but the Wild Places project is the most ambitious of the bunch. With an explicit interdisciplinary connection as well as opportunities for research, argument, and real-world writing application, this project uses place-based writing as a foundation to accomplish a variety of curricular goals in the service of preserving a natural area in (or near) your community.

It's completely normal if you find yourself wondering if this wouldn't be better suited to a science classroom. The emphasis on identifying a "wild place," pinpointing the things that threaten it, and formulating a proposal justifying its preservation may very well push you out of your comfort zone. This is one reason why we actually recommend teaming with (or drawing on the knowledge of) a science teacher in your school. That additional resource will provide your students with a richer experience. But, if we look at the writing processes we are required to teach (argument and research, especially) and take those in tandem with characteristics of authentic writing that encourage students to become invested in it (especially choosing a topic that matters and seeing its real-world application), there isn't a good reason to discount writing *about* science if it helps our students engage more meaningfully with our subject. Not to mention this project opens up a range of additional classroom possibilities, from encouraging students to write creatively about their wild place to connecting it to literature that has nature as a focal point.[2] The Wild Places project is a science-based assignment that has a natural home in the English language arts classroom.

The Assignment

Because this Wild Places project potentially has so many moving pieces, we find it helpful to return to the synopsis we mentioned a paragraph ago. In short, your students identify a natural place in their own community that they think is—or could be—in danger. In the interest of students having as much agency as possible, we hesitate to identify what this looks like, but it could include any of the natural spaces we identified earlier: woodlands, fields, marshes, rivers or streams, meadows, desert areas, and so on. Much of this selection process will obviously depend on the area in which you teach, but we encourage you not to put too many limitations on the areas your students select. If you don't have many truly natural places in your community from which to choose, a student may have to select a vacant lot seen on the bus ride to school, a copse of trees that has somehow remained standing despite the urban growth that surrounds it, or even a city park whose natural beauty seems threatened in some way.

One method that could help students identify their wild place is to share a story from your own life describing a wild place that fell prey to development. For example, our community in suburban Atlanta continues to grow, and this has resulted in the loss of several previously "wild" areas near us. A wooded area on Rob's drive to school was razed and turned into student housing and storage lockers. An open field near our home was recently turned into a massive complex for the sale, service, and storage of recreational vehicles. Most recently, one section of a secluded nature trail on which we like to walk our dog was demolished and an office building constructed in its place. No matter where you live, you probably have stories similar to these worth sharing.

There's one additional thing that can help students think through which area to choose: *threat* can take a variety of forms. Our examples involved the actual destruction of natural places, but we can see the environment despoiled in other ways. You might tell them to be on the lookout for places where litter seems to accumulate or where an excess of human or vehicular traffic is having—or could eventually have—a negative impact on a natural place. As a practical example, we recently learned that it will take hundreds of years for Joshua Tree National

Park to recover from the damage done to it during the early 2019 government shutdown (Boucher, 2019). Or maybe it is development adjacent to a natural place that could be the problem: the encroachment of commerce or industry on a previously pristine environment. What we hope is obvious is that there is a wide variety of ways students could approach this topic, and we encourage you to provide them with as much freedom as possible to select a wild place that matters to them.

A visit to an actual "wild place" is the first step in helping students work independently with the location they've identified. Because this project will likely be different from anything you've asked them to do previously, we consider this step essential. Your students should explore the location, making some general notes and observations about the sensory experience. What do they see and hear? How does the area make them feel? What lies just beyond the boundary of the natural space? Some low-stakes reflective and observational writing can help them get a general sense of the value of the place.

Given the nature of the project, you'll also want them to do additional focused writing as a second stage to the visit. These specific prompts should be tailored to the actual content you want them to address in their final project, and the initial writing might inform some of their responses. For example:

- What is the value of this location? What does it offer people, tangibly as well as intangibly?
- Why is it worth preserving?
- What are some potential threats that could put this wild place in jeopardy?
- Prioritize these threats. Do any of them seem more immediate than others?
- What ideas do you have for preventing these threats?
- What resources might you need to implement one or more of these ideas?

As we mentioned previously, it would be ideal to partner with one of your science teacher colleagues for this visit, especially if science isn't your forte. Your colleague could talk to your students about the location they're visiting prior to or during the visit, and this could shed more light for them on the area's specific ecology. They could also discuss the thinking that emerges from the above questions, and the science teacher could talk in a more nuanced way about the benefits of the area as well as the threats posed to it and the potential viability of your students' ideas for its preservation. Such a conversation could clarify your students' own thinking on the project, but it also provides them with a window into the real-world scientific application of this kind of discussion and writing. In other words, it isn't just an intellectual exercise; the preservation of our natural spaces is a legitimate career path for students who find themselves particularly interested in it.

Back in the classroom, your students will need to settle on the specific location they intend to write about, and you'll need to define for them the assignment's components as well as the form the final product will take. We encourage you to require your students to make at least one visit to their self-selected wild place in order to replicate some of the reflective and observational writing they conducted with the rest of the class. Their field notes and any other writing can be submitted at the end of the project.

To get to that point, we recommend making this a two-tiered assignment: further research on their wild place that will ultimately inform an argument-based final product that ideally maps onto a real-world writing genre. The research component comes first and will involve your students learning more about the location they choose:[3] its ecosystem, its benefits (which could include environmental, aesthetic, and recreational benefits, among others), the threats that endanger it (both humanmade and natural), and possible methods of preservation. This component of the project will address many of the research and inquiry components of your curriculum, and, depending on each student's wild place, could also extend to conducting interviews, adding further depth to the final product.

The exact nature of that product will depend on what you want your students to create. There's obviously room for a traditional research- or argument-based assignment, but, because the subject of the students' work exists in the real world and presumably involves real-world solutions to potential real-world problems, it makes sense, as Dyrness (2011) mentions, to look for ways students can produce real-world writing. A grant proposal, the script of a "preservation pitch" to the city planner, a letter to an environmental group, a pop-up museum whose exhibits are themed on "Protecting Our Wild Places"—there's a range of products at your disposal. As always, your choice will largely depend on your specific aims for this assignment and the particular skills or understandings you want to assess.

It's important to note that, if the final product doesn't allow for the natural incorporation of research (or if it won't be easy for you to tell how and where the research appears), you might ask your students to submit a separate document that reflects on the nature of their research, how it appeared in their final product, what choices informed that process, and so on. Similar to the notes pages recommended by Romano (1995) as part of his multigenre research project (discussed in Chapter 1), this reflective writing would more fully illuminate your students' learning as it pertains to their developing research skills.

Logistical Considerations

Because the Wild Places project requires students to make one or more independent place-based visits, you'll need to consider how to mediate those situations in which students don't have the opportunity to make a separate visit for the purpose of observation and writing (due to family commitments, transportation issues, or any number of other factors). One thing we recommend in such cases is allowing these students to base their projects on the common location visited with the entire class. The resulting work may not be as agentive and personally relevant as the work of those students who have been able to choose a site of their own, but it's one way of working around a complicated problem that often is no fault of the student's.

Another possible solution for these students is simply to eliminate the required visit portion of the assignment and allow them to conduct their research about a place they may have seen but have never actually visited. We recommend resorting to this option sparingly as it eliminates the place-based nature of the project and essentially turns it into a traditional research project with an advocacy component. That's certainly not the worst thing in the world, but we believe one of the strengths of this particular project is the way it encourages the students to make a personal connection with their wild place, experiencing it in real time so they come to a greater understanding of why it needs to be preserved. We can all make intellectual arguments about preserving natural spaces; the act of visiting one, however, makes it personal. And as we know, personal writing is often *better* writing.

Supplemental Lessons

If you've read our extended lesson ideas in the previous chapters, you'll no doubt recognize some supplemental lessons that would also be appropriate for the Wild Places project, such as:

- Chapter 3—Developing Research Questions and Observations and Interviews
- Chapter 4—The Rudiments of Genre and Reflecting on the Process

If you skipped straight to this chapter, we encourage you to consult those earlier chapters for ideas in addition to the one we describe next.

Writing a Grant Proposal

Of all the different real-world genre possibilities for this project, the grant proposal might be the most beneficial for your students to try. It's not only a genre they might very well find themselves employing for personal or professional reasons at some point in the future; it's one that requires them to attend to details they might not otherwise have considered. In our experience with grant writing, most proposals require at a minimum these different categories:

- cover letter—broadly introducing the proposal
- summary or abstract—a more detailed overview of the proposal, including what you need
- statement of need—specifically identifying the problem you want to solve
- goals and objectives—a clear identification of what you intend to achieve
- methods or strategies—how you intend to meet the goals stated above
- assessment or evaluation—how you'll know you've met your goals
- budget—a detailed account of the resources you need (including money) and how it will be used[4]

We hope you can start to see how elements of both research and argument are necessary to write a quality proposal. The students' research should be evident in their Statement of Need as well as the Goals and Strategies sections. The proposal itself is a form of argument wherein students have to convince their readers that there is not only a problem, but that their methods of solving it are worth funding. Additionally, where some students confuse argument with persuasion,[5] the pragmatic nature of the proposal forces them to think about the logical arguments necessary to convince their readers.

In a classroom setting, lessons on writing a grant proposal can obviously focus on clarity and specificity—What exactly is the problem? How exactly do you intend to solve it? Why exactly is your solution the appropriate one?—but, by contemplating how they'll know they've met their goals, your students are at least partially anticipating counterarguments from those who might disagree with them. The Wild Places project gives students an opportunity to write for real-world purposes, and the grant proposal gives them a real-world genre in which to do it.

Summing Up

We recognize the Wild Places project may be a discomfiting idea that pushes you off-balance. Of all the ideas we describe in this book, it's the one that seems to fall most outside the purview of what we do as English teachers. But, if we want our students to think intentionally about their relationships with the environment and the ways in which they can start to make small changes in their own communities, this project is one of the few that can accomplish that ambitious goal in concrete ways. Additionally, it provides us with the rare opportunity to help our students see how writing can be used to effect change in positive ways through the use of real-world genres. We realize the Wild Places project may require us to rethink the role of the English language arts curriculum and our own relation to it. In our opinion, it's long overdue.

Intended Benefits
- personal
- agentive
- engaging
- audience oriented
- promotes change

Interdisciplinary/Cross-Curricular Connections
- In addition to the obvious connection with your science department, there may also be opportunities for your art teacher to get involved. If you ask your students to design an exhibit for a pop-up museum or a visual display for a proposal pitch, the art teacher can help your students consider ways of representing aspects of their arguments through visual means.

Writing about Literature and Other Texts

To return to an idea we discussed in Chapter 4, it can be difficult for readers to connect with the physical location of a text if they've never experienced it firsthand. While you can compensate for some of the gaps in understanding by taking students to locations similar to those described in texts you're currently reading, in other instances, there's just no getting around the fact that actual experience will stay out of reach. Verona, Italy. The Alaskan wilderness. A tropical island in the Pacific Ocean. Barring some extreme good fortune, it's unlikely these notable literary settings (and others like them) will be viable options for place-based writing. Even so, by getting students out of the classroom and into natural spaces, you can begin to address some of the issues at the heart of texts you're reading—even if the settings themselves are impractical to visit.

Thoreau, Romanticism, and/or Writing about Nature

One day shortly after the start of the school year, Amanda came home with a story of having to teach her fourth graders how to play during recess. Whereas we both remember living for those moments when we could escape outdoors to play and explore, Amanda's students seemed at a loss for what to do when they made it to the playground. While we may want to attribute this to the uncomfortable truth that students' worlds are increasingly virtual in nature and online experiences often seem more real than physical ones, we also have to realize that some of our students' neighborhoods (like the ones in which some of Amanda's students live) may not be safe enough to allow outdoor play. In either case, teaching texts like Thoreau's (1854/2017) *Walden* presents us with some challenging issues. Even though *Walden* is a staple of American Literature classes, if our work is primarily conducted in the classroom—and if many of our students rarely experience the outdoors on their own—how do we ever expect Thoreau's desire to "live deep and suck out all the marrow of life" (p. 73) to make sense?

For rural and suburban teachers—or even teachers in urban settings who have an outdoor classroom or nearby park at their disposal—the answer can be as simple as getting your students outside to do some quiet writing. The finished product can vary depending on your aims for the activity, but the heart of the exercise should be taking your students to a natural space, asking them to quietly make some observations[6] about their surroundings, and then write. Because this activity can easily be completed in a single class period, we know several teachers—elementary, middle, and high school alike—who engage in it on a semi-regular basis. Sometimes, the goal is for students to write a poem based on their observations; in other instances, they write a reflective piece on how they're personally responding to the environment.

If Thoreau isn't your thing, a connection can also be made to the Romantic poets. After studying the techniques of Wordsworth, Coleridge, or Keats, students can venture outside to observe nature and craft their own Romantic poems. Or, if you're reading another text set in the outdoors, you can stage an activity wherein your students complete some observational writing that incorporates the stylistic techniques of the author in question. This encourages them to use mentor texts to create an original piece of writing based in a natural space in their own community.

Intended Benefits
- personal
- engaging

Interdisciplinary/Cross-Curricular Connections
- We'll mention this here, but it's true of every activity in this chapter: inviting a science teacher to discuss the ways scientists observe and write about nature can provide your students with a new vocabulary to conduct similar work of their own. Such a partnership will also appeal to those students who have existing (or developing) interests in science as a subject or career goal.

The Nature of Survival

Humankind versus nature. If there's one literary trope we learn (and read) about early in our schooling, it's this one. One or more individuals overcoming adversity in the immensity of the natural world has long been a popular dramatic device. From canonical literature (e.g., Ernest Hemingway's *The Old Man and the Sea* or William Golding's *Lord of the Flies*), to young adult literature (e.g., Gary Paulsen's *Hatchet* or Roland Smith's *Peak*), to memoir and literary nonfiction (e.g., Jon Krakauer's *Into Thin Air* or Cheryl Strayed's *Wild*), to popular contemporary fiction (e.g., Andy Weir's *The Martian* or Yann Martel's *Life of Pi*), there's something about this particular conflict that appeals to readers on a primal level.

Even though we're obviously not going to abandon our students in a natural place and leave them to fend for themselves (although we've heard of worse ideas for the last period of the day on Fridays), we can use natural places to get our students thinking about the methods of survival used by characters in the texts we're reading. For instance, taking your students to a forested setting could be one way of making a connection to *Into the Wild*, Krakauer's (1996) nonfiction account of the short life of Chris McCandless, or, for younger students, Paulsen's (1987) wilderness survival story *Hatchet*.

A simple scenario could guide your students' observation and writing: If you found yourself stranded in this natural place with only the clothes you're currently wearing, what would you need to accomplish first? What would ensure your survival until you could be rescued? What natural resources would be at your disposal to help you endure the elements? What other environmental factors would you need to consider (e.g., weather, wildlife, nutrition)?

By giving your students an opportunity to explore the area and make notes of the details they'd need to consider in an actual survival scenario, they can more readily appreciate what's at stake for the characters in the literature they're reading. As a follow-up activity, you could ask your students to evaluate the character's survival plan: Considering your own experience with wilderness survival, what did the character do well? What should they have done instead of, or in addition to, the existing plan? What do these choices and/or missteps reveal about character? In the process, your students are conducting character analyses based on their own outdoor experiences.

Finally, for a creative project, your students could collaboratively create a survival guide for the location they visited as a class, or for a separate location of their own choosing. The guide could incorporate a range of tips for the area they explored: what to forage, how to protect yourself from the elements, where to look for help, and so on.

Intended Benefits
- personal
- engaging
- audience oriented

Interdisciplinary/Cross-Curricular Connections
- With basic survival skills at the center of the activity, a discussion of Maslow's (1943) "hierarchy of needs" could provide your students with additional angles through which to explore the natural space and deepen their understanding of what's essential for survival.
- Mapping skills could also come in handy for this activity. As a component of their survival guides, the students could be required to provide a map of the natural place in question. A practical illustration of the location could allow the students to provide more specific directions in their written text. Teaming with a social studies teacher or community member conversant in mapmaking techniques could make the activity even more authentic.

Transposing Setting

What would happen if *Lord of the Flies* were set in a remote section of the Mojave Desert instead of a tropical island? How would *Heart of Darkness* change if Marlow hiked part of the Appalachian Trail to find Mr. Kurtz? What if Richard Connell's (1924/1990) classic short story "The Most Dangerous Game" took place in Louisiana marshland instead of on a Caribbean island? These seem like obvious questions to answer—setting is so hardwired into these books' DNA that changing them would seemingly change *everything*—but it's also interesting to consider just how much of plot and character is contingent upon the location in which a book is set. Consider the *Lord of the Flies* example we just mentioned. We know the book's literal "beast" is (spoiler alert) a downed parachutist, but how does the Beast's symbolic nature change when removed from the oppressive humidity of the jungle? Does it hold less power without the jungle to shroud it? And if *that* changes, what are the likely implications for the boys who, in Golding's (1954/1988) original text, allow themselves to become dehumanized in the name of protecting themselves from the Beast? We can consider these questions and others by simply transferring a text from its current setting to a new one.

For this activity, make that transformation literal. For any book that has location positioned as a catalyst for action, ask your students to consider how things would change in a new setting you visit as a class. As we've recommended elsewhere, give them time to explore the new location so they can make observations, take notes, and do some low-stakes reflective writing. The focus for this work should be thinking about how setting impacts both plot and character, so, to that end, you might focus their observations by first brainstorming sections from the text where the physical environment plays a pivotal role.

The final product could be a traditional essay exploring some aspect of the novel that would be influenced by a change in setting. But, returning once again to the notion that essays aren't the only means by which to assess students' thinking, a more engaging product would be to have your students rewrite a sequence or event from the text, placing it in the new setting. This would allow you to see the same things as the traditional essay, but it would also likely see more student buy-in while also providing you with some insight into your students' facility for narrative writing and all it entails (e.g., description, dialogue, character building, etc.). Finally, if you want to add a multimedia component to the assignment, Google Maps has a feature that allows users to pin locations on a custom map and add narrative comments. Students could pin their transposed settings (as in Figure 6.1, placing *Lord of the Flies* in a community park) and add detail justifying why this new location is (or could be) roughly equivalent to the setting in the source novel. This could serve as a form of prewriting for the assignment, or could even accompany the final product as a visual element for those unfamiliar with the new location.

Intended Benefits
- personal
- engaging

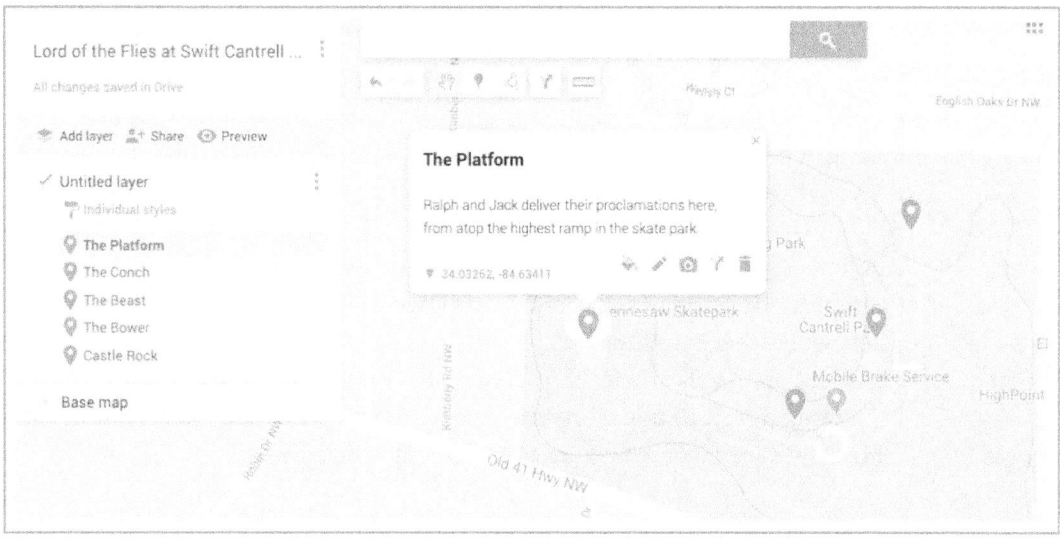

FIGURE 6.1. Using Google Maps to transpose the setting of a novel to a local place.

Variation to Add an Authentic Audience
- Because stories have implied audiences, it would be valuable for your students to share their rewritten sections of the text with each other or as part of some other storytelling event. Hearing what one another wrote would also reveal to them the range of interpretive possibilities present in a single text and using a single setting.

Writing Arguments

There are obvious arguments to be made about natural places. For example, there's urgency in arguing *for* their preservation generally or *against* individual human habits that endanger them specifically. The Wild Places activity we described at the beginning of this chapter centers on such important conversations. However, we also recognize that sometimes we need to structure activities with lower stakes in order to teach the simple mechanics of argument. Natural places allow for this kind of writing, too, which underscores the flexibility and adaptability of place-based writing. Whether you want your students to grapple with complicated arguments surrounding environmental advocacy (such as in the Wild Places assignment) or construct more simple arguments that mimic real-world writing genres (like the activity we describe next), the natural places in your community can serve as a productive venue for both approaches.

Creating Tourist Ads

One of the most effective ways we've found to teach argumentation is through the use of print and video advertisements. As we know, ads—whether we're talking about ads for products, charities, or politicians—exist only to persuade the viewer to do something: buy a car, donate money, vote for (or against) this person. They're not pure arguments, because they frequently rely on appeals to emotion; however, students often demonstrate deft analytical skills when asked to identify the strategies at work in effective TV commercials or print ads. We can leverage this in natural places to help students think about constructing an argument that "sells" their place to tourists.

During a visit to a local natural place, students can start to consider some critical questions when it comes to creating the ad, such as:

- Who is the intended audience?
- Why would this place appeal to that audience?
- What about it would you specifically want to emphasize?
- What aspects of the place will you want to downplay or omit?

When it comes to creating the ad itself,[7] students can use these questions as a foundation, but, as with any argument, they should also think about the claim they're making and the evidence they're providing that warrants it. Finally, because of this activity's specific real-world corollary, you'll also want to talk about the importance of acknowledging their target audience and allowing for the inclusion of emotional or ethical appeals so their final product will more closely align with real-world examples (Crovitz & Montgomery, 2015).

We realize the contradiction inherent in promoting a natural space for tourist traffic in a book that also advocates for environmental preservation and stewardship. Therefore, an alternate approach to this particular assignment (which isn't too far removed from the Wild Places activity) would be to write an "anti-tourism" ad. The argumentative skills you teach would remain the same; they'd just be employed in the service of arguing why a particular area *shouldn't* be opened for tourism.

Intended Benefits
- personal
- agentive
- engaging
- audience oriented

Variation to Add an (Even More) Authentic Audience

- Even though an authentic audience is already built into this activity, you might take it one step further by allowing students to make thirty-second video spots for their ads. These could, at a minimum, be shown to the class, but you might also explore other avenues for involving parents or community members in an evening of short films.

Writing Narratives, Poetry, and Scripts

Just as we can readily use natural spaces to forge connections between the environment and the literature we read, we can also use natural spaces to help students create their own literature. We all know one of the common complaints we hear from our students is that they don't have anything to write about. While we fundamentally disagree with them, we also understand their reticence. Sometimes (even many times), it takes someone else to show us how we can build on our own experiences and contexts to create original writing. By taking students to natural spaces in the community, you can help them generate ideas that can ultimately be turned into stories worth sharing.

Bringing a Scientist's Eye to Creative Writing

In previous chapters, we discussed ways of using outdoor locations as grist for the narrative and poetic mills. These activities largely consist of broad observations—looking at different locations (and the people who inhabit them) as productive settings in which to situate stories and poetry. While you can certainly modify those activities for use in natural places, they can also be taken one step further by zeroing in on minute details that help students think about capturing precise images in poetry or prose.

In a visit to a natural place, observation is once again at the fore of the students' work. This time, however, they should avoid the tendency to describe the location in broad strokes; instead, ask them to think small by adopting the perspective of a scientist. Rather than describing the forest, describe the pattern and texture of a single tree's bark, the veins of its leaves, the grain of the soil at its base. How would they describe a single blade of grass? The look of a pebble as a stream eddies around it? The ladybug that alights on their shirtsleeve? Your students' goal should be to look for those small details we often ignore in our tendency to look only at the big picture. The devil's in the details—so, too, is effective writing.

With these observations as their foundation, your students can write either narratives or poetry, depending on your aims. A self-contained activity would be to ask them to write a series of haiku about the place they just visited, but you could just as naturally extend the activity so that their observations have to be worked into an original narrative.

Intended Benefits
- personal
- engaging

Variation to Add Agency
- There may be other areas that your students find more inspiring to observe and write about. Rather than requiring all your students to write about the natural place you visit as a class, you could give them the option of observing another location on their own. Anyone who chooses to do this could be required to provide a photo of the place, so you'd have a frame of reference, but there's no reason to think the place you visit should be the only reasonable spot in which your students can be inspired to write.

Variation to Add an Authentic Audience
- As we've mentioned throughout this book, we're fans of providing different avenues for students to share their writing. For example, you could stage an in-class coffeehouse-style poetry reading—which, of course, is an event that would also require students to think about the *sound* of their work, a trait often omitted when students are primarily asked only to submit their writing to the teacher.

Interdisciplinary/Cross-Curricular Connections
- Given the specific lens for this activity, it would probably be a missed opportunity *not* to invite a science teacher to talk about how scientists approach observations of the natural world.

Be a Social Media Coordinator

Although social media originally existed primarily for personal use, its promotional potential was quickly (and understandably) seized upon by entities looking to sell things. Products, causes, politicians, even places—they all have accounts in multiple online locations with a single purpose: to get us to buy what they're selling. The social media accounts of physical places are particularly interesting because they're intended to sell *the feeling* of a place, as communicated through photography and captions, in the hope that you'll travel there. For example, we follow a Facebook account for Scotland's Isle of Skye. The photos highlight such things as Skye's immense physical beauty, the abundance of its wildlife, and the quaint, picturesque villages found on the coast. The captions are often humorous, using Scottish idiomatic language (e.g., referring to a photo of a border collie as a "wee dug") or references to local customs or history. Celebratory in nature and appealing to both potential tourists as well as those who already love the area, it's clear to see how this page quite successfully impresses upon viewers the notion that Skye is a unique location with a sense of place distinct from anywhere else in Scotland. Many similar sites for other locations exist throughout social media and could be seized upon as mentor texts for your students.

For this activity, in which your students will act as the administrator for the social media page of a natural place, first share with them some social media accounts for a variety of physical places. This will give them a sense of what makes those accounts distinct from other social media pages, including the way photos and text often work in tandem. You can also use this step of the activity to discuss the differences between social media accounts and the kind of targeted campaigns central to the Creating Tourist Ads activity described previously. Then, visit a natural place in your community so the students can explore, observe, and take notes and photos. Have them look at the place from different angles, including observing some things close up. They should also do some reflective writing on questions like these:

- What about the place would be worth sharing with others?
- How can its natural beauty be effectively communicated?
- Could some posts take the form of a short narrative description written from the point of view of an inanimate object (or animal) *in* the natural place?
- How about poetry?
- What photos would you take, and what text would accompany them?

The final product for this activity would be for your students to create a series of posts designed for one or more social media outlets. The assessment criteria can be broad—maybe you want them to write in a specific number of genres or include photos in a set number of posts—and will be determined by your goals for the activity. However, just as students have a range of personal uses for social media, we encourage you to provide them with the flexibility to take ownership of their own natural space "page." The ultimate goal is for students to share observational writing about the natural place that is descriptive enough to complement the spot's natural beauty. While not true narrative writing, this activity nonetheless incorporates aspects of it that could be expanded in subsequent assignments.

Intended Benefits
- personal
- agentive
- engaging
- audience oriented

Variation to Add an Authentic Audience
- An outside audience is certainly already implied, but, given the potential dangers of unfettered social media use, you might want to think about other ways of allowing students to publicize their work. One option might be to create a class blog in which their individual posts could be housed.

Writing for Research and Inquiry

One thing we readily acknowledge is the degree to which research activities conducted in natural places will probably not resemble anything we typically expect to find in an English language arts classroom. Some of this is down to the authenticity of the project: by situating research in the real world, we're necessarily moving away from those traditional classroom-bound topics. But the other challenge is that, simply put, the typical content of the English classroom doesn't easily lend itself to researching aspects of natural places. That needn't be seen as an impediment or a drawback. If we remember, once again, that we should focus on the skills and knowledge we want our students to develop in the process of conducting research, we automatically grant ourselves the freedom to develop research activities that are likely to be more authentic than writing another author study or defense of a controversial issue.

Coexisting with the Land

In this activity, we return to an idea we first explored in Chapter 3: environmental impact. Whereas in that activity (Making the School More Environmentally Friendly), students were tasked with making modifications to their school's existing structure and processes, here we're asking students to think from the ground up. Consider this scenario:

> The Rachel Carson Society is awarding a substantial monetary award to the team that designs a home most likely to blend organically with its surroundings. As a member of that team, your job is to collaboratively design that award-winning house. What environmental factors will you need to consider? How will you handle such variables as electricity, plumbing, and transportation to and from your home? How will the structure's appearance naturally blend with its surroundings? Your team will be responsible for writing a proposal that details the dwelling's design, and you should also develop a visual representation of the house consisting of at least its exterior and one room that highlights its environmentally sustainable features.

Any natural place will work with this scenario, although it could be interesting to problematize it by selecting a natural place that might not easily lend itself to the construction of a house. A meadow is almost too easy; if possible, think about presenting your students with a more challenging environment, such as a forest, marsh, or hillside.

A visit to the natural place you select will give the students an opportunity to think about crucial issues such as aesthetics and transportation, but savvy students will also likely start to think about issues like nearby water sources or the availability of direct sunlight (if they plan to install solar panels). We hope the research angle is obvious. Each team will have the agency to design a house that aligns with its vision, but writing the proposal will require unavoidable research into environmental sustainability and home design.[8]

The final product is built into the scenario. Each collaborative team will present their proposal along with the visual representation of the house they've designed. There's a range of ways to provide your students with an authentic audience, from inviting local architects, contractors, or city planners to hear their proposals to presenting them to parents, teachers, or community members in a night themed around the environment and innovation.

Intended Benefits
- personal
- agentive
- engaging
- audience oriented
- promotes change

Variation to Add an Argument Component
- Since a proposal is a form of argument (essentially, convincing a panel of reviewers that a project is viable), you could emphasize that aspect by specifically asking your students to consider the various claims they're making, the evidence they're providing to support those claims, and the counterarguments with which a proposal review panel might challenge them.

Interdisciplinary/Cross-Curricular Connections
- Given the inherent STEM focus of this project, there are obvious opportunities to partner with your science colleagues, as well as with community members who have experience and expertise in the environment, architecture, or construction.

Writing for Change

Throughout this book, we have discussed the potential for environmental stewardship and advocacy inherent in place-based writing, and we took up the issue most specifically in the Wild Places activity that opened this chapter. Helping students see the value in their environment increases the likelihood they will take care of it and speak out on its behalf. While this might be the most pressing (and most obvious) use for writing in natural places, taking students to unspoiled locations can also encourage them to think about *why we value these places at all*. What is it that natural places do for us? Why does their preservation matter? And, as we discuss in the next activity, how might we bring aspects of the natural world into the *un*natural world?

A Signature Location

Before we turn our attention to virtual places in Chapter 7, we wanted our final outdoor activity to merge several of the strands from earlier chapters—merging natural spaces with public places, argument with literature, and real-world genres with traditional academic writing. It isn't just to create a showstopper of a final activity (although, if you feel dazzled, don't let us stop you); it's to help students see that everything we discuss in *A Place to Write* is connected. It is, in some ways, fallacious for us to have compartmentalized things the way we have, and we've tried to point out where there's natural overlap. Certain activities can be facilitated in both museums *and* public places, and other activities can result in a traditional essay *or* a pop-up museum (or both!). As we've mentioned before, the beauty of place-based writing is how its very simplicity can be leveraged to incorporate a range of approaches and accomplish a range of goals. And that brings us to the Signature Location activity.

Most communities can claim a natural place as its trademark. In Georgia, the Chattahoochee River crisscrosses Interstate 75 just north of Atlanta, and the recreation area that accompanies it lends a natural flavor to this otherwise traffic-clogged metropolis. Further east, the marshes and tidelands make up the environmental character of Savannah and Tybee Island. Santa Barbara, California, bordered on the north by the steeply rising Santa Ynez Mountains and on the south by pristine stretches of Pacific Ocean coastline, finds its personality in these vastly different types of geography that are fewer than ten miles apart. Rural areas stretching from Ohio west through Nebraska are associated with flat panoramic views fringed by the tassels of corn stalks. Colorado's craggy mountains. Maine's rugged coastline. The lush forests and pristine lakes of Minnesota's Boundary Waters. Whatever the geographic region, these signature locations provide outsiders with easily recognizable images of specific communities. And, crucially, these images are responsible for imbuing each place with a sense of identity and ownership.

In your community, what's that place? The place many people would classify as your community's natural hallmark? Again, for us, it might be the Chattahoochee River, but we could also make an argument for the gently rolling North Georgia mountains mere miles away. Whatever place you identify in your community, take your students there and let them explore.[9] What makes this place special? What is it about this location that lends your community a sense of identity, or even local pride? How does the location make your students feel, and why do they think it makes them feel this way? The purpose of this visit is for your students to unpack these associations so they have a stronger sense of what causes them and why they're important.

Because we're focused on promoting change with this activity, we now want to turn our attention to a public place (revisit Chapter 5 for a list of possible locations) or to the school site itself. This will require a separate visit for more observation. At this location, ask your students to consider how well the public place reflects the sense of identity they associate with the signature location. To what degree does that signature location seem to have been considered or incorporated in the design of the public place? Do they associate the same sense of identity with the public place as they did with the signature location? And, most important, what specific changes might be made to the public place to more fully align it with the sense of identity inherent in the signature location?[10]

This activity blends our discussion of the value of natural places with our discussion in Chapter 5 about the artificial aesthetics of public places, and it asks students to bridge this gap. With the two visits (and their attendant observations, note-taking, and informal writing) as the foundation, your students will argue for specific ways the identity of the signature location can be more fully reflected in the aesthetics of the public place. As part of this conversation, you can even bring local history into the mix. Are there writers or artists whose work could also be incorporated in this rethinking of a public place? Is there a key historical figure or a crucial industry central to your town's history? These are all questions your students could consider, and you could even build in a research component to help them answer these (and other) emerging questions.

In practical terms (and to continue to use our own community), Rob's students came up with a plan to redesign the small park in downtown Kennesaw, Georgia, that incorporated aspects of the north Georgia mountains, the Chattahoochee River recreation area, notable Georgia authors (with quotes from Alice Walker and Flannery O'Connor), and the locomotive industry. Work of this kind asks students to consider local history, community identity, intentional aesthetic choices, the value of natural places, and a range of other possible topics.

What do the students submit at the end of all this? The probably unsatisfying answer is that it can be as broad or as narrow as your goals. Here are a few possible products your students could create as a result of at least two visits to different locations, informal writing, and some additional research:

- a letter or proposal to the town council
- a grant proposal soliciting funds for one or more of the proposed changes
- a visual display that includes a drawing or three-dimensional representation of their proposed changes
- a traditional explanatory essay that discusses the nature of community identity and how a town's public places contribute to it
- a social media page with multiple posts detailing the proposed changes

This is an activity that requires students to think big. We know thinking big is complicated. And messy. And not always easy to explain to test-obsessed administrators. But we'd argue that, for too long, school has shrunk the act of writing to a single point that's so constricting our students no longer see how it has anything to offer them. By thinking big, we're asking students to engage with the world, to see how their writing has a place in it, and to understand the power they possess as the next generation of leaders.

Intended Benefits
- personal
- agentive
- engaging
- audience oriented
- promotes change

Considerations for Students with Special Needs
- For activities incorporating social media, the more specific and clear you are with the type of social media post you would like students to produce, the better. Students can begin this assignment by identifying the key elements for the post they would like to create and determine why those elements are important. You may want to start with mentor posts that students can mimic using pictures and text they create independently. Memes are a quick, easy way to accomplish this. By following these exemplars, students are creating writing on their own while still having a clear goal for the finished product.
- While we want students to have autonomy to choose what they want to write, sometimes too many choices can cause paralysis for students and unnecessary stress for you as you try to provide support for a wide range of ideas. We recommend choosing one or two final product choices for your students and then providing them with vocabulary and mentor text support from there.

Considerations for English Language Learners
- Students could reimagine a work of literature that was originally written in their primary language, or about a culture with which they identify. Many great works of literature come from around the world, and, while finding these works in their original language may be a bit of a task, it is worth helping all students to understand and reimagine stories that they can feel empowered by.

- Showing students concrete examples of homes built to work with the environment around them will be essential in helping students understand what they should be thinking as they conduct research. You may consider showing them a video about the Leadership in Energy and Environmental Design initiative, or show them pictures of green homes from around the world. Some students may be able to provide a unique set of experiences they could share with the class in order to help all of your students understand the innovative ways people from around the world have found to work with the environment.

7

Writing in Virtual Places

Even though we hope we've impressed upon you the notion that place-based writing can be local and accessible (even facilitated, at times, on school grounds), we also recognize there may be a variety of reasons preventing you from venturing outside the classroom. Similarly, it may be that you want to scale your students up to true place-based writing by first doing something in a more controlled environment. It isn't a perfect solution, but we can look to technology—virtual places—as one way to replicate place-based writing without ever leaving your room.

Critically, though, this isn't a chapter about digital tools. There are many texts out there focusing on those tools written by people far more knowledgeable on the subject than we. The rapidly changing nature of technology also means any specific applications we mention here could be obsolete by the time you next pick up this book. While we do mention one or two tools later, this is primarily a chapter about *virtual possibilities*. It's up to you to decide which resources are most effective and readily available for your students. Underpinning this entire chapter is Hicks's (2009) contention that technology not supersede the writer or their writing:

> If we engage students in real writing tasks and we use technology in such a way that it complements their innate need to find purposes and audiences for their work, we can have them engaged in a digital writing process that focuses first on the writer, then the writing, then the technology. (p. 8)

In short, any references to technology in this chapter should be seen as a means, not an end.

Perhaps the most obvious use of these virtual places is the way we can use them to transport our students to far-off locations. They can still explore, conduct research, craft narratives, or write any other kind of text we might ask them to write in a physical location, but technology allows them to do so in a way that requires fewer logistical considerations than even a simple trip to a local park.

While the internet provides our students with an easy portal into remote locations, it's also important to remember that the online world is itself a place with distinct characteristics within and among websites and applications. Think back to Agnew's (1987) three characteristics of *place* that we first described in Chapter 1: *location* (its fixed address), *locale* (the components that constitute the place), and *sense of place* (its identity). Now consider a website like Facebook. It has a location (its URL). It has a locale (the timeline, the left-hand tabs, the icons across the top indicating likes and friend requests). And it certainly has a sense of place that distinguishes it from other social media outlets.[1]

Considering websites, especially social media sites built for interaction between users, as a type of place falls in line with the notion of "third spaces." Oldenburg (1991) defines these locations as "a generic designation for a great variety of public places that host the regular, voluntary, informal, and happily anticipated gatherings of individuals beyond the realms of home and work" (p. 16). It didn't take long for others to note similarities between certain virtual places and Oldenburg's physical third places (Rheingold, 1993), and more recently, researchers have concluded that online games like *EverQuest* or *World of Warcraft* also meet the definition of a "third space" (Moore et al., 2009; Steinkuehler & Williams, 2006). While we can certainly use the virtual world as a means to explore real or imagined physical locations, we can also start to think about the ways in which the virtual world itself is a place with distinct identifying features that can be leveraged for authentic writing.

Important to consider, too, is the way virtual places contain venues for authentic writing that our students may already be using. Blogging, fan fiction, discussion forums, online reviews, text-heavy social media sites like Tumblr—all of these could be practical ways to increase student engagement, as some of them are likely already immersed in these digital worlds. As a practical example, Lammers (2016) studied an online forum wherein adolescents and young adults wrote fan fiction about the video game *The Sims*. The participants used screenshots from the game as the foundation for written narratives about the game's characters. Lammers (2016) found that, if these young writers want their writing to be recognized and valued in this online context, they "need to attend to the grammars, structures, and expectations valued by their particular audiences" (p. 329). This aligns with our earlier observations about the agentive possibilities of place-based writing. If we want our students to write authentically, we need to empower them to make tactical choices about the pieces they compose. And one of the most effective ways to do this is by creating situations in which they can write for real audiences and purposes.

Using online places to facilitate writing also capitalizes on what Gee (2004) tells us about the value of affinity spaces, as well as what we know about literacy practices and what it means to adopt them as a framework for teaching (Barton, 2006; Beach et al., 2012; Pennycook, 2010). To connect these threads, they all involve the social, purposeful nature of language use as it happens naturally through engagement in a particular activity. At the core of an affinity space is the deep interest shared by its participants and the literacy practices (or social language use) that naturally emerge from that interest. The literacy practices embedded in an affinity space are purposeful—*authentic*—precisely because they are determined by (and grow out of) the activity. If we can create events like these in our classrooms—engaging activities that generate authentic, purposeful language use—we can help students understand the value of writing in the world beyond school precisely because they'll actually be engaged in it in a manner with which they're already familiar.

So what does this have to do with using virtual places as an approximation of place-based writing? In short, we know many of our students are already actively involved in (or at least familiar with) a variety of online spaces and their required discourses. On a mostly superficial level, there's the built-in engagement that often stems from utilizing media our students enjoy. If we can get them to write because they find online spaces to be more fun than traditional classroom spaces, that's not something we should ignore. More important, though, there's value in transparency. If we can help students understand how audience and purpose affect the language we use in a context in which they're already invested, there's a greater chance they'll start to see how audience and purpose should influence the decisions they make in all their writing.

The activities described in the following sections, then, approach virtual places in two very different ways. One way is to explore the online or digital versions of actual physical places in much the same way we've explored them in previous chapters. But the other way is to empower our students to more thoughtfully and strategically navigate the online spaces they regularly occupy, in the process seeing how that navigation can make them more nimble users of language in non-digital spaces, too.

Extended Lesson Idea: Creating a Virtual Tour

A few years ago, we treated ourselves to a summer vacation to Iceland. We didn't know much about the country except for the images that persist in the media: elven glades, thundering waterfalls, snowy crags, all soundtracked by the otherworldly sounds of Icelandic band Sigur Rós. It was helpful inspiration for a weeklong trip, but it wasn't much on which to base an itinerary. We knew we needed to look to travel guides to help us fill in the considerable gaps in our knowledge. Print-based travel guides (Fodor's, Lonely Planet, National Geographic, and the like) have traditionally been useful resources for travelers, their wealth of information about history, local culture, and popular sights giving the uninitiated a helpful overview of their destination.

In the last twenty years, however, the internet has given rise to a range of websites catering to tourists. From sites like Yelp and Tripadvisor, which allow users to review restaurants and hotels, to general travel guides, to sites sponsored by geographic regions or even entire cities, it's now easier than ever for tourists to learn more about their destination before they make a single reservation. Of particular note are sites that offer virtual tours. Using informational captions, photographs, video clips, and links to other helpful media (e.g., reviews, news stories, or blog posts), visitors are offered a multimedia bird's-eye view that can provide a seemingly comprehensive account of any location.

The catch of course is that these sites *aren't* comprehensive. As thorough as they might seem, they can't possibly include every sight worth seeing, every restaurant worth dining in, every tour worth taking, and every hotel worth a night's stay. Just as the contents of traditional travel guides are dictated by the author or editor, so too are these virtual tours dictated by the host website. And sometimes the contents are dictated by other forces. Which restaurants or attractions have paid to be featured on the virtual tour? Which ones offer discounts to patrons directed to them by the site in exchange for advertising? Existing partnerships like these and others might not be obvious to site visitors, nor might prospective tourists stop to consider which things have been *left off* the virtual tour due to space, funding, or other issues.

Just as we've asked students in other chapters to consider the voices omitted from museums and public displays, we can use the proliferation of virtual tours to consider what gets included in a tour of the local community as well as how that information could be presented in such a way to both educate viewers and promote the community to prospective visitors. Such a project can include elements of research, argument, and narrative writing. It can require the critical evaluation of existing websites. It can also ask students to consider how to effectively marry text with image. And all of this can be accomplished in authentic genres created for real audiences, without ever leaving the classroom.

The Assignment

Rather than thinking each student has to create an entire virtual tour of their own, we envision this as a collaborative project wherein each student will be required to create certain individual pieces that will be assembled into a cohesive whole. This will require some careful thought about the genres you want to include and the writing you want to assess, but the result of this forethought is the winnowing of a seemingly overwhelming endeavor into several key genres replicated in different ways by your students.

In practical terms, let's say you decide you want to include the following products in the virtual tour of your town:

- narrative pieces describing different aspects of the town or its surroundings (accompanied by photos)
- researched pieces detailing aspects of local history
- reviews of local restaurants, shops, attractions, etc.

All of these pieces could be organized by category on a blogging website, linked on an online map, or, if time and classroom technology allow, compiled using an actual virtual tour website. Rigell and Banack (2019) describe a project wherein an eighth-grade class wrote place-based poems, selected representative photographs of those places, and linked them all to pins using Google's Tour Builder platform. The resulting work helped the students reclaim the Appalachian community in which they lived and "instill a sense of pride that reached into" their classroom experiences (Rigell & Banack, 2019, p. 43).

Whatever form the final product takes, it would obviously be far too ambitious a project for individual students to construct their own personal tours. In a class of thirty students, however, with each student creating examples of *all three genres*, you suddenly have thirty options in each category from which to choose. This would result in either a detailed and complex depiction of your community (if you include every submission from every student) or a selective process whereby you choose representative samples for each category, making sure to include at least one product from each student in your class. In either case, the wealth of products created by students with different backgrounds, interests, and perspectives makes for a much fuller tour than one created by a single individual (or even a two-student partnership).

So where does all this start—especially given the absence of true place-based writing? In this case, the out-of-class experience is approximated by spending some time exploring a range of existing virtual tours. If, as we've mentioned elsewhere in this book, we want our students to write in a variety of genres (especially if those genres are unfamiliar to them), we need to make sure they're equipped to do so. Therefore, instead of venturing to a specific location to conduct observations and engage in some low-stakes exploratory writing, you'll provide your students with some time to make observations about one or more virtual tours. You can provide them with a list of possible sites to visit or allow the students to locate their own.[2] In either case, encourage them to click as many links as time allows and to write responses to some of the following questions:

- What kind of locations are linked in each tour? Where do the links take you?
- What do you notice about the writing included in the tour? What is its tone? What genres are included? What information does it provide?
- How are still images and video used in the tour? Are they always linked to text?
- Based on what you know about the tour's subject, does anything seem to be omitted? Did you expect to see something that was missing?
- What did you learn about the tour's subject from taking the virtual tour? What aspects of the tour were most and least helpful?

The purpose of this writing—and the conversation that follows—is to help students understand how virtual tours work in a broad sense, but it can also introduce them to the fact we mentioned earlier: a large-scale virtual tour, impressive as it might be, consists of a variety of smaller, more manageable artifacts created by a team of people—in this case, your students.

With this exploration of actual virtual tours serving as your foundation, the next step is for the class to determine the parameters of their own tour, which will largely depend on their existing knowledge of the community in which they live. It's also important at this stage for your students to remember the public nature of any virtual tour. It isn't a private document or something to be shared among a select group of people. It exists for education and promotion, to share knowledge about the community, and, with any luck, attract visitors. They can't include *everything*, so what makes the cut? They could consider questions such as these as a starting point:

- Which buildings or landmarks are essential to include?
- Which businesses should be reviewed?
- What are the natural spaces worth highlighting?
- What do you know about your town's history, and where should that information be shared? What do you still need to research?
- What are the lesser-known locations that deserve to be common knowledge?
- Which aspects of the town have been marginalized, and how should those places be represented?

This conversation will establish the boundaries for the project, but it also uncovers the tricky nature of curation (also discussed in Chapter 4). Including only *some* things necessarily involves omitting others. Such a discussion can be used to hone your students' skills in argumentation as they try to mount a compelling case advocating for the inclusion (or omission) of a particular aspect of the community. There are two tools that could help facilitate these early discussions. We mentioned Google's Tour Builder earlier in this chapter, and, in Chapter 6, we introduced the use of Google Maps' note-taking function. Both of these allow users to pin locations on a custom map and add narrative comments. Used collaboratively for the entire class, either resource could help students stake a claim for specific landmarks, but it could also provide a helpful visual depiction of your community to ensure you're not overlooking any particular areas.

Once you have made decisions regarding the locations and aspects of local history to include, the remainder of the project involves creating the artifacts that constitute the virtual tour itself. This will, in large part, be determined by your own goals, centering on the types of writing you want to teach and assess, and these goals will likely dictate the number of artifacts your students create. A quick sampling of virtual tours will reveal the different types of writing your students could do, but a few different genres leap immediately to mind (all of which, as indicated below, we have described in more detail elsewhere in this book):

- Reviews (Chapter 5)—One aspect of the virtual tour could be a selection of reviews of local restaurants (or businesses or attractions). Students could select a restaurant, eat there,[3] and write a review of the experience. This would allow you to assess your students' facility with argument in a real-world context, and would also, in its expectation that students eat at the restaurant they're reviewing, add a layer of actual place-based writing that doesn't exist elsewhere in the project.

- Local history (Chapter 4)—To add an element of inquiry, your students could research an event or historical figure with local significance and compose a succinct account of what they learn. Similar to the kind of information typically provided by tourist sites and guidebooks, this writing would broaden the scope of the tour by establishing the historical context that informs the community's present. It would also provide your students with practical experiences writing summary and paraphrase.

- Descriptive writing (Chapter 6)—Another way to bring your community to life is through the inclusion of descriptive writing (or a short narrative or even a poem) paired with a photo. If your students identify different landscapes that would make for evocative images, each student could take a photograph of their chosen location and compose a short piece to accompany it. The photo and writing could appeal to prospective visitors saying, in essence, "Here's what resonates with me about the town in which I live." And, again, by asking the students to take a photo of their selected location, it would add an element of place-based writing to this largely virtual project.

There are certainly other genres of writing that could also be taught and assessed in the context of this project. One thing consistent across all genres, however, is their public nature. Because the virtual tour is designed expressly for an outside audience, this project provides your students with a unique opportunity to explore the real-world impact of such rhetorical elements as tone and diction. Traditionally discussed only in the context of essay writing, the importance of such elements can be hard to notice when our students' writing never makes it past the teacher. The virtual tour, on the other hand, asks them to consider how their writing will be interpreted by complete strangers and to evaluate the likelihood that it will accomplish their intended purposes.

Logistical Considerations

In addition to deciding which written genres to include, probably the single most important factor to determine beforehand revolves around which places to include in the tour. Will each student be required to create one or more individual artifacts for unique locations (i.e., with no places duplicated between students), or will it be permissible for multiple students to create artifacts about the same locations? If it's the former, how will you decide who gets to "claim" certain locations? If it's the latter, and you have several students creating artifacts about a single location, how will you decide which student's work ultimately appears in the tour? Will your students be given the freedom to determine the contents of the tour themselves, or will you require that certain places or aspects of local history be included? We place no value judgments on any of these decisions. The size of your class, the opportunities in your community, and the number of written pieces you want your students to create will all play a role in deciding how to handle this aspect of the project.

Another essential variable is the appearance of the tour itself. How will your students ultimately be sharing their work? If this is your first experience with a project like this, you might try a blogging site that allows you to create different categories or pages. A page could be devoted to local history, another to reviews, and a third to narratives and photos. Additional pages could be created for other genres. This would be less visually impressive than some of the tours your students have explored, but it would also be more accessible and less technology intensive than attempting to create a tour that links all your students' writing to a panoramic photo.

That said—and mindful of the fact that we're still adamant about this not being a chapter devoted to online tools—Google's Tour Builder platform would certainly add a dimension of authenticity to your students' work. As with any other assignment, you need to decide which product will be the most effective showcase for your students' learning while also balancing what will be most realistic in your specific teaching situation.

Supplemental Lessons

You've no doubt recognized that some of our earlier activities could be used as supplemental lessons in the virtual tour project. We especially draw your attention to these activities:

- Chapter 4—Exploring Local History and Reflecting on the Process
- Chapter 5—Travel Blogging and The Aesthetics of Place
- Chapter 6—Creating Tourist Ads and Be a Social Media Coordinator

These specific activities could be worthwhile for you to consider in addition to the two we describe next.

Captions and Writing Summaries

Summarizing and paraphrasing source material can prove to be a tricky endeavor for some students. This is often one of the pitfalls of the traditional research paper, with students either failing to effectively recast their reading in the context of the paper or else inadvertently plagiarizing because they don't change enough of the original text to qualify as a true summary or paraphrase. The virtual tour becomes an effective venue in which to practice this skill, as insightful summary is one of the hallmarks of any tour. Whether it's a historical figure's biography, the background of a noteworthy public building, or the recounting of an important event, summary can be found all over most virtual tours.

To help your students get a better handle on not only how summaries are created but also how they function in a real-world setting, we recommend using some of the virtual tours your students discovered as mentor texts. In a guided analysis of image captions and other short explanatory passages, students can see how these sites present background information in an accessible way. Important, too, is the way the summaries sound. Students can consider issues of tone and word choice by identifying whether the summaries use such devices as evaluative language or humor, or if they stick to the kind of objective reporting we typically find in newspaper articles.

Once students have completed their own research, you can provide them with opportunities to practice writing their own summaries before they settle on the final version that will appear in the virtual tour itself.

Writing Reviews
We introduced the idea of the travel blog review in Chapter 5 and briefly mentioned the possibility of using mentor texts to familiarize students with the genre. That's a possibility with the virtual tour, too, especially if you specifically require your students to write a restaurant review. Most students won't have encountered this genre in any substantive fashion—and, if they have, it's likely in the context of a televised cooking competition like *Chopped*, *Top Chef*, or *The Great British Baking Show*—so bringing in published restaurant reviews would introduce your students to their structure, tone, and possible content.

There are certainly a range of reviews available online, from the haughty and highbrow (*The New York Times* or *Los Angeles Times* newspapers) to more casual blogging sites like *Roadfood* or *BlackboardEats*. In addition to thinking through the structure of the genre, these mentor texts can help students see the range of things to review in each restaurant, from the decor to the service to the quality of the food. And, if you carefully select a range of different reviews, students can also see how some reviewers maintain professional distance from their subjects while others effectively deploy snark and sarcasm to make their points.[4]

The review can be an engaging genre for teaching a form of argumentation, and its frequent appearance in real-world publications lends it an authenticity often missing from more conventional approaches to writing arguments.

Summing Up

One of the other unintended side effects of the virtual tour project is that it helps break down the notion that everything we do in the English classroom fits neatly into compartments or categories. The way standards and curricula define the subject—and the way we often teach it—can create that impression. There's literary text and there's informational text. There's explanatory writing and there's narrative writing. But the frequent reality is that there's overlap and bleed-through in all kinds of reading and writing, and both those activities are often engaged in for specific purposes that have nothing to do with school.

This is especially true of a project like the virtual tour. There's room in it for students to research and summarize, write descriptively, and argue. They can experiment with genre and tone. They can use images. If you wanted to push the concept a step further, why stop at simple captions that describe local landmarks? Could your students use podcasting technology or other digital tools to record their summaries as a form of audio guide? Might viewers of the tour click a link and actually *hear* your students displaying their research?

The virtual tour tackles many of the skills and understandings we want our students to have, and it does so in the context of individual authentic genres *embedded* in a larger authentic project. It's ambitious, true. But it's often the ambitious projects that resonate with our students and help them fully understand the value of what goes on in our classrooms.

Intended Benefits
- personal
- agentive
- engaging
- audience oriented

Interdisciplinary/Cross-Curricular Connections
- To supplement anything you teach about researching local history, a local librarian or archivist could talk to your class about how and where to most effectively conduct their research.

Writing about Literature and Other Texts

Literature and technology can often seem like strange bedfellows. Taking the vibrant worlds and vivid characters created solely through an author's rich use of language and finding ways to complement those things through impersonal- or distant-seeming virtual spaces can be challenging. It goes beyond the simple debate between print texts and e-readers to something we've been discussing all along: authenticity. Literary diehards—which is how we imagine many English teachers would characterize themselves—see dog-eared pages and broken spines as somehow more real, more valid than a finger scrolling a screen. We tend to agree. But, if we return to the idea that place-based writing allows us to incorporate writing *as it is actually used in the real world*, we have to contend with the fact that many—or even most—of our students will be more comfortable reading on, or aided by, an electronic device. Figuring out how to navigate this tension continues to be one of the most vexing problems of the twenty-first-century English classroom. We don't have the solution, but we've got at least one idea.

Do-It-Yourself eBook

Several years ago, Amanda was awarded a grant to purchase a set of e-readers for her students. She immediately saw an increase in her students' motivation to read, and the educational support provided by these devices—the ability to highlight and annotate text, word definitions literally at the readers' fingertips—was beneficial in helping her students gain a degree of reading independence. Regardless of what we think of these devices, there's no question that many students find them engaging and helpful. So, how do we capitalize on this without simply throwing more technology at our students?

One way is to have students think about the information that would be helpful to other readers by creating their own virtual texts. This could be accomplished through a common class text, small reading groups or book clubs, or even independent reading. Students look for places in a text where they could provide links[5] to the definitions of unfamiliar words, brief summaries explaining allusions or other important background information, or even relevant photographs or video. You could structure the activity as a catchall whereby your students link everything in a chapter or passage that would be helpful or interesting to a reader, or you could focus their work—and more specifically assess their understanding of a concept—by asking them to link particular things. For example, you might assign partnered groups different chapters and task them with explaining the allusions they find. Using Google Docs, each explanation could be created in a separate document and linked to the main text. This would assess your students' understanding of allusions, their ability to write an accurate summary, and could also possibly involve some basic research skills if the meaning of the allusion initially eludes them.

To connect this more specifically to place—although we refer you back to this chapter's introduction and point out that, in this activity, the virtual text your students are creating counts as a kind of place with its own rules, expectations, and genius loci[6]—you might want your students to think about setting or imagery. For instance, Chapter 1 of Golding's (1954/1988) *Lord of the Flies* is dense with description, as can be seen in this excerpt:

> Ralph stood, one hand against a grey trunk, and screwed up his eyes against the shimmering water. Out there, perhaps a mile away, the white surf flinked on a coral reef, and beyond that the open sea was dark blue. Within the irregular arc

of coral the lagoon was still as a mountain lake—blue of all shades and shadowy green and purple. The beach between the palm terrace and the water was a thin stick, endless apparently, for to Ralph's left the perspectives of palm and beach and water drew to a point at infinity; and always, almost visible, was the heat. (pp. 7–8)

To help students visualize a passage like this one, they could link photos of coral reefs or lagoons, a written summary of what a coral reef or palm terrace is, or even an attempted definition of troublesome vocabulary like *flinked*.

The purpose of such an activity is to connect reading and writing in a virtual text, but it is also to encourage a kind of thoughtfulness about digital spaces. The purpose of the activity isn't just to consider what *they* want to link in each passage; it's to consider what would be helpful *to another reader*. Such an exercise can create a sensitive or empathetic reading stance. And isn't that what we do as teachers? Anticipate what our students are likely to find challenging and figure out how to support their success?

Intended Benefits
- personal
- engaging
- audience oriented

Variation to Add an (Even More) Authentic Audience
- By asking students to consider other readers, an outside audience is already implied. Sharing this work on a class blog or through an online learning space (or even in a folder using Google Drive or your school's course management system) would take it even further into the realm of the authentic by allowing other readers to benefit from the work your students did in making the text more accessible.

Code-Switching and Online Correspondence

The notion of *code-switching*—changing one's language to reflect a particular context or rhetorical purpose (Devereaux & Wheeler, 2012)—can be a challenging concept for students who think there's only one way of talking or writing. But, if we leave it at that, we do our students a disservice. Modulating one's language to achieve a particular goal or to better "fit" a particular situation is a crucial skill for navigating the world, and the classroom provides us with ways to connect that concept to the literature we teach. By meeting this goal in the context of place-based writing, we also ask our students to think about various forms of communicative technology as individual spaces with rules of their own.

What do we mean by this? One of the primary ways in which we code-switch comes from different types of real-world correspondence, underscoring Dean's (2008) beliefs that "genres are social in how they function and in how they respond" and "part of the meaning [genres] carry resides in the social context that creates" them (p. 12). For example, the way Rob writes an email to a student is different from the way he texts a colleague. But the way he texts a colleague is different from the way he might *email* that same colleague, and all of those are different from the way he sounds when he sends a Facebook message or a text to one of his old college roommates. Similarly, Amanda's texts to her sister are markedly different from the way she responds to parents through her school's messaging application. However, those messages to parents are also different from the way she responds to her fourth-grade students who have managed to grab their mother's phone and message their teacher using the same app after the end of the school day. In other words, audience matters, but so does medium. And often overriding all these concerns is the actual purpose of the messages themselves. The choice to text a colleague instead of sending an email probably means there's an element of urgency—something work related that's time sensitive—whereas an email can be dealt with in a more leisurely fashion. But it might also indicate informality, something that's not urgent but also not work related. The point is that we constantly code-switch in virtual spaces, and we often do it unconsciously by "reading" the audience and purpose in order to settle on the most appropriate medium.

We can connect this to literature by thinking about point of view in the context of the books we read. Ask your students to choose several characters from the book you're reading and consider novel-related reasons why they might need to contact each other electronically.[7] Adopting these characters' perspectives, your students can then compose a series of messages between them in a variety of genres: email, text-speak, emoji, direct message, etc. You can ramp up the complexity of the activity by asking your students to justify their choices. In other words, in the process of studying Rick Riordan's Percy Jackson and the Olympians series, why did you choose to have Percy write Athena an email for one message while deciding it was most appropriate to write a text to Grover for another message? In the process, your students will write in different genres for different audiences and purposes. They'll also have to consider a character's point of view and, importantly for the concept of code-switching, how that point of view reveals itself across written genres. And, of course, the grander purpose for this entire exercise is that our students will start to see how they can modulate *their own language* to more effectively communicate in a variety of contexts, virtual and physical alike.

Finally, we want to conclude this activity by acknowledging the criticism that code-switching can legitimately be seen as a way of privileging "Standard" English over other dialects. That is not our intent. We want to encourage in all our students—regardless of home dialect—a greater degree of communicative and rhetorical awareness. We're not advocating that students abandon one dialect in favor of another. Instead, we merely want them to be sensitive to the ways in which they can tactically modulate their language for different audiences, purposes, and genres, even if their dialect otherwise remains unchanged. The goal is increased intentionality and rhetorical dexterity, not the erasure of dialect or identity.

Intended Benefits
- personal
- engaging
- audience oriented

Variation to Add an Authentic Audience
- Because audience is implied in this kind of correspondence, you might pair up students to write each other in character. Your students would still be demonstrating the same understanding of character, point of view, genre, and code-switching, but the act of *writing to* another person would lend the activity an added layer of authenticity.

Writing Arguments

Throughout this book, we emphasize the importance of using place-based writing to help students situate their arguments in authentic contexts as this is the way argument works in the real world. Arguing about virtual places, though, is a more challenging proposition. The places we visit online are both real and not real. They're real in the sense that they occupy a particular online space and, as we illustrated in the introduction to this chapter, demonstrate *location*, *locale*, and *sense of place*. But visiting a website about Yellowstone National Park obviously isn't the same thing as visiting the park itself. So we have to rethink how argument works in online places.

One way to do this is to consider the accuracy of the sites we visit. Even as long ago as the late 1990s, when Rob's students were first dabbling in online research, there was the concern that students visit reliable websites. However, this has lately taken on an even greater sense of urgency. Kohnen (2019) points out that the rapidly changing nature of the internet means that "teaching our students blanket rules about [online source] credibility" should be abandoned in favor of "teaching the critical thinking skills that will serve them no matter what websites, domain names, sharing platforms, or genres appear" (p. 29). Additionally, the proliferation of online propaganda and misinformation arguably reached critical mass in the 2016 and 2020 US presidential elections, and there remains a feeling in some circles that, even though we've acknowledged the problem, we haven't done enough to combat it. We can use argument writing as one way to encourage students to think critically about the online messaging they receive.

Just How Accurate Is Your School's Website?

Navigate to the websites of half a dozen different schools and you're likely to find similar information on each. Basic school information, such as bell schedules and mission statements. The academic subjects offered. Clubs and sports. Administration, faculty, and staff details. Maybe some resources like after-school tutoring or driver's education opportunities. But how closely have you and your students actually looked at your school's website?

Because our students often know the school grounds more intimately than we do, an assignment in which they analyze the school's website and identify its blind spots could result in an effective argument. In essence, they compare the physical place they inhabit with its virtual representation, and consider the following questions (among others):

- How accurate is the school's website? Do you recognize the school that's described on it?
- What's missing from the website? What information should be included to create a more thorough depiction of your school?
- Is there any information that seems unnecessary? What could be removed without losing anything substantial?
- Does it seem as though any particular voices are privileged on the website? If so, how can the site be revised to strike a more equitable balance?
- How do photographs or other images contribute to the website? What images would you add?
- To what audience does the website seem to be geared? Are there other audiences that should be considered?

Examining the school website as what it is—a public document representing just one version of the school—can help students see how all websites represent a particular perspective that may or may not be (but probably isn't) 100 percent accurate. Such a realization can encourage them to look at other online places with an equally critical eye.

Where does the authentic argument come in? One simple product is a variation on the letter to the principal. Students could write a letter arguing that specific changes be made to the school website to increase its accuracy. To be effective, these arguments would have to include claims, evidence, and the anticipation of the principal's counterarguments, in addition to the students' own proposed changes. A more sophisticated project could be to ask your students to actually design—online or on paper—revised webpages as they would like to see them. An accompanying reflective writing could further outline the information gaps in the current website and detail the reasoning behind their proposed revisions. Neither product is a formal essay, but both require the students to follow the same logic we would typically require in a more traditional assignment.

Intended Benefits

- personal
- engaging
- audience oriented

Evaluating Multiple Perspectives

As we mentioned in the previous activity, every website represents an individual perspective. This is glaringly obvious when we look at the way in which competing news websites report the day's events through their varying ideological lenses. But this bias—or point of view, to be more charitable—is also true even when we might consider a website's subject to be relatively noncontroversial.

To teach argument as well as help students understand the pervasiveness of this problem in a way that sidesteps any accusations of pushing a political agenda, we can ask students to analyze the way in which multiple websites represent a single location. While you might provide students with a list of national parks or major US cities (or cities of the world) or tourist attractions in the largest city in your state, we encourage you to let students choose a location that has personal interest to them so the ensuing work will be more relevant. Whichever method you use, after selecting a location, your students will explore a variety of websites focused on it. They'll be looking for commonalities across all sites, but the more illuminating thing to seek out would be the differences *between* sites—the aspect of a national park that shows up on only one website or the site that frames the subject in a decidedly unique way.

As a simple practical example, the Kennesaw Mountain National Battlefield Park, described by Amanda in Chapter 2 and just a short drive from her school, is represented across three different websites in three very different ways. Its National Park Service (NPS) page (https://www.nps.gov/kemo/index.htm) provides a comprehensive view of the park that includes details of the Civil War battle in question but also describes opportunities for hiking and other forms of recreation. On a website maintained by the American Battlefield Trust (https://www.battlefields.org/visit/battlefields/kennesaw-mountain-battlefield), the focus is exclusively on the battle, with detailed maps of individual skirmishes included on the main page. A third site (https://www.atlantatrails.com/kennesaw-mountain-trails), this one devoted to hiking and running, largely sidesteps the battle altogether. There are cursory references to the battle in the site's descriptions of available trails, but it's clear that the historical aspect of the park is not the main concern.

Students would quickly pick up on these differences, and this could be used as an entrance point to discussions about intended audience, tone, point of view, and bias, among other topics. For a final product, students could write a formal evaluation of the sites they visited and argue for one of them being the most helpful overall to visitors. While the differences between sites they visit on their own time may be more nuanced than what they've accomplished here, this activity can nonetheless introduce students to the notion of perspective and inherent bias.

Intended Benefits
- personal
- engaging

Variation to Add an Authentic Audience
- Instead of a formal evaluation, you might ask students to write to the organization behind one of the websites with suggestions for improvement. Similar to the previous activity, such a proposal would include the typical characteristics of an argument (making a claim, providing evidence, etc.), but, with this product, they would also have to consider how best to present these changes to an outside audience in a way that's perceived as helpful and not critical.

Writing Narratives, Poetry, and Scripts

One topic we've so far left unexplored is the natural overlap between storytelling and research. As we mentioned earlier, one of the failings of some approaches to teaching literature is the way we keep different types of writing at arm's length. We act as though research has no business showing up in narrative writing or that there can't be elements of storytelling in good explanatory writing. Some of this is a product of standards documents that create these artificial distinctions, but some of it is due to the fact that this complicates the nature of our work. And, as we all know, complication can be messy and laborious and time consuming.

But this particular complication is crucial for us to introduce. We've all read books in which the author's research is obvious, even in genre fiction. Dan Simmons's horror novel *The Terror* (2007) involves exhaustive research on nineteenth-century sailing and exploration, and Jennifer Egan's (2017) historical novel *Manhattan Beach* details the working conditions for divers—and especially women divers—in World War II–era shipyards. In both cases, the narrative's verisimilitude hinges on the research the authors have seamlessly woven into the story.

We can help students see where this research shows up in the texts we read, but the ease with which similar research can be conducted in online spaces also gives students a chance to try it themselves. In this way, virtual spaces can be used to facilitate the melding of inquiry with narrative.

Using Virtual Reality to Tell Stories

Just to reiterate, this isn't a chapter about tools. But it's inescapable that resources like Google Cardboard[8] have made virtual reality (VR) experiences accessible to students at a relatively low cost for schools. By using a mobile phone and a simple cardboard frame, students can take immersive VR tours of a variety of places that have relevance for the English classroom. Using photographic and video images of everything from natural landscapes to world cities to skydiving adventures to amusement parks, VR devices transport users to seemingly realistic worlds where they can enjoy complete 360-degree views of the environment. Students can travel to these locations and more without ever leaving the classroom.

One way we can use VR to conduct a variation on place-based writing is to have students make observations and take notes of what they're learning from their VR experiences, and write narratives set in those places. In a recent study set in an eighth-grade classroom studying *To Kill a Mockingbird*, Moran and Woodall (2019) noticed that VR devices "enhanced the literacy experiences of the students by helping them to think critically about the impact of setting on the novel's events" (p. 93). By modifying the activity slightly—writing an original narrative rooted in place as opposed to studying the effect of setting on an existing story—we can accomplish similar goals. Using a VR device, students can note details—about, say, climbing El Capitan or embarking on a safari—that would be useful in bringing that particular setting to life. This works in much the same way as our activity in Chapter 5 wherein students use a local public place as inspiration for an original narrative. We can require our students to use a certain number of details from the VR experience, and this still provides us with an opportunity to teach other lessons in narrative craft. Additionally, keeping in mind the connection between inquiry and narrative, you could require students to conduct additional research about their location, and some of those details could be infused in the narrative, as well.

Although this activity may seem more limited than basing a story on a visit to an actual location near the school, it has other clear benefits. While it's true that a VR experience doesn't allow students to experience any sensory details beyond sight, the range of possible VR locations from which to choose broadens the students' storytelling scope in other ways. In a VR-based story, students' stories aren't relegated to the local park or town square. They can take place on another continent or even in outer space, increasing the likelihood that students can tailor their stories to their personal interests.

Intended Benefits
- personal
- engaging

Variation to Add an Authentic Audience
- As we've mentioned elsewhere, it can be powerful to provide students with an authentic venue in which to share their stories. This particular activity might be especially suited for sharing on a class blog devoted solely to narrative craft—and, of course, on such a site students could embed photos or video of their chosen setting, lending it an additional multimedia perspective.

Found Poetry

Found poetry—selecting words from an existing text and rearranging them into an original poem—can be an engaging and low-stakes way to familiarize students with poetic conventions and artistic playfulness. The notion that poems lay bare the soul makes many students reluctant to pen their own. With found poems, however, the perception that we're simply repurposing other writers' words offers us a degree of camouflage that we don't otherwise have when writing original verse. This form also encourages experimentation, in that students not only have to select the words they want to use, but they also have to think about how to assemble them. Syntactic sense is just one consideration. Students can also experiment with stanza length, spacing on the page, unconventional word order, and so on. For less confident writers, playing with other people's words is safer than playing with their own.

A simple way this kind of writing can be facilitated in virtual spaces with a place-based writing element is to have students explore websites that pair nature photography with science writing,[9] whether it be descriptive, explanatory, or reflective. The goal for students is to compose a found poem that captures the essence of the image using only the text that accompanies it. In the process, they'll conduct some low-level research in an informational text, and the scientific details they ultimately select will be incorporated in a type of writing most students would consider to be decidedly nonscientific.

Intended Benefits
- personal
- engaging

Variation to Add an Authentic Audience
- This is the kind of product that practically begs to be displayed. The marriage of photo and poem is usually pleasing to the eye, and your school might be willing to let you hang the students' work as an art display in the front office or other prominent location.

Writing for Research and Inquiry

The close virtual proximity of the online spaces we ask our students to occupy with easily accessible research is another reason to consider using technology to approximate place-based writing. Since students are primarily conducting online research in other aspects of their schooling, it makes sense to leverage that fact into inquiry projects grounded in real places students explore virtually. As with the other activities in this chapter, it won't be quite as authentic as visiting the actual place, but there are ways to frame these assignments that go beyond the traditional.

Researching the National Parks

If one of our goals is to see our students become more environmentally conscious, but we can't actually get them out of the classroom and into nature, we need to look for ways to replicate that experience in the classroom. One way to accomplish this is to introduce a research project based in our national parks. Besides being the caretakers of arguably the most valuable natural resources in the United States, the NPS also hosts a website that serves as an exhaustive portal into the parks themselves (https://www.nps.gov). With options to search for individual parks, specific topics (e.g., "Accidents & Disasters," "Literature & Poetry," "Underground Railroad," etc.), or broad categories ("Discover History" and "Protecting the Natural World"), the NPS website presents teachers with a variety of ways to structure an inquiry project.

One relatively straightforward way to do it is simply to ask students to browse the list of parks until they find one that interests them. Students then develop a line of inquiry based on some aspect of the park about which they'd like to learn more. Crucially, such research wouldn't have to result in a simple report about the selected park. For example, a student exploring the site for the Harpers Ferry National Historical Park might ultimately decide to research the abolitionist movement. Similarly, a student researching Alcatraz Island could develop a general line of inquiry about its famous inmates or a more specific one about the life of Al Capone. As we have done elsewhere, we encourage you to give your students the latitude to develop a topic that engages them and about which they genuinely want to learn more. The park they select serves as their genesis and should still feature in the student's final product, but it doesn't have to be the focal point.

Central to the project is the understanding that the students' research shouldn't be confined to the NPS website. While some of their foundation will be established there—including learning about one or more specific parks serving as the project's inspiration—we would understandably want our students to consult additional sources proving to be more relevant to their specific research questions. The final product could take a variety of forms, from a traditional paper, to a poster session, to a short video connecting their research topic to park promotion. As always, this will largely depend on your individual goals for the project.

Intended Benefits
- personal
- agentive
- engaging

Variations to Add an Authentic Audience

- As we alluded above, you might consider requiring a final product geared toward an authentic audience. For instance, you could host a national parks celebration where students share what they learned about each park in a poster session or pop-up museum.

- Capitalizing on the virtual nature of the students' research, you might look for ways in which students can communicate directly with the national park they selected. Student work could be shared digitally with individual parks by creating a class blog, or videos could be hosted on a class YouTube channel.

Interdisciplinary/Cross-Curricular Connections

- Depending on the selected topic, there may be opportunities to involve colleagues from other disciplines. The students researching Al Capone or the abolitionist movement could have their learning supplemented by a social studies teacher, while another student researching the effects of climate change on North Carolina's Cape Hatteras National Seashore could consult a science teacher.

Video Games and World Building

As hesitant as we might be to acknowledge them—or even seriously consider their classroom implications—video games also represent virtual experiences. While it might be tempting to dismiss them as frivolous or useful only for entertainment, it's important to remember that these games' potential for student engagement is probably unmatched by anything else we could bring into the classroom. Whether played on a console, personal computer, or handheld device, video games are everywhere, and we're probably overdue in considering how we can use them to our advantage.

One of the most remarkable aspects of current video games, especially those played on consoles, is the intricate world building achieved by their developers. From the Old West of *Red Dead Redemption* to the ancient Greek civilization of *Assassin's Creed: Odyssey* to *Tomb Raider*'s ancient vaults, some developers have taken great pains to anchor their games in worlds—and places—we recognize. A potential project is to ask our students to develop one or more research questions originating in the world of a particular video game.

Before going any further, it's probably worth mentioning (especially in light of administrators or parents who might look at an activity like this with raised eyebrows) that video games have emerged in recent years as legitimate sources of instruction. Sherry and Lawrence (2019) have advocated for pairing video games and argument writing to help students become more conscious of ethical issues (including environmental stewardship). In the process, students learn more about selecting evidence, writing arguments for resistant audiences, and listening to other perspectives, all of which are skills that "may be important for those who will be . . . leaders in their own communities" (Sherry & Lawrence, 2019, p. 73). Additionally, Adams (2009) has explored strategies for teaching multimedia texts through video games, while Ostenson (2013) makes a case for using games to teach a variety of narrative features.

To head off another logical question, of course we realize it's unrealistic to devote class time to playing these games. But, with access to YouTube, you *can* find gameplay videos that give your students a portal into games without actually playing them. By devoting just five to ten minutes of class time, students can sample one or more videos for games they like (or have always wanted to play) and start to identify possible research topics about the world depicted in the game. How realistic is *Red Dead Redemption 2*'s depiction of the Pinkerton National Detective Agency? Are the structure and defenses of the sailing ships in *Assassin's Creed: Black Flag* true to form? How realistic is the science in the postapocalyptic survival game *The Last of Us*? As in the national parks project, the range of possible research questions is bounded only by what your students find resonant in the games they play.

Given the controversial nature of some games, you might want to develop a list of games you consider off limits, and, of course, you'd have to exercise caution when it comes to selecting the gameplay videos. One possible solution is to curate this particular assignment more heavily than usual by generating a nonnegotiable list of potential video games and one or more inoffensive gameplay videos for each. How heavy-handed you need to be will depend on your students (and their parents), but, if we want our students to come to research with genuine curiosity, we need to seriously consider the media they consume and how it can be leveraged for educational purposes.

A final product that incorporates a slightly more authentic audience than a traditional research paper would be a presentation that draws on screenshots or short video excerpts from the game in question. Your students would still demonstrate what they learned from their research, but it would be paired with media that illustrates their points, presented to an audience predisposed to be interested in the topic.

Intended Benefits
- personal

- agentive
- engaging

Interdisciplinary/Cross-Curricular Connections

- Depending on the student's topic, some supplemental information from a colleague could be helpful. For example, a student researching the historical accuracy of the ancient Greek world depicted in *Assassin's Creed: Odyssey* would find a world history teacher to be a valuable resource.

Writing for Change

We're not breaking any news by pointing out the toxicity of social media. From Twitter trolls to Facebook bullying to the racist, misogynistic, homophobic, ableist user comments that accompany so many YouTube videos, it's no wonder we often doubt the value of social media. However, such concerns are, as the saying goes, like closing the stable door after the horse has bolted. Social media isn't going anywhere, especially for our students. If we want the virtual spaces that our students inhabit to be civil and kind, we should think about the role we as teachers play in fostering such environments. Thinking about virtual spaces as just one step removed from physical reality can help our students understand that their personas are just as important in the digital world—and there's no reason to think online interactions should be any less respectful than the interactions they have face to face.

This I Believe (about Social Media)

Often, being the change we want to see in the world means recognizing and reckoning with that world's flaws. This activity centers on analyzing behavior in social media spaces and writing a proposal that identifies problems as well as solutions.

We acknowledge the logistical challenges inherent in such an activity. Many schools block social media sites for good reason. In some ways, though, this actually allows you to conduct a more focused activity. Rather than simply setting your students loose on social media—rarely a pedagogically sound idea—you can screenshot some examples of problematic social media behavior for your students to analyze. This, of course, allows you to weed out the more egregious examples of racist, sexist, homophobic, or ableist language, but it also means you can focus on more nuanced examples of troubling language.

After all, students will have no trouble recognizing insults and name-calling, and there's little to be learned from acknowledging why that kind of language is wrong. But denigrating people with language that doesn't involve obvious slurs or profanity? Or *gaslighting*?[10] Engaging in *whataboutism*?[11] These and others are all types of language that degrade the quality of communication on social media. Because they're often not as easy to identify, it's important that we help our students recognize them for what they are.

As a next step, ask your students to note what they see in their own social media use.[12] They can certainly record their own interactions, but it might make more of an impact if the goal is for them to specifically monitor what they see other people doing. Questions like the following can help guide their analysis and generate subsequent writing:

- What do you see happening in the comments of other people's Facebook pages, or what do you notice when you look at the replies on a celebrity's Twitter or Instagram account?
- What kind of posts seem to receive the most negative feedback, and how would you characterize the feedback itself? Is it critically substantive? Or does it simply consist of personal attacks?
- When arguments between users start *within* comments, what does that usually look like?
- Where do you see *positive* examples of online interactions? What do those look like, and how do other users react to them?

What we're actually asking our students to do here is to conduct a rhetorical analysis of real-world discourse, or examine how people actually use language in day-to-day life. Sometimes, we don't recognize the prevalence of something until we're faced with quantifiable data, so looking at social media interactions in this way can help students notice the many different ways language is used to harm others in a venue primarily used for entertainment. And, by noticing this, our hope is that our students—some of them, at least—will resolve to make a change.

The culminating writing is a variation on National Public Radio's *This I Believe* program. In a written statement, students acknowledge some of the existing problems they notice in the way social media is used and, more important, articulate the ways in which they can make a positive difference. Besides being a powerful vehicle for students to stake out their convictions, it also serves as a way of assessing the analysis they conducted as well as their ability to construct a logical argument.

Intended Benefits
- personal
- agentive
- engaging
- audience oriented
- promotes change

Variation to Add an Authentic Audience
- With the National Public Radio program as a model, the assignment could be even more powerful if students were given an opportunity to audio or video record their statements. These could then be hosted on the school's website as an example of students making a positive difference in their online communities.

Considerations for Students with Special Needs
- Focusing student research and writing on a place they are most familiar with will help scaffold their thinking about writing. Students can be encouraged to take pictures or videos of the place they will be writing about and to share those with one another. This can aid in allowing all students to feel like experts on the places they've selected as well as encourage a sense of community and connection as students see familiar places being chosen by their peers.
- A VR experience could be leveraged as a connection to one of the place-based writing experiences described in Chapter 4. Before a student takes a trip to a particular museum, you might introduce them to this place via a virtual field trip. VR can also be utilized to help students discuss life skills that may be dangerous or difficult to manage at school. For example, students could take virtual "walks" around their neighborhoods using Google Earth. In the process, they could write about such things as the meaning of specific street signs, or you could help them use certain grammar concepts effectively (prepositions, for instance) by asking them to describe the shortest route from home to school and back again.

Considerations for English Language Learners
- For the virtual tour activity, you may consider allowing your English language learners the opportunity to collaborate on pieces created by their peers in the role of translator. Such an accommodation can help all

students see the benefit of being multilingual. For the English language learners themselves, their translations can be treated as a valuable way to allow more members of the community to access places in multiple languages.

- Because the use of VR is relatively new to the world of education, it's helpful to know that some VR software comes with vocabulary support built in. These supports are often provided as a supplement to teachers, but sometimes they can be found embedded in the experience itself. It may be beneficial to utilize one of these tours in order to help scaffold a student's experience in the place.

Final Thoughts

Our goal in writing this book was twofold: to convince you of the effectiveness of place-based writing and empower you to do more of it yourself by demonstrating its flexibility and accessibility. There are certainly other variables to keep in mind when designing place-based writing experiences, but its central tenets are really no different from any other kind of writing we ask our students to do. We're teaching skills and knowledge, we're meeting specific learning goals, we're helping our students become more dexterous users of language. The only substantive shift is that we're also asking our students to consider the world in which they live by getting them out in it. Encouraging them to actively engage in and grapple with real-world issues and contexts will increase the likelihood that they actually see how their written words can impact the world.

At the same time, we know our zeal for place-based writing can create the impression that we favor the wholesale abolition of the traditional essay. That actually isn't the case. As teachers, we have a professional obligation to ensure our students have a facility with the traditional essay, as it is a form they will encounter repeatedly at all levels of formal schooling. We'd be doing our students a disservice if we discarded it altogether. What we're arguing for instead is the need to take a thoughtful, balanced approach to writing instruction that always has authenticity in mind.

At the beginning of this book, we said we wanted it to serve as a resource and a tool kit. Now, at the end, we also hope it will be the first step in a long-distance collaboration among teachers of various grade levels, subject areas, and geographic regions. As you experiment with place-based writing in your own classroom, we hope you'll feel comfortable sharing your successes and good ideas with us. Drop us an email or snag us at a conference. Bend our ears. Let us know how things are going. Our own understanding of this practice is still a work in progress (beginning in the 2015 Invitational Summer Institute of the Kennesaw Mountain Writing Project and continuing through the moment we wrote this conclusion), so *A Place to Write* certainly shouldn't be seen as the final word in place-based writing. Instead, opening a wide-ranging dialogue—what's working, what isn't, where you've taken students, how you've sweet-talked your administration into securing funding—will help all of us in our collective efforts to facilitate authentic writing by getting students out of the classroom and into the world.

Appendix

Garden and Composting Research Project

Note: These lessons were originally designed for Amanda's fourth-grade class; please feel free to modify them for your own context.

Day 1

Objective

- Students will identify, in writing, what they know and want to know about a new location.

Instructional Steps

1. Choose a part of the school that is relatively new to the students or that has a possibility to generate multiple questions. Before venturing to this location, provide students with a graphic organizer to help them separate their thinking into what they know and what they wonder. Students will also need a writing utensil and something to write on.
2. Lead students to the location and allow them to explore the area safely. As the students explore, circulate among them and aid students in their thinking by asking guiding questions, such as "What is this for?" or "What is the purpose of this?"
3. Return to the classroom. Discuss as a class what they noticed as well as any questions that arose or other things they were wondering about. This conversation can be facilitated by listing these ideas on two separate charts. One chart should focus on what the students identified as areas of knowledge and the other should be a collection of things they wondered about.

Assessment

- Class discussion and compilation of the two charts
- Graphic organizers checked, to ensure students have identified things they would like to know about the new location

Day 2

Objectives

- Students will discuss how their audience informs the presentation of information.
- Students will decide on an overall topic and audience for their research, based on the information gathered from the previous class, and then explore how they might present their future research.

Instructional Steps

1. Review the two charts from the previous class and highlight any common themes you noticed. For example, you might say, "I noticed that most of the wonderings centered around composting."
2. Based on how the final project will be presented (whole class, small groups, individual), have students decide on the topic for their research and choose an intended audience.
3. Lead the class through a discussion of how their audience should inform the choices they make for their final presentation. Some guiding questions for this discussion might include "What support might you need to provide your audience?" or "What might your audience be most engaged by?"
4. Provide various examples of informational final products (i.e., books, videos, PowerPoint presentations, speeches, etc.) and ask students to explore in small groups the positives and negatives of each type of product as it pertains to their selected audience. In this step, guide students in thinking about the topic they chose and how each type of presentation could help get their research across to their audience. You can select groups based on whom students will be working with or whom they are sitting closest to.

5. Have groups come back together as a class and share their thoughts on which product would best fit their topic and audience. Allow some conversational back and forth in order to encourage positive debate.
6. Conduct a quick exit ticket, whereby students must write down their topic, audience, and product type.

Assessment

- Class discussion and group discussion about audience and product
- Exit tickets checked, to ensure students have a clear idea of their topic, audience, and product

Day 3

Objective

- Students will explore the structure of the product they chose and create a list of features that will be important and engaging to include for their topic and selected product.

Instructional Steps

1. Provide students with multiple examples of the type of product they will be creating.
2. Distribute a graphic organizer for collecting ideas for key text features (e.g., a T-chart that captures text features on one side and benefits on the other). Model the type of thinking you expect students to engage in as they explore their products using the graphic organizer. Highlight guiding ideas such as "What features occur across multiple products?" or "What features do I find most engaging or helpful?" These questions should be on the graphic organizer for students to answer in writing.
3. Using the same student groups from the previous day, allow time to explore the products you've provided as you rotate through the room. Use the guiding questions from Step 2 to guide student discussion and writing in their groups.
4. Bring the class together to share one feature they would like to incorporate in their final product and an explanation of why it would be effective.

Assessment

- Graphic organizer with key text features identified for each student

Day 4

Objective

- Students will develop a set of questions that will become the focus of their research.

Instructional Steps

1. Reintroduce and discuss the questions that were gathered from the students' first trip to the school location. Ask students to discuss together (using think–pair–share or turn and talk) which of those questions would be the most important to focus on as they undertake their research.
2. If students are conducting this project as a class, guide the collection of these research questions carefully to ensure the questions do not overlap and no major areas of knowledge are missing. You will disseminate the question equally among the groups/students. If students are doing this research in small groups or individually, they should gather the questions for you to review before beginning their research.

Assessment

- Student discussion using think–pair–share or turn and talk
- Collected focus questions

Days 5–7

Objective

- Students will conduct research to answer their focus question(s) using multiple sources of information.

Instructional Steps

1. Gather multiple types of resources for students to use in their research. You should consider not only books and online articles but also videos, supervised visits to the original school area, and outside experts.
2. Provide students with their focus research questions, resources, and a scoring guide explaining the requirements for their final product (see, e.g., Figure A.1). Introduce the scoring guide and detail the steps students should take to complete each required element.
3. Send students off to begin their research using the elements you provided. Students will record their findings in writing as they research. You may find it helpful to create a graphic organizer that highlights the elements of the standards that you are focusing on. For example, I used a graphic organizer that asked students to identify key content vocabulary and text features as they researched (Figure A.2).
4. Meet with students, either in their small groups or individually, to guide them to resources that will be the most helpful in answering their research questions. If at all possible, you want to point students toward resources outside of the traditional books and articles in order to guide them away from simply copying information down. For example, when my students wanted to know why plastic was not allowed in a compost bin, I had them put a banana peel and a plastic spoon in the bin and go back the next day to see what happened. They used their observations as evidence in their research.

Assessment

- Student research and answers to the key questions you identified for your standard

Days 8–10

Objectives

- Students will synthesize the information they compiled in their research and create a final product in order to teach their intended audience.
- Students will present their research to their audience.

Research and Information		
Research Focus	The writer focused their research on the group question. They left out unimportant or off-topic information that did not help them provide a clear answer to their question.	/10
Research Sources	The writer used multiple sources for their research. The sources were not all the same type (ex. books, articles, videos, interviews, etc.).	/15
Research Use	The writer used the information from their research in their final product. There is clear evidence of facts and information from multiple sources in their final product. The group used research from all group members.	/10
Information	The writer taught their audience different things about their focus question using facts, quotes, and other details.	10
Organization	The writer organized their information in clear sections or paragraphs, grouping ideas together in a way that made sense. There is obvious thought to the order of the information provided and transition words were used to show how one piece of information connected to another.	/5

Group Participation		
Participation	Each member of the group worked together to contribute to the final product. No members of the group were left out of the work or were consistently off task.	/5
Group Survey	Each member of the group filled out the group survey. Points will be awarded or deducted based on the feedback of each member's contribution to the final product.	/10

Audience and Final Product		
Audience	The writer made an obvious effort to address their audience. They considered what their audience might already know and need to know about their question. They provided information in a way that would be engaging and informative to their audience.	/15
Text Features	The writer included at least three text features (bolded words, pictures with captions, illustrations, charts, graphs, maps, etc.) in their final product. These text features aided in conveying information to their audience.	/10

Conventions		
Spelling and Grammar	The writer used what they knew about word families and spelling patterns to spell and edit. They spelled words that were provided to them in their research correctly by going back to those sources for help. The writer also made sure their sentences followed appropriate grammar rules by checking for run-ons and fragments.	/5
Capitalization and Punctuation	The writer used what they knew about capitalization and punctuation rules to ensure all sentences began and ended appropriately. They were sure to use quotations when giving their audience information taken directly, word for word, from their research.	/5

FIGURE A.1. "Garden and composting" research project: Scoring guide.

Word	Definition	Sentence (from the source)

FIGURE A.2. Glossary graphic organizer.

Instructional Steps

1. Provide students with the materials they will require for synthesizing and completing their research project. Provide an exemplar of a final product that is easily accessible to students to use as references as they write.
2. Conference with groups/individual students throughout this writing process based on the standards and skills you wish to target.
3. Have students present their information to their audience based on the type of product they created. If you are not able to physically watch their presentation, students should provide video or picture evidence of their presentation.

Assessment

- Final product produced by each group or student
- Student presentation of their research to their audience

Notes

Introduction

1. *Rural Voices: Place-Conscious Education and the Teaching of Writing* (Brooke, 2003), *Place- and Community-Based Education in Schools* (Smith & Sobel, 2010), *Taking Inquiry Outdoors: Reading, Writing, and Science beyond the Classroom Walls* (Bourne, 2000), and *Writing America: Classroom Literacy and Public Engagement* (Robbins & Dyer, 2005) are four texts we commonly recommend.

Chapter 1

1. If you want a detailed, nuanced account of how our country got here, check out Ravitch's (2010) *The Death and Life of the Great American School System*.

2. Briefly, this approach "builds on the knowledge and experiences of your students, draws on the worlds they live in, and connects those worlds to texts, language practices, and critical issues" (Beach et al., 2012, p. 6).

3. The idea that humans are inextricably tied to place, and therefore students should be encouraged to research "answers that vex their communities" (Theobald, 1997, p. 134).

4. Not that there's anything wrong with that. We actually love taking our students outside to read and think it's worth doing any chance you have.

5. And here we're defining *outdoors* as literally anywhere that's not the classroom, as you'll see in Chapter 3.

Chapter 2

1. A popular initiative in recent years, the acronym stands for "science, technology, engineering, math."

2. Within these standards, ELAGSE is the acronym for "English Language Arts Georgia Standards of Excellence," 4 indicates the grade level, RI denotes Reading Informational, W stands for Writing, and the final number is the number of the standard itself.

3. All student names are pseudonyms.

4. This battle is especially notable as Sherman's sole defeat during his Atlanta campaign.

Chapter 3

1. Bishop (1999) provides a helpful list of criteria to support your students as they get a handle on ethnographic research.

2. We've found the second edition of Emerson et al.'s (2011) *Writing Ethnographic Fieldnotes* to be one of the most helpful, user-friendly guides to writing field notes.

3. If you need a crash course in this yourself, try the reissued edition of Spradley's (1979/2016) *The Ethnographic Interview*.

4. John Hughes's (1985) *The Breakfast Club* is a useful movie to explore in this regard. While the film presents certain stock character types (e.g., the jock, the troublemaker, the nerd, the loner, the princess), Hughes subverts the clichés to point out the characters' individuality and the ways in which they contradict others' expectations of them. In the process, what we initially view as stereotypes are eventually revealed as fully fleshed-out humans.

5. For those unfamiliar with Brandon Stanton's project, the Humans of New York website can be found at http://www.humansofnewyork.com.

6. Based on the concept of the pop-up restaurant, the *pop-up museum* consists of student-created "exhibits" that are temporary in nature and meant to be viewed by an audience for a limited time before being taken down.

7. Unless they're in the cafeteria or the home economics room, you might advise them not to taste anything.

8. We'll leave it up to you to decide if the restrooms are off limits, but it's probably a wise idea.

9. As a handy reference for more of these common mythological terms, try visiting the Greek Mythology page on *Encyclopedia Mythica* (http://pantheon.org/mythology/greek).

10. Starting with a basic clause, the cumulative sentence adds on—or accumulates—detail through the addition of phrases (e.g., absolute, participial, prepositional, etc.) at the end of the sentence.

11. This activity originated with Emily Wynn, an English education student of Rob's at Kennesaw State University (and currently a teacher at Mount Paran Christian School). We further modified it for use in other courses.

12. This activity can obviously be structured to tackle the issue of gentrification head on. We briefly introduced the value of exploring this topic in Chapter 1 and return

to it in more detail in Chapter 5. Those discussions can inform the shape of this particular activity in your own classroom.

13. We also believe students, in the name of authenticity, should be free to argue *against* the placement of more art, as long as they have compelling, logic-based reasons for doing so. "Art is dumb" won't cut it.

14. This is another place where the heuristic (Shor, 1996) we introduced in the School Safety assignment could come in handy.

15. As you contemplate these possibilities, we again encourage you to explore Dyrness's (2011) work with PAR.

Chapter 4

1. This can get tricky, because the research isn't always obvious. We recommend using Romano's (1995) method of requiring students to write a brief "notes page" to accompany the narrative. This page is a short reflective writing in which the students articulate exactly where in their narrative their research appears and why they made those choices.

2. As we mentioned in Chapter 3, try the reissue of Spradley's (1979/2016) *The Ethnographic Interview* as a handy resource for this process.

3. This question is loosely based on Peggy McIntosh's (1989) essay "Unpacking the Invisible Knapsack," wherein she considers those intangible advantages she unavoidably carries as a white, middle-class woman. While this question doesn't explicitly ask students to consider issues of race and ethnicity, religion, sexual orientation, etc., it opens up that possibility, adding another dimension to this project.

4. This activity could be conducted with other authors. Mary Shelley's *Frankenstein* is a novel-length work that incorporates suspense (and is stylistically similar to Poe's), but there's a wealth of accessible young adult literature—ranging all the way from Lois Lowry's dystopian fantasy *The Giver* (1993) to Jason Reynolds and Brendan Kiely's gritty, ripped-from-the-headlines *All American Boys* (2015)—that could also be used to study techniques that create suspense.

5. Even if you're using more contemporary texts, like those mentioned in the previous footnote, the historic home would still provide students with a potentially creepy backdrop for their suspenseful stories.

6. An interesting (albeit controversial, in some corners) approach to this idea would be to argue for the Southern general who was most significant to a losing cause.

7. A slight variation to this activity would be to ask students to rank items in their order of importance (e.g., the Top 5 scientific innovations in the museum, the Top 5 landscape photographers in the exhibit, the Top 5 most important campaigns in the American Revolution, etc.).

8. For the record, the best animated Disney movie is actually *Toy Story 2*.

9. "A literary description of or commentary on a visual work of art" (Merriam-Webster, n.d.).

10. It's probably worth mentioning that part of our job as English teachers—whether we're using place-based writing or not—should be debunking these "writing myths" by sharing the struggles of practicing writers (including ourselves).

11. If you feel particularly unskilled in this area, a helpful resource is Grierson and Orme's (2015) article, "Speak Out! How Ekphrasis Inspires Writing on the Edge."

12. We've found that paintings and sculptures often give the students more to work with, but, in terms of agency, we believe students should have the freedom to write about any piece of art that grabs them.

13. This activity wouldn't have to be confined to art museums. For example, we know that history museums can often represent a particularly Eurocentric cis male version of events, with women and ethnic minority perspectives minimized or excluded altogether. Students could easily (and sadly) find omitted voices in a variety of other museums, all of which would be fair game for this activity.

Chapter 5

1. Classifying these different types of places has caused no end of headaches. One specific type of place we struggled with classifying is the botanical garden. Neither fish nor fowl, it's too developed to be a natural place (see Chapter 6), too restrictive to be a public place (unless your local garden doesn't have an admission fee), and not technically a museum. Yet the botanical garden has aspects of all three general types of places. If you have one in your community, take advantage of it—somehow!

2. We use this word intentionally. Some writing is *bad*. This doesn't mean we think less of the student who wrote it, but it's important to acknowledge that everyone—your authors included—has written garbage. What's crucial is acknowledging bad writing as a valuable and often unavoidable first step in ultimately ending with good writing.

3. One of our favorite local parks features a running-walking trail, a playground, a dog park, a skate park, picnic areas, a water feature for children to play in, and a lot of open space. A class of students could observe in this space and not see their narrative approaches duplicated by anyone else.

4. If you haven't acquainted yourself with Noden's (2011) text *Image Grammar: Teaching Grammar as Part of the Writing Process*, we think you'll find it an invaluable resource for teaching imagery (and grammar).

5. Tina Fey's screenplay for *Mean Girls* (Fey & Waters, 2004) is an incisive and funny take on high school with a range of scenes you could examine in class, as is *Rushmore*, Wes Anderson and Owen Wilson's (1998) subtler take on the high school genre.

6. For obvious reasons, you'll want to have an introductory discussion with your students in which you establish some firm guidelines for ensuring they're respectful of the location. Similarly, you'll want to be sensitive to students who may have experienced a recent death in the family.

7. It can work with one location, but adding a second gives students some options when it comes to writing the final product.

8. What we mean here is that sometimes the accomplishment(s) identifying a public figure as worth commemorating can eventually be overshadowed by other elements in that figure's life. For some recent examples, consider how we've reevaluated certain artists' work in the #MeToo era.

9. The use of the plural here is important to note. Some students may find they need to argue that the restaurants are plentiful and varied, but the retail options are limited—in essence, making two claims. In this way, we might even consider some reviews more sophisticated forms of argument than the kind students are typically asked to write.

10. Let's face it: they usually are—and, in fact, they'd better be. Any book that reads exactly like real life would probably be too tedious to endure.

11. And yes, okay, it actually *is* ridiculous. But that doesn't mean it can't have classroom value.

12. There are obvious limitations to this activity, especially if you teach in an area where technology is scarce. Even though smartphones are increasingly common, you may need to explore other options for conducting this activity. For instance, you could simply ask your students to complete some first-draft writing in the actual location where they have immediate access to their subject.

13. For this activity more than any other in the chapter, the range of options for the location you select will depend entirely on your community, but it's important that the place you ultimately choose has seen change throughout your community's history.

14. At last count, in the metro Atlanta area, there were nearly forty farmers markets in a roughly thirty-mile radius of the city (Cameron, 2019). Even if you live in a smaller community, we imagine there's probably a farmers market close enough for you to use as a resource.

15. For this final question, we're thinking of the ingredient's significance to the larger food tradition of which it's a part. For our students, researching the prominence of okra or peaches in Southern cooking would be appropriate, but a student living in Minnesota or Wisconsin could research the Scandinavian cooking influence, and students in California or Arizona could explore a variety of spices or vegetables unique to southwestern cuisine.

Chapter 6

1. For example, see Making the School More Environmentally Friendly in Chapter 3, What's Missing in Your Community? in Chapter 4, and Community Means Everyone in Chapter 5.

2. Jon Krakauer's (1996) *Into the Wild*, William Golding's (1954/1988) *Lord of the Flies*, Henry David Thoreau's (1854/2017) *Walden*, and, for younger students, Gary Paulsen's (1987) *Hatchet*, Jack London's (1903/2008) *The Call of the Wild*, or Louis Sachar's (1998) *Holes* are just a handful of titles placing nature at the center that spring immediately to mind.

3. The specificity of this research will be determined by the area in which you live as well as by the place each student chooses. If you live in a clearly defined geographic region (e.g., the Shenandoah Valley, the Mojave Desert, the foothills of the Great Smoky Mountains), it will likely be easier to conduct this research. It will be more challenging (but not impossible) to research, say, rivers and streams of eastern Illinois.

4. Asking your students to consider the financial resources to enact their proposal might be a bridge too far. Instead, you might ask them to focus on the material needs required for their proposed solution(s) and leave economics out of it.

5. In short, an *argument* is a logical exercise, while *persuasion* can succeed solely through appeals to emotion and/or credibility without recourse to logic (Hillocks, 2011).

6. If you're going to make the direct connection to Transcendentalism and its emphasis on the individual, it actually becomes an important component of the activity that the students don't share or collaborate while they write.

7. It will be up to your discretion if all your students have to create an ad for the place you visit. Instead, you may want to merely use that place—and the writing your students do there—as an inspirational model and allow them to choose a location of their own for the ad itself.

8. Unless you have a student whose parent is an architect or contractor, which could be either a pro (a valuable resource) or a con (minimizing that team's need for research).

9. With enough time and flexibility, you might open this up to your students. What natural place do *they* think is your community's signature location? This could be a valuable discussion with which to begin the activity (and even one that results in some low-level argumentation).

10. In contrast to the student feedback we suggested you solicit in choosing the signature location, you might choose the public place on your own. This can ensure that the students aren't choosing a public place that actually aligns quite nicely with the signature location, thus rendering the activity sort of pointless.

Chapter 7

1. This particular point becomes especially fascinating when you consider what a site like Facebook "means" to different people and how that affects its sense of place. Some people see it as a harmless vehicle with which to share photos and stay connected with friends and family. Others view it as an isolating influence on social interaction. Still others, in light of the role Facebook played in the 2016 and 2020 US general elections, see it as a pernicious outlet for propaganda, disinformation, and foreign influence on American politics.

2. Even a cursory online search using the terms *virtual tour*, *city virtual tour*, or *museum virtual tour* results in a lengthy list of tours for students to explore, from local colleges to the Smithsonian Museum of Natural History to major cities like New York and London.

3. Student finances are obviously a potential issue, and it would be unfair of us to assign work that our students could not reasonably complete due to the expense involved. This is where you'll use your professional judgment and consider ways of adjusting the workload for some students (maybe by asking them to double up on one of the other genres and skipping the review).

4. Pete Wells's (2012) takedown of Guy Fieri's Times Square restaurant ("As Not Seen on TV") is a thing of ill-tempered beauty. Similarly, Chris Nuttall-Smith's (2014) review of Donald Trump's America restaurant ("America at the Trump Hotel: The Food Is Amazing but You Shouldn't Eat Here—Ever") is a good example of how to eviscerate a business's service while still loving its food.

5. These could be actual links if you're able to conduct this activity through word-processing software or an application like Google Docs. If that technology is impractical or unrealistic, you could photocopy or print out short passages from the text and the "links" could simply be underlined or highlighted in the text itself, with the students' supplemental material appearing in hard copy form (in the margin or on another paper).

6. Roughly, "sense of place." See Chapter 5 for a detailed exploration of this concept.

7. Even though this activity centers on contemporary forms of communication, we'd argue that the setting of the books themselves doesn't actually matter. Did Bilbo Baggins use email? Did Ponyboy Curtis own a cell phone? Of course not. But it's okay to suspend our disbelief for this one activity.

8. At this point, it might be reasonable for you to wonder if we're receiving a kickback from Google for all the times we've plugged their resources. We're not. Whatever you think of the tech giant's ubiquity (and potential overreach), their various platforms remain some of the most accessible and inexpensive in the electronic marketplace.

9. If you're unsure where to start, the National Geographic website provides a wealth of stunning nature photography paired with quality science writing. And, if you have old print copies of *National Geographic* (or a similar magazine), there's nothing preventing you from doing this activity in a nonvirtual setting.

10. Manipulating someone with so much false information they begin to question their own memory or sanity.

11. Pointing out the flaws of others in order to dodge criticism levied at you or someone you're defending.

12. We recognize that not everyone—especially younger students—uses social media (or that their parents will be accepting of such an assignment). In these cases, you can provide additional screenshots for students to analyze.

Works Cited

Adams, M. G. (2009). Engaging 21st-century adolescents: Video games in the reading classroom. *English Journal, 98*(6), 56–59. https://www.jstor.org/stable/40503460

Agnew, J. A. (1987). *Place and politics: The geographical mediation of state and society.* Allen & Unwin.

Anderson, J. (2005). *Mechanically inclined: Building grammar, usage, and style into writer's workshop.* Stenhouse.

Anderson, W. (Writer & Director), & Wilson, O. (Writer). (1998). *Rushmore* [Film]. Buena Vista Pictures.

Applebee, A., & Langer, J. (2011). A snapshot of writing instruction in middle schools and high schools. *English Journal, 100*(6), 14–27. https://www.jstor.org/stable/23047875

Armbruster, K., & Wallace, K. R. (Eds.). (2001). *Beyond nature writing: Expanding the boundaries of ecocriticism.* University Press of Virginia.

Augé, M. (1995). *Non-places: Introduction to an anthropology of supermodernity.* Verso.

Barton, D. (2006). *Literacy: An introduction to the ecology of written language.* Blackwell.

Bautista, M. A., Bertrand, M., Morrell, E., Scorza, D., & Matthews, C. (2013). Participatory action research and city youth: Methodological insights from the Council of Youth Research. *Teachers College Record, 115*(10), 1–23.

Beach, R., Share, J., & Webb, A. (2017). *Teaching climate change to adolescents: Reading, writing, and making a difference.* Routledge.

Beach, R., Thein, A. H., & Webb, A. (2012). *Teaching to exceed the English Language Arts Common Core State Standards: A literacy practices approach for 6–12 classrooms.* Routledge.

Beers, K., & Probst, R. E. (2012). *Notice & note: Strategies for close reading.* Heinemann.

Berg, P. (Writer & Director), & Cohen, D. A. (Writer). (2004). *Friday night lights* [Film]. Imagine Entertainment.

Berry, W. (1977). *The unsettling of America: Culture and agriculture.* Sierra Club Books.

Bishop, S. (2003). A sense of place. In R. E. Brooke (Ed.), *Rural voices: Place-conscious education and the teaching of writing* (pp. 65–82). Teachers College Press.

Bishop, W. (1999). *Ethnographic writing research: Writing it down, writing it up, and reading it.* Heinemann.

Bitton-Jackson, L. (1997). *I have lived a thousand years: Growing up in the Holocaust*. Simon Pulse.

Blau, S. (2003). *The literature workshop: Teaching texts and their readers*. Heinemann.

Bomer, R. (2007). The role of handover in teaching for democratic participation. In K. Beers, R. E. Probst, & L. Rief (Eds.), *Adolescent literacy: Turning promise into practice* (pp. 303–10). Heinemann.

Boucher, A. (2019, January 28). Joshua Tree National Park "may take 300 years to recover" from shutdown. *The Guardian*. https://www.theguardian.com/environment/2019/jan/28/joshua-tree-national-park-damage-government-shutdown

Bourne, B. (Ed.). (2000). *Taking inquiry outdoors: Reading, writing, and science beyond the classroom walls*. Stenhouse.

Bridge, S., & Common, D. (2020, September 8). The future of school may be outdoors, even after the pandemic. *CBC News*. https://www-cbc-ca.cdn.ampproject.org/c/s/www.cbc.ca/amp/1.5535039

Brooke, R. E. (Ed.). (2003). *Rural voices: Place-conscious education and the teaching of writing*. Teachers College Press.

Bruce, H. E. (2011). Green(ing) English: Voices howling in the wilderness? *English Journal*, *100*(3), 12–26. https://www.jstor.org/stable/25790054

Buell, L. (Ed.). (1995). *The environmental imagination: Thoreau, nature writing, and the formation of American culture*. Harvard University Press.

Bull, K. B., & Dupuis, J. B. (2014). Nonfiction and interdisciplinary inquiry: Multimodal learning in English and biology. *English Journal*, *103*(3), 73–79. https://www.jstor.org/stable/24484156

Cameron, C. W. (2019, March 19). Your complete guide to 2019 metro Atlanta farmers markets. *Atlanta Journal-Constitution*. https://www.ajc.com/lifestyles/food-cooking/where-find-2019-farmers-markets-around-metro-atlanta/1PIXc6Y2FXovYV3PJGUpDM

Cammarota, J., & Fine, M. (2008). *Revolutionizing education: Youth participatory action research in motion*. Routledge.

Casal, R. (Writer), Diggs, D. (Writer), & López Estrada, C. (Director). (2018). *Blindspotting* [Film]. Summit Entertainment.

Case, J. (2017). Place-based pedagogy and the creative writing classroom. *Journal of Creative Writing Studies*, *2*(2), Article 5. https://scholarworks.rit.edu/jcws/vol2/iss2/5

Centers for Disease Control and Prevention. (2020, September 11). Deciding to go out. Retrieved September 16, 2020, from https://www.cdc.gov/coronavirus/2019-ncov/daily-life-coping/deciding-to-go-out.html

Chandler, D. (2002). *Semiotics: The basics* (2nd ed.). Routledge.

Christensen, L. (2015). Rethinking research: Reading and writing about the roots of gentrification. *English Journal*, *105*(2), 15–21. https://www.jstor.org/stable/26359349

Collins, S. (2008). *The hunger games*. Scholastic.

Connell, R. E. (1990). *The most dangerous game*. Creative Education. (Original work published 1924)

Conrad, J. (2012). *Heart of darkness*. Penguin. (Original work published 1899)

Cortez-Riggio, K.-M. (2011). The Green Footprint Project: How middle school students inspired their community and raised their self-worth. *English Journal, 100*(3), 39–43. https://www.jstor.org/stable/25790059

Cresswell, T. (2015). *Place: A short introduction* (2nd ed.). Wiley Blackwell.

Critchfield, R. (1991). *Trees, why do you wait? America's changing rural culture*. Island Press.

Crovitz, D., & Devereaux, M. D. (2016). *Grammar to get things done: A practical guide for teachers anchored in real-world usage*. Routledge.

Crovitz, D., & Montgomery, R. (2015). Imagining the impact of images: Visual scenario-based approaches in English language arts. *Ubiquity: The Journal of Literature, Literacy, and the Arts, 2*(1), 7–53. http://ed-ubiquity.gsu.edu/wordpress/crovitz-and-montgomery-2-1

Dean, D. (2008). *Genre theory: Teaching, writing, and being*. National Council of Teachers of English.

Dean, D. (2010). *What works in writing instruction: Research and practices*. National Council of Teachers of English.

Deveraux, M. D., & Wheeler, R. (2012). Code-switching and language ideologies: Exploring identity, power, and society in dialectically diverse literature. *English Journal, 102*(2), 93–100. https://www.jstor.org/stable/23365404

Dewey, J. (1990). *The school and society and The child and the curriculum* [Combined volume]. University of Chicago Press. (Original works published 1899 and 1902)

Duke, N. K., Purcell-Gates, V., Hall, L. A., & Tower, C. (2006). Authentic literacy activities for developing comprehension and writing. *The Reading Teacher, 60*(4), 344–55. https://doi.org/10.1598/RT.60.4.4

Duncan-Andrade, J. M. R., & Morrell, E. (2008). *The art of critical pedagogy: Possibilities for moving from theory to practice in urban schools*. Peter Lang.

Dyrness, A. (2011). *Mothers united: An immigrant struggle for socially just education*. University of Minnesota Press.

Elkins, J. (2008). Introduction: The concept of visual literacy, and its limitations. In J. Elkins (Ed.), *Visual literacy* (pp. 1–10). Routledge.

Emerson, R. M., Fretz, R. I., & Shaw, L. L. (2011). *Writing ethnographic fieldnotes* (2nd ed.). University of Chicago Press.

Esposito, L. (2012). Where to begin? Using place-based writing to connect students with their local communities. *English Journal, 101*(4), 70–76. https://www.jstor.org/stable/41415476

Fecho, B. (2004). *"Is this English?": Race, language, and culture in the classroom*. Teachers College Press.

Fey, T. (Writer), & Waters, M. (Director). (2004). *Mean girls* [Film]. Paramount Pictures.

Fitzgerald, F. S. (2013). *The great Gatsby*. Scribner. (Original work published 1925)

Freire, P. (2000). *The pedagogy of the oppressed* (30th anniv. ed.; M. B. Ramos, Trans.). Continuum. (Original work published 1970)

Freytag, G. (1968). *Freytag's technique of the drama: An exposition of dramatic composition and art* (6th ed.; E. J. MacEwan, Trans.). Scott, Foresman and Company. (Original work published in German 1894)

Gallagher, K. (2011). *Write like this: Teaching real-world writing through modeling and mentor texts*. Stenhouse.

Gee, J. P. (2004). *Situated language and learning: A critique of traditional schooling*. Routledge.

Geertz, C. (1973). *The interpretation of cultures*. Basic.

Georgia Department of Education. (2015). Grade 4 English Language Arts Georgia Standards of Excellence. In *English Language Arts Georgia Standards of Excellence (GSE) K–5*. https://www.georgiastandards.org/Georgia-Standards/Pages/ELA-K-5.aspx

Golding, W. (1988). *Lord of the flies*. Perigee. (Original work published 1954)

Grierson, S., & Orme, S. (2015). Speak out! How ekphrasis inspires writing on the edge. *English Journal, 104*(6), 47–54. https://www.jstor.org/stable/24484433

Gruchow, P. (1995). *Grass roots: The universe of home*. Milkweed.

Gruenewald, D. A. (2003). The best of both worlds: A critical pedagogy of place. *Educational Researcher, 32*(4), 3–12. https://doi.org/10.3102/0013189X032004003

Hemingway, E. (1997). Hills like white elephants. In *Men without women* (pp. 50–55). Simon & Schuster. (Original work published 1927)

Hicks, T. (2009). *The digital writing workshop*. Heinemann.

Hillocks, G., Jr. (1995). *Teaching writing as reflective practice*. Teachers College Press.

Hillocks, G., Jr. (2002). *The testing trap: How state writing assessments control learning*. Teachers College Press.

Hillocks, G., Jr. (2011). *Teaching argument writing: Grades 6–12*. Heinemann.

Hughes, J. (Writer & Director). (1985). *The breakfast club* [Film]. Channel Productions.

Hurst, H. (2015). Dodging the "R" word: Research as a tacit process. *English Journal, 105*(2), 96–101. https://www.jstor.org/stable/26359362

Intergovernmental Panel on Climate Change. (2018, October 8). *Special report: Global warming of 1.5 °C* (SR15). https://www.ipcc.ch/sr15

Jacobs, E. (2011). (Re)place your typical writing assignment: An argument for place-based writing. *English Journal, 100*(3), 49–54. https://www.jstor.org/stable/25790061

Jardine, D. W., Friesen, S., & Clifford, P. (Eds.) (2006). *Curriculum in abundance*. Lawrence Erlbaum.

King, M. L., Jr. (1963). "Letter from a Birmingham Jail" and "I Have a Dream" [Pamphlet]. Southern Christian Leadership Conference.

Kinloch, V. (2010). *Harlem on our minds: Place, race, and the literacies of urban youth*. Teachers College Press.

Kirby, D. L., & Crovitz, D. (2013). *Inside out: Strategies for teaching writing* (4th ed.). Heinemann.

Kittle, P. (2008). *Write beside them: Risk, voice, and clarity in high school writing*. Heinemann.

Kixmiller, L. A. S. (2004). Standards without sacrifice: The case for authentic writing. *English Journal, 94*(1), 29–33. https://www.jstor.org/stable/4128844

Kohnen, A. M. (2013). The authenticity spectrum: The case of a science journalism writing project. *English Journal, 102*(5), 28–34. https://www.jstor.org/stable/24484089

Kohnen, A. M. (2019). Teaching online research as a critical literacy skill. *English Journal, 108*(5), 25–30.

Krakauer, J. (1996). *Into the wild*. Villard.

Lammers, J. C. (2016). "The Hangout was serious business": Leveraging participation in an online space to design *Sims* fanfiction. *Research in the Teaching of English, 50*(3), 309–32. https://www.jstor.org/stable/24889924

Lee, H. (2002). *To kill a mockingbird*. HarperCollins. (Original work published 1960)

Lewis, J., & Aydin, A. (2013, 2015, 2016). *March* (Books 1–3; N. Powell, Illus.). Top Shelf Productions.

Lewis, M. A., & Rodesiler, L. (2018). Between being and becoming: The adolescent-athlete in young adult fiction. In I. P. Renga & C. Benedetti (Eds.), *Sports and K–12 education: Insights for teachers, coaches, and school leaders* (pp. 135–50). Rowman & Littlefield.

Lindblom, K., & Christenbury, L. (2018). *Continuing the journey 2: Becoming a better teacher of authentic writing*. National Council of Teachers of English.

Lipsyte, R. (2016). Sports culture [Foreword]. In A. Brown & L. Rodesiler (Eds.), *Developing contemporary literacies through sports: A guide for the English classroom* (pp. xv–xvii). National Council of Teachers of English.

London, J. (1986). *To build a fire and other stories*. Bantam. (Original work published 1908)

London, J. (2008). *The call of the wild*. Puffin. (Original work published 1903)

Maslow, A. H. (1943). A theory of human motivation. *Psychological Review, 50*(4), 370–96. https://doi.org/10.1037/h0054346

Marsico, K. (2018). *Johnny Clem's Civil War story*. Lerner.

McCann, T. M. (2010). Gateways to writing logical arguments. *English Journal, 99*(6), 33–39. https://www.jstor.org/stable/20787663

McCann, T. M., Johannessen, L. R., Kahn, E., & Flanagan, J. M. (2006). *Talking in class: Using discussion to enhance teaching and learning*. National Council of Teachers of English.

McIntosh, P. (2003). White privilege: Unpacking the invisible knapsack. In S. Plous (Ed.), *Understanding prejudice and discrimination* (pp. 191–96). McGraw-Hill.

Merriam-Webster. (n.d.). Ekphrasis. In *Merriam-Webster.com dictionary*. Retrieved September 14, 2020, from https://www.merriam-webster.com/dictionary/ekphrasis

Moore, R., Gathman, E. H., & Ducheneaut, N. (2009). From 3D space to third place: The social life of small virtual spaces. *Human Organization*, *68*(2), 230–40. https://doi.org/10.17730/humo.68.2.q673k16185u68v15

Moran, C. M., & Woodall, M. K. (2019). "It was like I was there": Inspiring engagement through virtual reality. *English Journal*, *109*(1), 90–96.

Moynihan, K. (2016). Bringing Edward Hopper's paintings into the English language arts classroom. *English Journal*, *105*(5), 68–74. https://www.jstor.org/stable/26606375

National Council of Teachers of English. (2019, March 1). Resolution on literacy teaching on climate change [Position statement]. https://ncte.org/statement/resolution-literacy-teaching-climate-change

Noden, H. R. (2011). *Image grammar: Teaching grammar as part of the writing process* (2nd ed.). Heinemann.

Nuttall-Smith, C. (2014, November 28). America at the Trump hotel: The food is amazing but you shouldn't eat here—ever. *The Globe & Mail*. https://www.theglobeandmail.com/life/food-and-wine/restaurant-reviews/america-at-the-trump-hotel-the-food-is-amazing-but-you-shouldnt-eat-here-ever/article21833277

Ogle, D. M. (1986). K–W–L: A teaching model that develops active reading of expository text. *The Reading Teacher*, *39*(6), 564–70. https://www.jstor.org/stable/20199156

Oldenburg, R. (1991). *The great good place: Cafés, coffee shops, community centers, beauty parlors, general stores, bars, hangouts, and how they get you through the day*. Paragon.

Ostenson, J. (2013). Exploring the boundaries of narrative: Video games in the English classroom. *English Journal*, *102*(6), 71–78. https://www.jstor.org/stable/24484129

Owens, D. (2001). *Composition and sustainability: Teaching for a threatened generation*. National Council of Teachers of English.

Pagliano, P. (1998). The multi-sensory environment: An open-minded space. *British Journal of Visual Impairment*, *16*(3), 105–9. https://doi.org/10.1177/026461969801600305

Paris, D. (2012). Culturally sustaining pedagogy: A needed change in stance, terminology, and practice. *Educational Researcher*, *41*(3), 93–97. https://doi.org/10.3102/0013189X12441244

Paris, D., & Alim, H. S. (2017). What is culturally sustaining pedagogy and why does it matter? In D. Paris & H. S. Alim (Eds.), *Culturally sustaining pedagogies: Teaching and learning for justice in a changing world* (pp. 1–21). Teachers College Press.

Paulsen, G. (1987). *Hatchet*. Simon & Schuster.

Pearce, K. (2000). Writing out. In B. Bourne (Ed.), *Taking inquiry outdoors: Reading, writing, and science beyond the classroom walls* (pp. 126–36). Stenhouse.

Pennycook, A. (2010). *Language as local practice*. Routledge.

The Princess Bride. (1987). Story by William Goldman, directed by Rob Reiner, Twentieth Century Fox.

Probst, R. E. (2004). *Response and analysis: Teaching literature in secondary school* (2nd ed.). Heinemann.

Purves, A. C., Rogers, T., & Soter, A. O. (1995). *How porcupines make love III: Readers, texts, cultures in the response-based literature classroom* (Rev. ed.). Longman.

Ravitch, D. (2010). *The death and life of the great American school system: How testing and choice are undermining education*. Basic.

Ray, K. W. (2006). Exploring inquiry as a teaching stance in the writing workshop. *Language Arts, 83*(3), 238–47. https://www.jstor.org/stable/41962104

Reid, L., & Smith, N. (1993). John Wayne meets Donald Trump: The Lower East Side as wild West. In G. Kearns & C. Philo (Eds.), *Selling places: The city as cultural capital, past and present* (pp. 193–209). Pergamon.

Rheingold, H. (1993). *The virtual community: Homesteading on the electronic frontier*. HarperCollins.

Rigell, A., & Banack, A. (2019). Where we're from: Poetry, placemaking, and community identity. *English Journal, 109*(1), 38–44.

Robbins, S., & Dyer. M. (Eds.). (2005). *Writing America: Classroom literacy and public engagement*. Teachers College Press.

Rodesiler, L., & Kelley, B. (2017). Toward a readership of "real" people: A case for authentic writing opportunities. *English Journal, 106*(6), 22–28.

Romano, T. (1995). *Writing with passion: Multiple genres, life stories*. Heinemann.

Rosenblatt, L. (1995). *Literature as exploration* (5th ed.). Modern Language Association.

Sachar, L. (1998). *Holes*. Farrar, Straus and Giroux.

San Pedro, T. J. (2017). "This stuff interests me": Re-centering indigenous paradigms in colonizing schooling spaces. In D. Paris & H. S. Alim (Eds.), *Culturally sustaining pedagogies: Teaching and learning for justice in a changing world* (pp. 99–116). Teachers College Press.

Seale, T. (2014). Creating synergy beyond the English hall. *English Journal, 103*(3), 12–14. https://www.jstor.org/stable/24484140

Shepard, D. L. (2018). Student-athlete identity formation and the relationship between an athletic subculture and academic success. In I. P. Renga & C. Benedetti (Eds.), *Sports and K–12 education: Insights for teachers, coaches, and school leaders* (pp. 77–88). Rowman & Littlefield.

Sherry, M. B., & Lawrence, A. M. (2019). Put me in the game: Video games and argument writing for environmental action. *English Journal, 108*(6), 69–76.

Shipka, J. (2005). A multimodal task-based framework for composing. *College Composition and Communication, 57*(2), 277–306. https://www.jstor.org/stable/30037916

Shor, I. (1996). *When students have power: Negotiating authority in a critical pedagogy*. University of Chicago Press.

Shrake, K. (2000). It started with a stream. In B. Bourne (Ed.), *Taking inquiry outdoors: Reading, writing, and science beyond the classroom walls* (pp. 61–75). Stenhouse.

Smith, G. A., & Sobel, D. (2010). *Place- and community-based education in schools*. Routledge.

Sobel, D. (2004). *Place-based education: Connecting classrooms and communities*. Orion Society.

Spradley, J. P. (2016). *The ethnographic interview* (Reissue ed.). Waveland Press. (Original work published 1979)

Steinkuehler, C. A., & Williams, D. (2006). Where everybody knows your (screen) name: Online games as "third places." *Journal of Computer-Mediated Communication*, *11*(4), 885–909. https://doi.org/10.1111/j.1083-6101.2006.00300.x

Sweney, M., & De Liz, A. (2018, February 16). "Parents killed it": Why Facebook is losing its teenage users. *The Guardian*. https://www.theguardian.com/technology/2018/feb/16/parents-killed-it-facebook-losing-teenage-users

Theobald, P. (1997). *Teaching the commons: Place, pride, and the renewal of community*. Westview.

Thomas, A. (2017). *The hate U give*. Balzer + Bray.

Thoreau, H. D. (2017). *Walden and Civil disobedience* [Combined volume]. Penguin. (Original works published 1849 and 1854)

Walker, L. (2005). I belong to this place: Claiming a neighborhood landmark. In S. Robbins & M. Dyer (Eds.), *Writing America: Classroom literacy and public engagement* (pp. 74–82). Teachers College Press.

Wells, P. (2012, November 13). As not seen on TV. *The New York Times*. https://www.nytimes.com/2012/11/14/dining/reviews/restaurant-review-guys-american-kitchen-bar-in-times-square.html

Whitney, A. E. (2011). In search of the authentic English classroom: Facing the schoolishness of school. *English Education*, *44*(1), 51–62. https://www.jstor.org/stable/23238722

Whitney, A. E. (2017). Keeping it real: Valuing authenticity in the writing classroom. *English Journal*, *106*(6), 16–21.

Wiesel, E. (1960). *Night* (S. Rodway, Trans.). Bantam.

Wiggins, G. (2009). Real-world writing: Making purpose and audience matter. *English Journal*, *98*(5), 29–37. https://www.jstor.org/stable/40503292

Williams, T. T. (2001). *Red: Passion and patience in the desert*. Pantheon.

Williams-Forson, P., & Counihan, C. (Eds.). (2012). *Taking food public: Redefining foodways in a changing world*. Routledge.

Woodhouse, J. L., & Knapp, C. E. (2000). *Place-based curriculum and instruction: Outdoor and environmental education approaches* (ED448012). Clearinghouse on Rural Education and Small Schools, Appalachia Educational Laboratory.

Wright, R. (1998). *Black boy*. HarperCollins. (Original work published 1945)

Index

The letter *f* following a page locator denotes a figure.

Adams, M. G., 174
advocacy, local, 128
affinity spaces, 152–53
agency, 16–17, 29
Agnew, J. A., 10, 11, 69, 152
Anderson, J., xiv
Applebee, A., 1–2
arguments, writing
    accuracy in, 165–67
    art, making room for, 56–57
    community, preserving or developing the, 55–56
    curation, defending, 83–84
    heuristic for, 54
    innovation, arguing the, 81–83
    multiple perspectives, evaluating, 167–68
    in museums, 81–84
    in natural places, 139–41
    in public places, 109–13
    real-world applications, 111–13
    reasons for, 53
    in school locations, or nearby, 53–57
    school safety, thinking about, 53–55
    school websites, accuracy of, 166–67
    tourist ads, 140–41
    travel blogs, 111–13
    in virtual places, 165–68
    weakness in teaching, 53
art
    making room for, 56
    writing about, 85–86
assessment, 2–3, 38
audience
    authenticity and, 5
    orienting to the, 19–20
Augé, M., 95
authenticity, 4–7, 17, 22, 153
author's style, adopting, 49–50

Banack, A., 155
Beach, R., 8, 64
Beers, K., xiii
Bishop, S., 127
Blau, S., xiii, xiv
Bomer, R., 20
Brooke, R. E., 21
Bruce, H. E., 64

Chandler, D., 34
change, writing about
    community, what's missing in your, 91–92
    community means everyone, 121–23
    the costs of, 96–97, 117–19
    making the school more environmentally friendly, 63–65
    in museums, 90–92
    in natural places, 146–49
    place-based writing and, 20–21
    in public places, 121–23
    in school locations, or nearby, 63–65
    a signature location in, 146–49
    social media and, 175–77
    in virtual places, 175–77

character, honoring through epitaphs, 106–8
characters, creating, 102–3
character sketch, 51–52
choice, 16–17
Christenbury, L., 4, 7
Christensen, L., 96–97
climate change, 64
code-switching, 163–65
community
    change in, 96–97
    gentrified, 96–97
    meaning of, 121–23
    preserving or developing, arguing for, 55–56
    writing about what's missing in, 90–92
    writing promoting, 20–21
correspondence, online, 163–65
Cortez-Riggio, K.-M., 127
creative writing, 98, 141–42
Cresswell, T., 10, 95
Crovitz, D., xiv, 4, 34
culture, ethnographic thick descriptions of
    the assignment, 42–43
    descriptive writing, 46
    foundational lessons, 46
    goal of, 41
    interpretation in, 47
    introductory activities, 44–45
    logistics, 44
    note-taking in, 46
    observations and interviews, 46
    opportunities for, 46
    requirements, 42
    research questions, developing, 45
    summing up in, 47
    supplemental lessons, 44–47
    understanding culture in, 44–45
curation, defending, 83–84
curricular scarcity, 9

Dean, D., 42, 164
Devereaux, M. D., xiv
Dewey, John, 8, 9
dialogue, crafting believable, 103–4
Duke, N. K., 4

Dyrness, A., 38, 62, 131

ebooks, do-it-yourself, 162–63
education, place-based, 9–12
ekphrasis, 85–86
Elkins, J., 34
empathy, building, 43
engagement, writing promoting, 17–18, 23, 24–26, 29
English language learners, writing in
    museums, 93
    natural places, 149–50
    or near school locations, 66–67
    public places, 123–24
    virtual places, 177–78
environmental education and advocacy, 10–12, 126–27, 145–46, 172–73. *See also* natural places, writing in or about
environmental school design, 63–64
epitaphs, honoring character, honoring through, 106–8

Facebook, 152
feedback, 5
foodways and food traditions, 120–21
found poetry, 170–71
Freire, P., 11
Freytag, G., 105
functional authenticity, 6

Gallagher, K., 4
games, online, 152
Garden and Composting Research Project, 26–33, 181–87
gardens, sensory, 24–25
Gee, J. P., 152
Geertz, C., 41
genius loci, 95, 108
genre, exploring local history, 74–77
gentrification, 96–97
Goldman, William, 104
Grammar to Get Things Done (Crovitz & Devereaux), xiv
graphic organizers, 105
Gruchow, P., 71
Gruenewald, D. A., 117

hero's journey, writing about the, 50–51
Hicks, T., 151
Hillocks, G., Jr., xiv, 2, 53, 83
history, exploring local
    the assignment, 71–73
    logistics, 73–74
    process, reflecting on, 76–77
    purpose of, 70–71
    rudiments of genre, 74–75
    summing up, 77–78
    supplemental lessons, 74–77
    what is home? 75
home, 71, 75–76
Hurst, H., 73

identity, 11
imagery, using, 101–2
innovation, arguing the, 81–83
instructional frameworks, inauthentic, 8
internet as place, 152
interpretation, learning, 47
The Interpretation of Cultures (Geertz), 41
interviews, learning about, 46

Jacobs, E., 127
Jardine, D. W., 9

Kelley, B., 4
Kennesaw Mountain National Battlefield Park, 33–36
Kinloch, V., 11, 96–97, 117
Kirby, D. L., 4
Kittle, P., xiv
Kixmiller, L. A. S., 4
Kohnen, A. M., 6–7, 21, 166

Lammers, J. C., 152
Langer, J., 1–2
latent authenticity, 6
Lawrence, A. M., 174
Lewis, M. A., 43
Lindblom, K., 4, 6
Lipsyte, R., 43
literature and other texts
    author's style, adopting, 49–50
    character, honoring through epitaphs, 106–8

character of a place, 108–9
code-switching, 163–65
cumulative sentence character sketch, 51–52
do-it-yourself ebook, 162–63
grounding in the real world, 79–80
the hero's journey, 50–51
in museums, 78–81
myth, 50–51
in natural places, 134–39
nature, 135–36
online correspondence, 163–65
in public places, 106–9
purpose of, 78–79
romanticism, 135–36
in school locations, or nearby, 48–52
setting, 137–39
survival, nature of, 136–37
suspense, building, 80–81
virtual places, 161–65
The Literature Workshop (Blau), xiv
locale, place and, 10–11, 69–70, 152
location, place and, 10–11, 152

Maslow, W., 137
McCann, T. M., xiv
Mechanically Inclined (Anderson), xiv
Montgomery, R., 34
monuments, context and, 110–11
Moran, C. M., 169
museums, stories set in, 88–89
museums, writing in or about, 68–93
    arguments in, 81–84
    art, poetry and prose, 85–86
    change, 90–92
    community, 91–92
    curation, defending, 83–84
    ekphrasis, 85–86
    for English language learners, 93
    exploring local history (extended lesson), 70–78
    goal of, 69
    innovation, arguing, 81–83
    literature and other texts in, 78–81
    missing voices, 89–90
    narratives, poetry, and scripts, 84–89
    perspective, thinking about, 87–88

reasons for, 69–70
research and inquiry in, 89–90
stories set in museums, 88–89
for students with special needs, 92–93
suspense, building, 80–81
myths, writing about, 50–51

narrative, rooting in place, 98–106
the assignment, 99–100
beginners, requirements for, 101–2
believable dialogue, crafting, 103–4
characters, creating, 102–3
difficulty of, 70–71
graphic organizers for, 105
imagery, using, 101–2
logistics, 100–101
pop culture for, 104
sketching the structure, 105
summing up, 105–6
supplemental lessons, 101–5
narratives, poetry, and scripts, writing
bringing a scientist's eye to, 141–42
ekphrasis, 85–86
found poetry, 170–71
in museums, 84–89
in natural places, 141–44
perspective, thinking about, 87–88
poetry and prose about art, 85–86
in public places, 113–15
in school locations, or nearby, 58–60
school map, 58–59
social media for, 142–44
stories set in museums, 88–89
virtual places, 169–71
virtual reality to tell stories, 169–70
voice and point of view, 113–14
writing marathon, 59–60
writing poetry from a new angle, 114–15
narrative writing, 98–99
national parks
Kennesaw Mountain National Battlefield Park, 33–36
researching the, 172–73
natural places, defined, 127
natural places, writing in or about, 125–50

arguments in, 139–41
bringing a scientist's eye to creative writing, 141–42
change, 146–49
for English language learners, 149–50
examples of, 125–27
land, coexisting with the, 145–46
literature and other texts in, 134–39
local advocacy in, 128
narratives, poetry, and scripts in, 141–44
nature, 135–36
place-based opportunities, 126
research and inquiry in, 144–46
romanticism, 135–36
setting, 137–39
a signature location in, 146–49
social media for, 142–44
for students with special needs, 149
survival, nature of, 136–37
tourist ads, creating, 140–41
value of, 126–27
Wild Places project (extended lesson), 128–34
nature writing, 135–36
Noden, H. R., 102
non-places, 95, 108
note-taking, 46
Notice & Note (Beers & Probst), xiii–xiv

observations, ethnographic, 46
Oldenburg, R., 152
On the Chopping Block project, 61–63
Ostenson, J., 174
outdoors, defined, 189n5
Owens, D., 11
ownership, writing creating, 16–17

Pagliano, P., 25
paintings, reading, 34–35
Paris, D., 16
participatory action research (PAR), 12, 38
Pearce, K., 127
the personal in place-based writing, 15–16, 38
perspective, thinking about, 87–88

perspectives, evaluating multiple, 167–68
place
    aesthetics of, 116–17
    characterizing, 108–9
    defined, 10
    internet as, 152
    locale in, 10–11, 69–70, 152
    location in, 10–11, 152
    sense of place in, 10–11, 152
place-based education, 9–12
place-based writing
    authenticity in, 4–7
    benefits of, xiii, 20–23, 36
    defined, xiii, 9–10
    final thoughts, 179–80
    flexibility of, 37–39
    hallmark of, 14
    implementing, 12–14, 22–23, 40
    strengths of, 12
    theory supporting, xiii–xiv
    uniqueness, 15
place-based writing, traits of
    agentive, 16–17
    audience oriented, 19–20
    change, promoting, 20–21, 39
    engaging, 17–18
    personal and purposeful, 15–16, 38
place-based writing activities. *See also* museums; natural places; public places; school locations; virtual places
    adapting, 37
    additional resources, 38
    Garden and Composting Research Project, 26–33, 181–87
    Kennesaw Mountain National Battlefield Park, 33–36
    malleability of, 12–13
    School Tour, xi–xiii
    sophisticated, elements creating, 21–22, 22f, 23f
Poe, Edgar Allan, 80–81
poetry, writing. *See also* narratives, poetry, and scripts, writing
    about art, 85–86
    found poetry, 170–71
    from a new angle, 114–15
politics, 12, 42–43, 110–11

pop-up museums, 190n6
Probst, R. E., xiii
process, reflecting on, 76
public places
    accessibility to, 97–98
    displacement from, 96
    places classified as, 94–95
    term usage, 94
public places, writing in or about, 94–124
    aesthetics of place, 116–17
    arguments in, 109–13
    change, 117–19, 121–23
    character, honoring through epitaphs, 106–8
    character of a place, 108–9
    community, 121–23
    for English language learners, 123–24
    literature and other texts in, 106–9
    local foodways and food traditions, 120–21
    monuments and context, 109–10
    narratives, poetry, and scripts in, 113–15
    poetry from a new angle, 114–15
    research and inquiry in, 115–21
    rooting narrative in place (extended lesson), 98–106
    for students with special needs, 123
    travel blogging, 110–13
    voice and point of view, 113–14
purpose, writing promoting, 29

Ray, K. W., 29, 32
real world, grounding writing in the, 79–80, 161–62
research and inquiry writing
    aesthetics of place, 116–17
    change, cost of, 117–19
    on land, coexisting with the, 145–46
    on local foodways and food traditions, 120–21
    on missing voices, 89–90
    in museums, 89–90
    narratives, poetry, and scripts in, 87–88
    national parks, researching the, 172–73
    in natural places, 144–46

in public places, 115–21
school locations, in or near, 61–63
video games and world building, 173–75
virtual places, 171–75
research papers, 41–42, 61, 93–94
research questions, developing, 45
reviews, writing, 111–12
Rigell, A., 155
Rodesiler, L., 4, 43
Romano, T., 6, 98, 132
romanticism, 135–36

San Pedro, T. J., 16
school locations, writing in or near, 37–67
arguments in, 53–57
art, making room for, 56–57
author's style, adopting, 49–50
change, writing for, 63–65
community, preserving or developing the, 55–56
concerns, 40
cumulative sentence character sketch, 51–52
for English language learners, 66–67
ethnographic thick description (extended lesson), 41–48
hero's journey, 50–51
literature and other texts in, 48–52
making the school more environmentally friendly, 63–65
on myth, 50–51
narratives, poetry, and scripts in, 58–60
On the Chopping Block project, 61–63
research and inquiry in, 61–63
school map, 58–59
school safety, thinking about, 53–55
School Tour activity, xi–xii
for students with special needs, 66
writing marathon, 59–60
school map, 58–59
schools, making more environmentally friendly, 63–64
school safety, thinking about, 53–55
School Tour activity, xi–xiii
school websites, accuracy of, 166–67

scripts. *See* narratives, poetry, and scripts, writing
Seale, T., 39
sense of place, 10–11, 108–9, 152
Sherry, M. B., 174
Shipka, J., 38
Shor, I., 16, 54
Shrake, K., 63
Signature Location activity, 146–49
Smith, G. A., 20, 127
Sobel, D., 9, 15, 20, 127
social media, 142–44, 175–77
stories
set in museums, 88–89
using virtual reality to tell, 169–70
structure of narrative, rooting in place, 105
students with special needs, writing in
museums, 92–93
natural places, 149
public places, 123
school locations or nearby, 66
virtual places, 177
summing up, learning about, 47
survival, nature of, 136–37
suspense, building, 80–81

Talking in Class (McCann et al.), xiv
The Testing Trap (Hillocks), 2
text-self connection, 35f
Theobald, P., 10
This I Believe (about social media), 175–77
Thoreau, Henry David, 135–36
tourist ads, creating, 140–41
travel blogging, 111–13

video games and world building, 173–75
virtual places, writing and, 151–78
accuracy in, 165–67
affinity spaces, 152–53
arguments in, 165–68
benefits of, 153, 170
challenges, 161–62
change, 175–77
code-switching, 163–65

do-it-yourself ebook, 162–63
for English language learners, 177–78
found poetry, 170–71
literature and other texts in, 161–65
multiple perspectives, evaluating, 167–68
narratives, poetry, and scripts in, 169–71
national parks, researching the, 172–73
online correspondence, 163–65
research and inquiry in, 171–75
school websites, accuracy of, 166–67
social media and, 175–77
for students with special needs, 177
technology for, 151
video games and world building, 173–75
virtual reality to tell stories, 169–70
virtual tour, creating a (extended lesson), 153–61
websites, considerations, 152
virtual reality, using to tell stories, 169–70
virtual tour, creating a
   the assignment, 154–58
   captions and writing summaries, 159–60
   considerations in, 153–54
   logistics, 158–59
   reviews, writing, 160
   summing up, 160–61
   supplemental lessons, 159–60
voice and point of view, 113–14
voices, missing, 89–90

websites, accuracy of school, 166–67
websites as place, 152
Whitney, A. E., 4, 5, 14
Wiggins, Grant, 3, 4
Wild Places project
   the assignment, 129–32
   grant proposals, writing, 133
   logistics, 132
   summing up, 134
   supplemental lessons, 132–33
Williams, Terry Tempest, 12
Woodall, M. K., 169
world building, video games and, 173–75
Write beside Them (Kittle), xiv
writing
   bad, 98–99, 192n2
   closed-circuit model of, 5
   descriptive, 46
writing instruction, 1–4, 15, 99
writing marathon, 59–60
Wynn, Emily, 190n11

youth participatory action research (YPAR), 38, 92

Authors

Rob Montgomery is a former high school English teacher and is now associate professor of English and English education at Kennesaw State University. In his current position, he works with preservice English education candidates, and he codirected the Invitational Summer Institute of the Kennesaw Mountain Writing Project for several years. He has also worked with the Georgia Film Academy and serves on the editorial board for *Teachers, Profs, Parents: Writers Who Care*, a blog maintained in conjunction with the National Council of Teachers of English's English Language Arts Teacher Educators Commission on Writing Teacher Education.

Amanda Montgomery currently teaches third grade at Park Street Elementary School in Marietta, Georgia. She received her teaching certification and master's degree at the University of Georgia, Athens. In the past few years, she has actively participated in the Kennesaw Mountain Writing Project as codirector of the Invitational Summer Institute.

This book was typeset in TheMix and Palatino by Barbara Frazier.

Typefaces used on the cover include Freeland and Akzidenz-Grotesk.

The book was printed on 50-lb. White Offset paper by Seaway Printing Company, Inc.

www.ingramcontent.com/pod-product-compliance
Lightning Source LLC
Chambersburg PA
CBHW080745250426
43673CB00062B/1896